D1499772

Romance and Chronicle

823.2
M29
F45

5.º

62624

P. J. C. FIELD

Romance and Chronicle

A STUDY OF MALORY'S PROSE STYLE

BARRIE & JENKINS
LONDON

LC 75-130262

© 1971 by P. J. C. Field
First published in 1971 by
Barrie & Jenkins Ltd
2 Clement's Inn
London WC 2
Reprinted 1971

ISBN 0.214.65230.0

Printed in Great Britain by
Robert MacLehose and Co. Ltd
The University Press, Glasgow

TO MY PARENTS

Contents

Abbreviations

"Arthur"	"The Tale of King Arthur," in V.
AM	*Annuale Mediaevale*
A.V.	*The Holy Bible....* London, 1611.
BJRL	*Bulletin of the John Rylands Library*
B.M.	The British Museum, London
B.N.	The Bibliothèque Nationale, Paris
Bodl.	The Bodleian Library, Oxford
CL	*Comparative Literature*
E & S	*Essays and Studies*
EA	*Etudes Anglaises*
EETS	The Early English Text Society, London
ES	*English Studies*
FMLS	*Forum for Modern Language Studies*
"Gareth"	"The Tale of Sir Gareth of Orkeney . . . ," in V.
"Grail"	"The Tale of the Sankgreal . . . ," in V.
JEGP	*Journal of English and Germanic Philology*
L	*Le Roman de Balain*, ed. M.D. Legge. Manchester, 1942.
"Lancelot"	"The Noble Tale of Sir Launcelot du Lake," in V.
"Lancelot & Guenivere"	"The Book of Sir Launcelot and Queen Guinevere," in V.
"Lucius"	"The Tale of the Noble King Arthur that was Emperor . . . ," in V.
MÆ	*Medium Ævum*
MED	*A Middle English Dictionary*, ed. H. Kurath and S. Kuhn. Ann Arbor, 1953- . In progress.
MLN	*Modern Language Notes*
MLR	*Modern Language Review*
Morte	*Le Morte Darthur*
"Morte"	"The Most Piteous Tale of the Morte Arthur Saunz Gwerdon," in V.
MP	*Modern Philology*
MS	*Mediaeval Studies*
Mustanoja	Tauno F. Mustanoja, *A Middle English Syntax*. Helsinki, 1960.
N & Q	*Notes and Queries*

NED	*A New English Dictionary on Historical Principles,* ed. Sir James Murray *et al.* Oxford, 1888-1933.
PBA	*Proceedings of the British Academy*
PQ	*Philological Quarterly*
REL	*Review of English Literature*
RES	*Review of English Studies*
Rom	*Romania*
RS	*Research Studies*
S	*Le Morte Darthur by Sir Thomas Malory, the Original Edition of William Caxton now Reprinted* . . . , ed. H.O. Sommer. 3 vols. Oxford, 1889-91.
SN	*Studia Neophilologica*
SP	*Studies in Philology*
STS	The Scottish Text Society, Edinburgh
Sommer	*The Vulgate Version of the Arthurian Romances,* ed. H.O. Sommer. 8 vols. Washington, 1909-16.
Tilley	M. P. Tilley, *A Dictionary of the Proverbs in England in the Sixteenth and Seventeenth Centuries.* Ann Arbor, 1950.
"Tristram"	"The Book of Sir Tristram de Lyones," in V.
TSE	*Tulane Studies in English*
UNS	*University of Nebraska Studies*
V	*The Works of Sir Thomas Malory,* ed. Eugène Vinaver. Second edition. 3 vols. Oxford, 1967.
v.	*vide,* "see".
ZRP	*Zeitschrift für Romanische Philologie*

Preface

Nearly all the readers of the *Morte Darthur* have been attracted and impressed by its style: even Malory's first biographer, Edward Hicks, allowed himself to be drawn into a chapter on the subject. In recent years the need for a full-length study of the subject has been increasingly felt, and has been voiced by, among others, two distinguished medievalists each of whom has written a survey of the current state of Malory scholarship: Derek Brewer in *Forum for Modern Language Study* (1970) and Larry Benson in *Critical Approaches to Six Major English Works*, ed. R. M. Lumiansky (University of Pennsylvania Press, 1968). I have allowed these two articles and the bibliography in Professor Eugène Vinaver's 1967 edition of Malory to excuse me from documenting fully those aspects of the *Morte Darthur* not immediately relevant to my argument.

The help of others is a *sine qua non* of scholarly achievement. My indebtedness to many of my predecessors is revealed in my notes and bibliography, but I must single out from amongst them for special mention Professor Vinaver, whose edition has greatly eased the labours of all who have worked on Malory since it first appeared. My gratitude is also particularly due to the Principal and Fellows of Brasenose College, Oxford, and the Council and Senate of University College, Bangor, whose financial support has made my research possible; to Dr Robert Shackleton and Miss M. A. Muir, who put their greater expertise in Old French at my disposal; to Professor J. A. W. Bennett, Dr D. S. Brewer, Miss Vivien Cook, Professor Norman Davis, Dr Alastair Fowler, Miss P. O. E. Gradon, Douglas Gray, Dr Caterina Maddalena, B. D. H. Miller, and Dr Lawrence Wright, who read drafts, answered questions, and set standards for imitation; and to Dr Isobel Murray, without whose criticism, encouragement, and help this book would have come into being with many more faults, if it had come into being at all. I owe thanks to the Bibliothèque Nationale in Paris which made its manuscripts of the French prose *Tristan* available to me, to Mrs S. M. Gordon-Rae and her assistants on the staff of the Bodleian Library who responded heroically to endless demands for books, and to Mrs E. Read who provided typing of unparalleled accuracy. I am grateful to Mr R. W. Burchfield and Professor Norman Davis for their permission to use the Early English Text Society's photographs of the Winchester manuscript of *Le Morte Darthur*, to Messrs Faber and Faber for permission to reprint the passage on page 6 from T. S. Eliot's *Essays*, and to the editor of *Speculum* for permission to reuse part of an article which first appeared in his journal.

Inevitably some valuable books have appeared too late to be used: notably the most recent parts of the *Middle English Dictionary*, and the dictionary of Middle English proverbs compiled by B. J. and H. W. Whiting.

I hope, however, that even without them I have helped to make more evidently applicable to the *Morte Darthur* those words which Sir Francis Bryan added a little later to *The Golden Boke of Marcus Aurelius*, which had also found its way through a variety of languages into English: "A ryghte precious meate is the sentences of this boke: But finally the sauce of the sayd swete style moveth the appetite. Many bokes there be of substanciall meates, but they be so rude and so unsavery, and the style of so small grace, that the fyrste morselle is lothesome and noyfull: And of such bokes foloweth to lye hole and sounde in Libraries, but I truste this wylle not."

                                                                           P. J. C. FIELD
University College
Bangor
North Wales
September, 1970

Preliminaries

When we talk of style, in a work of art or elsewhere, we are thinking of a kind of variation which distinguishes the object we are considering from a norm established by other members of its class. A world in which all members of each class of objects and events were uniform would be a world without style. Style in literature is made possible by synonymy in language; by the fact that there are different ways of saying the same thing. This is a very approximate statement: a little reflection reveals that a different manner of expression may make "the same thing" into something very different. The language we use breaks up experience into certain patterns which set limits to what we can say in it, as the difficulties of translation into another demonstrate. But when we come to use a language, we find that although the language has already made some choices for us, there are still others which we need to make ourselves. And what we ordinarily mean by style is the variation between individuals which is the product of these choices.[1]

The conclusions which we draw from these variations, and to some extent the kind of variation we look for, will depend on what we understand by literature. And on this there is no convenient agreement. The variety of possible attitudes to literature is very large, and each position has its stylistics, implicit or explicit. And so we find a bewildering number of definitions of style competing for our attention and acceptance. We are urged to consider style as variation, as expression, and as choice; as ingratiation, as transubstantiation, and as *l'homme même*; as the effective value of organised language, and as the aggregate of contextual probabilities.[2] There are definitions of style based on the point of view of the writer, definitions based on the impressions of the reader, and definitions which presuppose objective analysis of the text itself. Which definition appeals to us will commonly depend on what we feel a work of literature as such to be.

If, for instance, we consider that literature is in its essence the expression of genius, then our literary criticism will be an attempt to explain that genius. We may assess the structure of a work largely in terms of originality, and its message as the product of its author's life. In our treatment of its style, we will look for the linguistic habits peculiar to the writer, and attempt to discover how they are bound up with his experience and personality. We may well be silent about the writer's audience, and feel his work compromised by any discernible attempt to please them. A position like this was typical of the Romantic movement, when the touchstone of literature was no longer the judgement of the readers (or alternatively, the best readers) of all ages. And so we are not surprised to find Matthew Arnold, the characteristic voice of Victorian England, explaining style in terms of the temperament of individual authors. He feels that the remarkable intensity of Milton's writing comes from a surging yet bridled excitement in the poet; that Shakespeare's manner is the product of instinctive unregulated impulse; and that Luther's prose displays the coarse courage and honesty of the typical German.[3]

Though somewhat out of fashion in Anglo-American literary criticism, this is a valid way of approaching literature, and in our own century has been given a more up-to-date philosophic underpinning by the aesthetic of Benedetto Croce. Under his influence, a number of linguists have come to look on language as a process of creative self-expression. The stylistic criticism of the most distinguished member of this school, Leo Spitzer, is marked by a strong individualistic and psychological bias. In an outstanding essay on Diderot's prose, he relates one aspect of Diderot's style, his characteristic rhythms, to his nervous temperament and his philosophy of mobility.[4] Style is not viewed in isolation, but is shown to be the product of the author's personality and opinions.

This is not, however, the approach which will be followed in this book. Here I shall be concerned primarily with the way in which Malory's style contributes to the meaning of the *Morte Darthur* as a whole, not with the way in which it expresses his personality. There is no necessary conflict between these methods, since "meaning" in this large sense is *a priori* likely to express the dominant interests and attitudes of the author. But a psychological interpretation introduces two avoidable difficulties, one of methodology and one of literary theory. The former is that we would have to commit ourselves to opinions on the author of the book which we have no evidence outside the book itself to verify: indeed, it is not certain which of the fifteenth-century Thomas Malorys wrote it.[5] And a work of art may reflect only part of its author's personality, and that indirectly; particularly if it is a work of conscious artistry, or written in a strong tradition, or, like the *Morte Darthur*, heavily dependent on other works for its matter. Any of these factors might prevent a book from being a "natural" reflection of its author's psyche and falsify our deductions about it.

The theoretical difficulty is that the work is prior to the author, at least in the reader's mind. We are interested in Malory because he wrote the *Morte Darthur*, not in the *Morte Darthur* because Malory was its author. In contrast, most of us would lose interest in Shakespeare's hypothetical laundry bills if they were found to describe someone else's washing. And so, however interesting it might be to relate the book to its author's personality, it should be possible to find and appraise a focus of interest in the work itself without venturing on the uncertain ground of biography. Such a focus of interest would be a more properly literary one.

We may find a clue to the nature of this in Stendhal's definition of style: "le style est ceci: Ajouter à une pensée donnée toutes les circonstances propres à produire tout l'effet que doit produire cette pensée."[6] Behind such a statement lies the assumption that a work of art embodies its "donnée" in an organic whole, and that in a successful book all the parts of this whole work together harmoniously to help to produce the total effect. Clearly, style is one of these parts, and a modern critic has succinctly outlined some of its possibilities and its function:

> A heavy dependence on abstraction, a peculiar use of the present tense, a habitual evocation of similarities through parallel structure, a tendency to place feelings in syntactical positions of agency, a trick of underplaying casual words: any of these patterns of expression, when repeated with unusual frequency, is a sign of a habit of meaning, and thus of a persistent way of sorting out the phenomena of experience.[7]

It is the habit of meaning which matters: the higher the frequency with which a feature of style occurs in a work, the more significant it is. Moreover, since a language is the possession of all its users, whose uses of it define its possible meanings, and amongst whom any single author, however able, is negligible, a feature of style is significant in a work not only in direct proportion to its frequency there, but also in inverse proportion to its frequency in other contexts. The contexts will include the author's other writings, related sub-genres and genres, the literary output of the language, its non-literary expressions, and perhaps also the literary and non-literary output of other languages. Part of the meaning which is carried by the style of Pope's *Dunciad* comes from its differences from as well as its similarities to Virgil's *Aeneid*. The style characteristic of a particular work is the result of a very large number of very small choices, which in their totality create what has been called the final elaboration of meaning.[8]

The major divisions of my treatment of Malory's style will correspond to the different modes of the *Morte Darthur* itself—narrative, descriptive, dialogue, and commentary— to see what each one contributes to the book, and whether each assists towards the same effects. In analysing the commentary in the book, I shall make use of the familiar critical distinction between the narrator whom we meet in the book and Sir Thomas Malory the man, and for reasons which I have already suggested, I shall not be concerned with the extent to which they resemble one another.

But despite some of the more ascetic modern critics, I shall not debar myself from mentioning the author's name and his discernible intentions where this seems helpful. A perfect work of art stands free of its creator, and needs no explanation in terms of him; but an imperfect one does not. And the *Morte Darthur*, though a great work, is an uneven one. There is no aspect of it in which every detail fits into an organic unity. There are small anomalies in its style, as in its structure, characterisation, and scale of values, which only a dishonest ingenuity could disguise, and which cannot be accounted for except as deficiencies in their author's grasp of the central idea of his own work. If they are accepted in that way, such flaws dwindle to a proper insignificance, and the *Morte Darthur* displays a substantial unity of form and meaning.[9]

It is not for me to judge the success of this method, but it would be superfluous to justify the attempt. One of the founders of English literary criticism thought the *Morte Darthur* to be the prose analogue of Chaucer's poetry and the greatest (if not the most original) prose work before Bacon's *Advancement of Learning*.[10] Later scholars have agreed on the book's stature while they disagreed violently over its nature. And its style has been universally praised but never analysed. To attempt to define it may be thought foolhardy: the effort disregards the experience of Malory's most recent editor, who considered that "his unexpounded miracle of style" escaped analysis.[11] But no close analysis of Malory's style has ever been published, and his manner of writing ensures that anything but a close examination will fail even to apprehend the facts. Malory's style is unusually interesting in combining a strong demand for emotional response with a quite exceptional degree of self-effacement by the author within the story. But because Malory's style is emotionally evocative, those critics who find it successful have all too often been seduced into describing their own reactions to it rather than the style itself.[12] This short-circuits criticism.

At this stage we may conveniently make a point which arises from two competing descriptions of style, and which will help to establish what use we can make of other texts. It has been pointed out that choice must be at the basis of any expressive theory of style, and that the tones and overtones of a work are controlled by the selection of the most appropriate of several similar meanings.[13] And the author, not the narrator, is clearly the maker of the choices. But to define style as choice, though strictly true, can be misleading. It not only leads the attention back from the book itself to the author and his intentions, but suggests that the author selected the means he used, consciously and in full awareness of the consequences, from the whole language. Whereas an author may choose a style without being aware of all its effects, yet those effects still follow inescapably. The style of *The Pilgrim's Progress* and its effect upon its readers is unaffected by how much or how little Bunyan knew of the fashionable literary manners of his time. If he knew no other way to write, or was unable to write in other ways which he knew existed, it would be difficult to say that he "chose" his style. And yet we can call it (roughly) pious and popular because we can set it against other works which are neither. Since an author may not have a total grasp of the language of his time, and certainly cannot have such a grasp of the language of the future, it may be more profitable to think of style as variation rather than choice, varying about norms provided by the language itself, rather than choosing from the resources of an author's mind.

One such set of norms is provided by Malory's sources, French as well as English; another by his English contemporaries. A close comparison with his sources and contemporaries will show what Malory's style is, and what range of expression was available in his day. But some further comparisons will be made to sketch in a little of the wider framework in which we in the twentieth century must see it. Five centuries of literature have made our awareness different from that of Malory's first audience. This is what T. S. Eliot meant when he argued:

> The existing monuments form an ideal order among themselves, which is modified by the introduction of the new (the really new) work of art among them. The existing order is complete before the new work arrives; for order to persist after the supervention of novelty, the *whole* existing order must be, if ever so slightly, altered; and so the relations, proportions, values of each work of art toward the whole are readjusted.... Whoever has approved this idea ... will not find it preposterous that the past should be altered by the present as much as the present is directed by the past.[14]

A great many "really new" works of art have appeared since Caxton printed the *Morte Darthur*. Our expectations of prose have been greatly altered by the Augustan age. It is fitting therefore that we should turn to the most magisterial of the Augustans to have the principles involved set out with force and clarity.

> To works, however, of which the excellence is not absolute and definite, but gradual and comparative; to works not raised upon principles demonstrative and scientifick, but appealing wholly to observation and experience, no other test can be applied than length of duration and continuance of esteem.... Demonstration immediately displays its power, and has nothing to hope or fear from the flux of years; but works tentative and experimental must be estimated by their proportion to the general and collective ability of man, as it is discovered in a long succession of endeavours. Of the first building that was raised, it might be with certainty determined that it was round or square, but whether it was spacious or lofty must have been referred to time. The Pythagorean scale of numbers was at once discovered to be perfect; but the poems of *Homer* we yet know not to transcend the common limits of human intelligence, but by remarking, that nation after nation, and century after century, has been able to do little more than transpose his incidents, new name his characters, and paraphrase his sentiments.[15]

This is relevant to Malory not merely because he is the first major prose writer of English fiction, and because his value has been confirmed by time. But, less obviously, the very facts upon which that judgement of value is based, are themselves partly the creation of time. When the *Morte Darthur* first appeared it could easily have been discovered how many monosyllabic words it contained, but whether its sentences were long or short must, as Johnson said, be "referred to time". The fifteenth-century reader or hearer had of course a standard valid for him, by by which a sentence seemed long or short, since the book did not appear, like Johnson's hypothetical building, *ex nihilo,* but it was not necessarily the same as ours. It is because we have become used to literary prose that we feel Malory's to be colloquial. The contrast makes the judgement. In this study of Malory's style, I have therefore attempted to set Malory against the background both of his age and of ours, in the hope that the more enduring facts and values might emerge more clearly in perspective. We cannot be sure of the precise impression which the *Morte Darthur* made on readers in the age in which it was written, but the evidence, as we shall see, points to some surprising similarities with the impression it makes in our own age.

One more point remains. In the following pages, I have often been compelled to speak as if the literary characteristics of the *Morte Darthur* were the result of conscious art. This has saved many a series of clumsy periphrases. The reader must accept as the price of this convenience "devices" which were not devised, and "effects" which became effective by being tested on Malory's pulses rather than his judgement. It is no part of my contention that he was a conscious artist: rather the reverse.

II

Background

During the middle ages, French literature exercised a cultural hegemony over English. Like so many other works, Malory's *Morte Darthur* is based on French originals. But it is not simply a translation from the French. Malory was trying to give the whole story of the rise and fall of Arthur's court more comprehensively, and at the same time in briefer compass, than had been done before. The various romances which told of Arthur and his knights had not all been written with the aim of being consistent with one another, and some of them flatly contradicted others. But between 1450 and 1475 there were two attempts to make an authoritative collection of stories. One was the French collection now preserved in the Bibliothèque Nationale in Paris as MS B.N. fr. 112, made by Micheau Gonnot for Jacques d'Armagnac.[1] The other was an English translation made by Sir Thomas Malory. Gonnot took material from half a dozen stories, put them roughly in the order of probability of happening, and tried to tidy up some of the loose ends. Malory did something of the same, working a slightly smaller body of material rather more thoroughly into a unity. The skeleton of Malory's story was provided by the most widely read and most influential group of Arthurian prose romances, which modern scholars call the Vulgate Cycle.[2] The five romances of the cycle gave accounts respectively of the early history of the Grail up to Arthur's time; the legendary wizard Merlin who established the Round Table; Lancelot's rise to be its most famous knight and his love for Arthur's wife; the search of the knights of the Round Table for the Grail, in which Galahad was successful; and the death of Arthur in the wars caused by the discovery of Lancelot's adultery. Malory selected from the Vulgate Cycle, and added to his selection at those places at which it seemed to him that they would make the most coherent whole, stories and parts of stories from at least three other romances. One of these was a long French romance, the prose *Tristan*, and the other two were poems in English, the alliterative *Morte Arthure* and the stanzaic *Le Morte Arthur*. There may be others. It is possible for instance, that the Chapel Perilous episode in "Lancelot" may be derived from the French prose romance *Perlesvaus*.[3] But of some parts of his book we do not know whether they are Malory's own invention or whether they depend on sources which are now lost. The longest of these is his tale of "Gareth", for which we know of no source, and which most critics have felt it unlikely that Malory made up on his own.

The sources for the major sections of the *Morte Darthur* are as follows: for "Arthur", the French prose *Merlin* and *Suite de Merlin*, which together make up an expanded version of the second of the five Vulgate Cycle romances;[4] for "Lucius", the alliterative *Morte Arthure*; and for "Lancelot", the prose *Lancelot* (the third of the Vulgate Cycle romances) and possibly a short section of the *Perlesvaus*. No source is known for "Gareth";[5] but the "Tristram" comes from the French prose *Tristan*; the "Grail" from the *Queste del Saint Graal*, fourth of the Vulgate Cycle romances; and "Lancelot & Guenivere" and the "Morte" mainly from the *Mort Artu*, the last romance of the Vulgate Cycle, and the stanzaic *Le Morte Arthur*.[6] So, of the eight tales into which Vinaver has divided the *Morte Darthur*, five have French sources, one an English source, and one a source in each language. Given this, it was clearly possible that Malory's style would simply reflect that of his sources, particularly that of the great mass of French material.

That this did not happen seems to have been more accidental than deliberate. One of the most striking characteristics of Malory's work is the extent to which he shortened the tales he found in his sources. Once again, Gonnot did the same for his manuscript, but less thoroughly than Malory.[7] As Caxton remarked in his preface to the first edition, the noble volumes in French had been "drawen oute bryefly into Englysshe" by Malory.[8] Malory's stories vary from a half to an eighth of the size of those which inspired them.[9] His story of Balin, for instance, has been reduced to some 11,000 words, where the nearest French equivalent to his source is about 38,000 words.[10] Obviously, one of Malory's foremost intentions must have been sheer condensation of material, and although his motives for this are unknown, some of its effects are clear. Had he turned the French prose romances which make up the bulk of his sources into the same quantity of English, it would have been difficult for him to avoid the word-for-word translations which many of his contemporaries produced in the same circumstances. But a much shortened version allowed him to find his own way of telling the story. His changes were decisive and affected his style radically. Even in his early work we can see an individual style developing which foreshadows his later mastery of story-telling. The result is stories which are good in a rather different way from the French.

Malory retold the story in his own manner, and in style as well as in other ways, his story looked to the past rather than to the future. Briefly, we may say that his sources are relatively literary in style, and he made them relatively colloquial. The NED defines colloquial as "proper to common speech as opposed to elevated or formal language." This does not take us far. We need to find out what the properties of common speech actually are, and these are best revealed by a consideration of the differences between speaking and writing. Three important factors affect style. Firstly, the speaker has various aids, some of them non-linguistic like gesture and facial expression, some of them linguistic like pitch and stress and speed of delivery, which are denied to the writer, except for such rudimentary assistance as the latter can get from punctuation and typography. These resources are available in formal as well as common speech, but the use of nearly all of them will be restricted on nearly all formal occasions by various social proprieties. In the written language they are not available at all. The weight of the spoken meaning, therefore, cannot be fully transcribed on paper. Secondly, ordinary speech, especially dialogue between two or more people, is always tentative. A sentence begun can be altered to end in soft words in the face of anger, or amplified in the face of misunderstanding. The writer must make his attempt at communication once and for all, without a guiding response from his reader. Thirdly, speech, and especially informal speech, is composed much more quickly than writing, even with modern mechanical aids like the typewriter. The speaker, therefore, has proportionately less time to select and place each word. It is in the interest of the writer to use complex constructions and subtle relationships, to reduce the number of words and hence the time spent to a minimum. To load every rift with ore will also help the writer to provide a substitute for the aids to understanding which he has lost.

We can therefore expect the syntactic basis of the spoken language to be relatively simple and diffuse, and the syntax of the written language to tend to a more complex lucidity. But the spoken language, as modern linguistics reminds us, is prior to the written language. This is so in societies as well as in individuals, and we should expect to find the literary style developing from the colloquial. We can see this happening in English, in the prose written in the fourteenth and fifteenth centuries. The first stirrings of this new development are isolated and uncertain, and found at first only in the writings of the most highly educated, those whose daily work is on and in the written word. In the middle ages, there were few of these in the vernacular languages. However many people were technically literate, paucity of books had meant a literature limited in concentration and complexity by being composed for reading aloud. There are exceptions in the work of occasional writers whose personal inclinations made them want to press their medium to its limit. In prose, we can find sermons by clerics for clerics which must have required a high degree of trained attention to absorb, and in verse, there are passages of *Piers Plowman* which are undeniably concentrated and complex. But as long as literature was normally read aloud, the medium itself rather discouraged than encouraged complex organisation of the detail of the language. The only works which are exceptional as a class are the mystical treatises, which presumably were for private reading, and these we shall have to return to later. Malory seems to think of reading aloud as the norm, and we see it in the aristocratic English society pictured in Chaucer's *Troilus and Criseyde*.[11]

Few people under these circumstances could have been at ease with reading and writing. All but a few medieval people seem to have read more slowly than we do, and to have mouthed the words to themselves as they read. The very mistakes made by professional scribes suggest that they took the words they were copying one at a time, pronouncing them aloud.[12] In sixteenth-century England, Henry VIII himself was not at home with writing; he wrote to his Cardinal and chief minister in 1519:

> Myne awne good Cardinall, I recommande me unto yow as hartely as hart can thynke. So it is that by cause wryttyng to me is somewhat tedius and paynefull, therefor the most part of thes bysynesses I have commyttyd to our trusty counseler thys berrer to be declaryd to yow by mowthe, to whyche we wollde yow shulde gyff credens.[13]

Nor did the aristocracy seem to care about improvement. Sir Thomas

Elyot in the early sixteenth century speaks of ignorance and contempt for learning among the English aristocracy,[14] and the French aristocracy seems to have been much the same. In the fifteenth century, Alain Chartier remarked that the French courtiers thought it a disgrace to their rank to be able to read and write, and in the next century Castiglione said that the French noble thought it insulting to be called a clerk.[15] It was in this society that Malory lived and wrote. A brief look at the historical background will help us to understand why he wrote as he did.

The Anglo-Saxons had written the best vernacular prose in Europe. But the Norman Conquest put an end to the English achievement. The kings of England after the Conquest ruled or tried to rule lay and ecclesiastical princes who spoke Latin, French, and Welsh, and for whom literature of high quality appeared in all three languages. We do not know of anything comparable in English until the fourteenth century, when English was again firmly established as the language of the English ruling classes.[16] The best of the second-rate material in English in the interval bears the marks of an oral tradition. A few beautiful songs remind us that literature is not confined to the literate, and an occasional line of irony or forceful metaphor from Layamon's *Brut* shows that someone is still trying to compose a form of the old alliterative poetry. But while the subject and audience of Layamon's poem may still have been noble, its medium had atrophied. It may well be, as most scholars believe, that poetry of the classical Anglo-Saxon kind was still being composed in some parts of England. It is difficult to explain the fourteenth-century revival of alliterative poetry on any other assumption. But there is no evidence that any of the lost poems of the intervening period were ever written down.

In the circumstances of the time, it was inevitable that prose should suffer even more than poetry. Poetry had a greater intrinsic interest; men could and would memorize it, value it, and try to compose more like it. It could earn both prestige and perhaps some sort of a living, while to a superficial consideration, there was nothing to prize in prose. It was only ordinary speech written down. An oral tradition would quickly lose those qualities which gave the best prose its expressive power: precision, power of suggestion, and complex organisation. Although the Old English classics were still being copied out in the century after the Conquest, there was little need or opportunity to practise original writing of the old West Saxon literary English, which was being replaced by Latin in its original strongholds, the monasteries.

Education was now in the medium of two other languages with greater prestige; and first Latin and later Anglo-Norman became the language of the law. For these reasons and others, the syntax and vocabulary of English changed with alarming speed, until the spoken language became entirely divorced from the old language of Wessex. English prose suffered cultural amnesia.

Only in one area of life was the tradition of English prose continuous: in the sphere of homiletic writing. The fundamental work on this, although it has since been challenged several times, is R.W. Chambers' monograph.[17] Chambers argued that English religious writing had been continuous from the time of King Alfred to Sir Thomas More. Whether or not this is true without reservation, it would certainly be misleading to apply the word tradition to any but religious prose in the middle ages. Tradition suggests not only a continuous output, but also a certain quality maintained by conscious understanding of the principles of the relevant art. Such understanding may be achieved by constant practice or imparted by instruction. Few except the clergy had the time or interest for either. Those who wrote in English in the early middle ages were urged on by the desire to save souls, especially in religious communities of women, which could be reached only through English. In this movement the sermon had a prominent place. In the thirteenth century, the Fourth Lateran Council laid a new emphasis on the preaching of sermons. Preaching to the laity in their own language was the indispensable beginning of spreading the rudiments of doctrine, and doctrine was a matter of eternal moment. Even elementary knowledge could not be taken for granted. Robert Grosseteste, writing about 1235, assumes that his priests will have to teach their parishioners in their sermons the ten commandments, the seven deadly sins, the seven sacraments, and the importance of baptism and the sacrament of penance.[18] Many of the laity must have lacked even the simplest knowledge, and the campaign to instil it through sermons became a great educational movement.[19] One of the by-products of this movement was the appearance of books of homilies designed to provide ready-made sermons for priests who were incapable of producing a proper sermon on their own. A number of these books of homilies were in English, and we might perhaps look for the development of the prose virtues there.

But the sermon is not the best genre in which to develop a highly organised prose. To an even more exclusive degree than the rest of medieval literature, sermons were meant for oral delivery, and even if the preacher composed them in writing, there would be small point in his trying to exploit the full potentialities of his medium when they would have been wasted on a congregation which received his words aurally. The importance of the exemplum, essentially a short narrative, in medieval vernacular sermons may be a sign that preachers or their congregations or both preferred to avoid the more complicated uses of language which abstract argument would have forced upon them. But at least the clergy were writing English prose, particularly it seems in the West Midland region, and they kept up a tradition of a kind which continued through the mystical writers of the fourteenth century, and broadened out into the translations of the Bible and Capgrave's history. And, moreover, in the *Artes Praedicandi* they discussed the best way of expressing what they had to say.[20]

It was also the clergy who compiled, copied, and had easiest access to the other two kinds of handbooks which were concerned with style, the *Artes Dictaminis* for letter-writing, and the *Artes Poeticae* for poetry. And there is some evidence that, within the tradition of religious writing as a whole, the narrower tradition of lyrical prayer and mystical writing which seems to stem from the *Ancrene Riwle* in the early thirteenth century is influenced by styles and habits derived ultimately from Latin rhetoric.[21] Here more than in any other English prose in the middle ages we find both a sufficient output and a conscious understanding of the art in question, which together will provide for English prose a tradition in the fullest sense. That it should be a rhetorical tradition may be partly explained by the effort to communicate the incommunicable, and the responsiveness to style of introspective minds. The devotional and mystical writers have clearly read their predecessors and have the training to be able to use rhetoric. There is a revealing difference here between Lady Julian of Norwich and writers like Richard Rolle and the author of *A Talking of the Love of God*.[22] Rolle's early writings in English, especially his *Meditations on the Passion*, are packed with most of the figures of the rhetoricians, and he gradually learns later to use them more discriminatingly to give emphasis where he wants it. The antithetical style of the *Cloud of Unknowing* and the treatises associated with it is also sharpened by a pervasive use of rhetorical figures, particularly figures based on word-repetition[23] and the alliteration of key words. Julian, though widely read in Latin religious writing, seems to have had no formal education in rhetoric, and to have picked it up from writings in the mystical tradition. Her use of rhetorical figures like anaphora and isocolon is deliberate but not expert, and a natural good taste seems to have kept it sparing throughout her work.[24]

Rolle and his school were the most popular English authors of the middle ages, but we shall deceive ourselves if we think of this thin-spun tradition as comparable, for instance, with that of the nineteenth-century novel. On religion, the most important of all subjects, the total output was small, and the English part small within the total, and without printing or modern publicity, the circulation of any given work was very restricted. In poetry, many of the best works have survived only in a single manuscript. Books were valuable and rare enough to be entailed in wills.[25] Literature was still half private, and authors isolated and unco-ordinated. We can see this in the common phenomenon of multiple translation. Among the most popular works of the end of the middle ages, there were seven or eight translations made of St Bridget's *Revelations* and *Life*, the same number of Friar Laurent's *Somme des Vices et des Vertus*, four of the *Secreta Secretorum* and the *Life of Alexander*, and three of "Mandeville" and the *Imitation of Christ*, each translator unaware of the duplication.[26] The public at large must have known even less about what was being written, and most writers of prose must have had to translate and compose without much in the way of examples in front of them.

Moreover, unfortunately for English prose, the clergy produced their most ambitious works, both as to content and form, in Latin. John of Salisbury, Roger Bacon, and William of Ockham were figures of European stature who naturally wrote in the language of Europe. The theoretical linguistics of the middle ages was nearly all both in and on Latin. Even the histories of England, like Matthew Paris's, were written in Latin. Among the intellectually important figures only Reginald Pecock and John of Ireland, neither of them of the first rank, were prepared to stoop to writing in English. And the philosophers among the clergy wrote, as John of Salisbury complained, with very little regard for style.[27] It was inevitable that this should have a bad effect on the vernacular. English was unlikely to develop far while the ablest of those who had time for intellectual matters were arguing with one another about theology in another language. Indeed, it was possible for a cleric to be so steeped in Latin as to feel uneasy in the vernacular. John of Ireland himself, in a book addressed to the King of Scotland about 1490, confesses to having some difficulty with the vernacular in which he wrote it, and implies that the half dozen works he had written in Latin for the king's father had cost him less trouble than this one in

English.[28] Even in the early seventeenth century, it was said of John Overall, Regius Professor of Theology at Cambridge, and later Bishop of Norwich, that he was not given to preaching because he had spoken Latin so long that it was troublesome to him to speak English in a continued oration.[29]

The prevailing Latinity had some compensations. The learned language was written in a great many different ways, but complex organisation of language, for instance in the use of apposition or various kinds of subordination, was an obvious and important part of most good Latin, and it was a constantly available model to the most intellectual part of the literate public. It has already been suggested that the style of the mystics may derive ultimately from rhetorics which only existed in Latin.

But although these rhetorics did deal with the low style and condensation, they all emphasised decoration, expansion, and the high style.[30] The stress of the rhetorics on tropes and figures and the detail of language could divert attention from the clarity and proportion of good prose. It seems to have had this effect on Rolle's early writing in English. There were lessons to be learnt from a less showy Latin than that encouraged by manuals of rhetoric. But although Latin was available as a model, it was not often used as such, and good Latin and bad English were found together in the same man well after the fifteenth century. Late in the reign of Henry VIII, John Palsgrave translated a comedy called *Acolastus* into English and dedicated it to the king. In his epistle dedicatory, he spoke of certain scholars who could write, speak, and versify well in Latin, but could neither translate nor compose in the vernacular.

> They be not able to expresse theyre conceyte in theyr vulgar tonge, ne be not suffycyente, perfectly to open the diversities of phrases betwene our tonge and the Latyn (whiche in my poore judgemente is the veray chiefe thynge that the schole mayster shulde travayle in). In so moche that for want of this sufficient perfection in our owne tongue, I have knowen dyverse of theym, which have styl continued theyr study in some of your graces universities, that after a substanciall encrease of good lernynge, by theyr great and industrious study obteyned, yet whan they have ben called to do any service in your graces commen welthe, eyther to preach in open audience, or to have other administration, requiringe theyr assiduous conversantynge with your

subjectes, they have then ben forced to rede over our Englyshe
auctours, by that meanes to provyde a remedy unto their evident
imperfection in that behalfe.[31]

But not all English clerics found their grasp of English atrophying as
their command of Latin increased. And whether by the constant use of
Latin or by their greater practice in English, vernacular prose written
by the more highly educated clerics shows throughout the middle ages
a better grasp of structure than that written by laymen. The process
was no doubt reciprocal: they wrote better because, for many reasons,
they thought better; but one of the most important reasons why they
thought better was that they had learnt to handle and control the
language which embodied their thoughts. We can see their superior
grasp exemplified in the work of several fifteenth-century clerics who
show little concern with rhetorical devices.

William Thorpe wrote down the story of his examination for heresy
before Archbishop Arundel soon after it took place in 1407. It was first
printed in the *Actes and Monuments* (1563) of John Foxe,[32] who said he
had had a version from Tyndale, who had had Thorpe's own manuscript, slightly modernised but "some thing savering the old speach of
that time". We can see what Thorpe has gained from Latin in his
effort throughout at a grasp of the whole sentence, and attempts which
go with this to make his statements all-embracing. Neither of these is
always successful, but his partial success would have been impossible
without his use of apposition, antithesis, and parallelism. This is evident
at times in the reported speech of the examination proper, but even
clearer in the argument of the preface.

> And I was than greatly comforted in all my wittes, not only for
> that I was than delivered for a time from the sight, from the
> hearing, from the presence, from the scorning, and from the
> manasyng of myne ennemies: but muche more I rejoysed in the
> Lord, because that thorowe His grace, He kept me so, both among
> the flattering specially, and among the manasing of mine adver-
> saries, that without hevinesse and anguishe of my conscience I
> passed away from them.[33]

It was the ability to organise thoughts and words which he shows here
that enabled him to defeat the Archbishop's attempt to drive him into
admitting his undoubted heresy. Thorpe in this passage stands out as

superior to most of his contemporaries in two ways which show this control. Firstly, when he accumulates terms in parallel, nearly all add something to the meaning of the passage. Secondly, he is able to suspend constructions, insert complex subordinate units, and carry on afterwards. He is not always as successful as this.

> I know my soden and unwarned apposing and answering that al they that wil of good hart without faining able them self wilfully and gladly after their conning and their power to folow Christ paciently, traveling busily, prively and apertly in worke and in word, to withdrawe whosoever that they maye from vyces planting in them (if they may) vertues, comforting them and furthering them that standeth in grace: so that therwith they be not born up into vain glory, thorow presumpcion of their wisdom, nor enflamed with any worldly prosperitie: but ever meke and pacient, purposing to abide stedfastly in the Wil of God, sufferyng wilfully and gladly without anye grutching whatsoever rodde the Lord will chastise them wyth, than this good Lord will not forget to comfort all such men and women in all theyr tribulacions, and at every poynt of temptacyon that any ennemy purposeth for to do against them.[34]

Behind this sentence there is a drive to agglomerating comprehensive statement not uncommon at the time. Thorpe loves to accumulate parallels like this into an annihilating completeness, and he can usually control his syntax while he is doing it. Here he has slipped. There is no verb or compliment to follow "apposing and answering": we cannot tell whether Thorpe had meant to say that he knew that his "answering" was true, or that it would please God, or that it would infuriate the Archbishop. And he has almost lost control of the next clause. His syntax is not picked up properly from his first "they", after the enormous relative clause which makes up the major part of the sentence. Instead of saying that they "will be comforted" by the Lord, Thorpe here draws on the resources which less ambitious writers used all the time. He claps on a paratactic "then" and a couple of its commonest demonstrative concomitants: a "this [good Lord]" and an "all such [men and women]" to reassure the reader that he is still treating the same subject, although both author and audience may by now be unclear about the way in which beginning and end are related.

There are other matters which do not fall as definitely as leaving out the complement of a verb into the class of mistakes, in which Thorpe's touch is not always sure. His doublings of statements sometimes make him seem clumsy, as do the changes of construction from a series of infinitives to a series of present participles, and the frequent (and occasionally conflicting) prepositions which order the elements of his long sentences. In the face of this, the high praise he has sometimes received is unjustified,[35] but he can control a complicated whole despite the conspicuous effort and occasional mistakes, and his control marks the future trend of English prose.

The most individual prose writer of the fifteenth century was Reginald Pecock, who produced the first good philosophical disquisition in English. His claim to fame relies on his ability to produce not merely a sentence but a whole book which is foreseen in advance, where each paragraph has its appointed place, and the argument proceeds massively through *pro* and *contra* to its conclusion.[36] Latin is an inspiration to Thorpe, but a model to Pecock. He thinks in scholastic Latin though he expresses himself in English. Since the English of his time was not adequate to express what he wanted to say, he had to coin words from Latin, French, and English to embody his ideas, and borrow Latin structure to relate them to one another. But the Latin which he borrows from is not any Latin, but the highly structured Latin of medieval philosophy. Pecock's sentences become long and crowded with proliferating dependents so that no side issue is left to the imagination. Typical is his introduction to his defence of the curious Franciscan habit of handling money with sticks to avoid touching it:

The justifying of the iij^e governaunce spokun bifore in the xij^e chapiter of this present v^e partie schal be in ij causis, of which the firste is this: Whanne ever eny deede or thing is to be forborn or left, for that it is yvel, or for that it is perilose, or for eny other good cause, it is alloweable, yhe, and preiseable forto forbere the neighing and the entermeting and the homelynes with the same thing; as whanne evere and where ever fleischli love to a womman is to be forborn, it is preiseable forto forbere the nyghing and the homeli cumpeniyng with hir; and in lijk maner, for that Adam and Eve oughten have forborne the eting of the appil in Paradise, it hadde be good and preisable if thei hadden forborn the entermeting which thei maden aboute the appil in it biholding, handling, taasting, ymagynyng, and questiouns theraboute moving.[37]

We notice that the organisation of the sentence is tight and logical: general principle, examples, and detailed application of the principle to the examples. The sequence of tenses is sound, and the distinctions between "allowable" and "praiseable", "evil" and "perilous" are neat and meaningful. The list with which the sentence closes does not merely produce a forceful-sounding climax by repetition, but distinguishes and names all the dangerous elements of "entermeting". Nothing is redundant.

This sentence introduces a subtle and acute argument on the friars' odd way of dealing with money, which, though finally unconvincing (since we know the weakness of all men), yet persuades us that it might be a useful devotional practice to men who were of the good will which he assumes, and not just an occasion for conspicuous hypocrisy, as it is assumed to be in Chaucer's *Summoner's Tale*. Its ability to persuade is the product of its organisational power, and reveals the mental grasp of the vain, tactless, sincere, scholarly, religious man who wrote it.

The eccentric style of Reginald Pecock is a linguistic sport. More central in his time is the writing of Nicholas Love, who writes a more consistently beautiful prose than any other English author of the late middle ages. Before 1410, he translated and expanded parts of the Latin *Meditationes Vitae Christi*, a gospel paraphrase attributed to St Bonaventure, and presented it to the same Archbishop Arundel who had examined William Thorpe. This book, the *Mirror of the Blessed Lyf of Jesu Christ*, became the most popular single English book in the fifteenth century.[38] Like the two writers' just examined, his style is markedly influenced by Latin, but unlike Thorpe he is in control all the time, and unlike Pecock's, his style is governed primarily by linguistic rather than logical criteria. Among fifteenth-century translators he is unique in that he can write as well as his source, in the same style, handling syntactic relationships with apparent ease.[39] He can use complex formal parallels to clarify his matter, as here:

> Children haven nede to be fedde with mylke of lyghte doctrine, and not with sadde mete of grete clergie and of highe contemplacioun.[40]

A scholastic precision is sometimes evident in his terms, as well as in the structure of his exposition. Apposition, subordination, and things omitted but to be understood come easily to him. In this and in his use of participles, relatives, and other pronouns he is inspired by Latin. Sometimes what he has to say is directly modelled on Latin, but even then Love can alter and expand while preserving the general structure of his original:

> Now take we here entente to the manere of hym in this clepinge and gederinge of his disciples, and of his conversacioun with hem; hou lovely he speketh to hem, and how homely he scheweth hym selfe to hem; drawynge hem to his love withynneforthe by grace and withouteforthe by dede; famylierly ledynge hem to his moder house, and also goynge with hem often to her dwellynges, techynge and enfourmynge hem; and so in alle other manere beinge as besy aboute hem, and with as grete cure as the moder is of hir owne sone.[41]

The patterns of repetition in the English are a little different from those in the Latin:

> Considera ergo et conspice eum in predictis vocationibus et conversatione cum ipsis; quam affectuose vocat eos reddens se eis affabilem, modestum, benignum, et obsequiosum: intus et extra; ducens eos ad domum matris et familiariter vadens ad domos eorum. Docebat etiam eos et curam de ipsis habebat precipuam sicut mater de unico filio suo.[42]

Love has run the two sentences of his source into one, so diffusing the influence of the closing simile over the whole pattern of clauses; cut the string of adjectives stressing Christ's condescension down to the adverb "homely"; and expanded "intus et extra", which must surely mean "indoors and out", into the different contrast of the worlds of grace and nature. We need not pursue the reasons why he might want to do this; for our purpose the important consideration is that he is able to.

He is equally in control when writing on his own, as when he closes his discussion of the grace of silence:

> Where of and othere vertuouse exercise that longeth to con- templatyf lyvynge, and specially to a recluse; and also of medled lyf, that is to saye somtyme actyfe and somtyme contemplatyf as it longeth to dyverse persones that in worldely astate haven grace of goostly love, who so wole more pleynely be enformed and taught in Englisshe tonge lete hym loke the tretys that the worthy

clerke and holy lyvere maister Walter Hyltoun, the chanoun of
Thurgartun, wrote in Englische by grace and highe discrecioun;
and he schal fynde there, as I leve, a sufficient scole and a trewe
of alle thise: whose soule reste in evere lastynge blisse and pees, as
I hope he be ful highe in blisse, joyned and knytte with outen
departynge to his spouse Jesu by parfite use of the beste parte that
he chase here with Marye, of the which parte he graunt us
felawschippe, Jesu oure lorde God.[43]

Until this level of competence spread more generally, there would be
things which Englishmen could not say in their own language.

English prose was undoubtedly influenced by Latin, and it may well
have been influenced by French too. And French prose, when it
developed, was more likely than the learned language to affect the
laity. "Mandeville" said that he put his travels in French and English to
make them available to "lordes and knyghtes and othere noble and
worthi men that conne not Latyn but litylle".[44] But in the nature of
things, French influence is harder to detect than Latin. Until the
fourteenth century, French was the dominant language of the English
ruling classes, and this brought a great many French words and phrases
into the English vocabulary. The influence of French in vocabulary is
clear and important. But the French influence on syntax and organisation of language is more difficult to assess. Individual words are easily
adopted from one language to another, and even in large quantity need
not be accompanied by any change in the structure of the debtor
language.

In the early middle ages, there was an additional restricting factor.
Little French prose was written either in England or France, and what
there was was of an elementary kind. Most of what was written for the
Anglo-Norman aristocracy was written in verse, and most commonly
in short couplets which gave little scope for the characteristic virtues of
prose. French prose did not really get under way, even in France, until
the thirteenth century. But by the fourteenth century, continental
French prose, like that of the other major Romance languages, had
developed a competence and complexity which was well ahead of
English.[45] And this was reflected in some of the French prose written
in England, notably in Duke Henry of Lancaster's *Les Seyntz Medicines*,
written in 1352.[46] And it may well have provided a model to some
writers of English prose as well.

The model was certainly accessible. A great deal of French was read in England in the later middle ages as in the earlier. Before 1400, French books seem to have been commoner than English ones.[47] A list of books owned by Richard II in 1385 includes a very high proportion of French romances and no identifiable English books at all.[48] His court seems to have shared his tastes. And towards the end of the next century the Pastons, much lower in society, still had some French books among their English ones.[49] But any assessment of the influence of French prose on English is complicated by the fact that the French achievement is very close to the English potential. In contrast, Latin influence can be irrefutably demonstrated by the appearance of Latin locutions, especially participial constructions which have never had a natural place in English. French influence would produce very few of these, and mainly a tauter grammar and longer, better organised sentences, which might have been evolved without it. And the proportion of French-derived words, as we have seen, has no necessary connection with the influence of French syntax. A recent close investigation of the influence of French on English phrasing could come to no firmer conclusion than that by the fifteenth century the English language had begun to settle down as a new and more stable mixture, but that the new patterns eluded dogmatic statement.[50]

It has been argued by one of the most learned medievalists of recent times that the literature of the middle ages was dominated by rhetoric.[51] This is certainly true of court poetry in English, both the newer verse written under continental influence, and, in its own way, that in the old alliterative tradition. It is true also of a good deal of Latin prose. In the darkest of centuries on the Continent we can find a few writers who can be called "mannerist",[52] and in England in the twelfth century, Gervase of Canterbury clearly has a conception of style in mind by which he distinguishes the chronicler like himself from the historian proper:

> Historicus diffuse et eleganter incedit, cronicus vero simpliciter graditur et breviter. "Proicit" historicus "ampullas et sesquipedalia verba;" cronicus vero "silvestrem musam tenui meditatur avena".[53]

And in the fifteenth century there was a revival among writers of Latin of a more flowery prose full of rhetorical tropes, exemplified in the writings of John of Whetehamstede, Abbot of St Albans.[54] His contemporary Thomas Bekynton, who seems to have acquired some feeling for classical literature in the household of Humphrey of Gloucester, was very rude about Whetehamstede's prose,[55] but it manifested greater linguistic ability than was found in the contemporary vernacular.

Except in a few writers, nearly all in the mystical tradition, we do not find the rhetorical impulse full-blown in English medieval prose, which is practical in intention and usually prosaic in both senses. Far from being able to superimpose the additional patterns of rhetorical tropes and figures on their writings, the writers all too often had insufficient control of the patterns of the language itself. Even famous writers like Lydgate could produce sentences which were a tangle of subordinate clauses with no main clause to centre on. In this matter, English translation is very revealing.[56] Translations were very popular, and five-sixths of the printed books published in English in the fifteenth century were translations. The translators felt no sense of responsibility towards the *ipsissima verba* of their texts, and some of them say explicitly that they intend to reproduce the thoughts rather than the words of their originals. They add or leave out what they please, but when they do reproduce their originals, they almost all, with remarkable unanimity, follow them word for word. The translators as a body obviously had little confidence in English prose or in themselves. The only common impulse towards change is a tendency slightly to simplify the most complicated syntax of their originals. Word-for-word translation allows the translators to preserve some remarkably subtle and complex patterns from Latin and French, in sharp contrast to the syntactic chaos which ensues when they interpolate passages of their own composition. Caxton and Berners are eminent examples of this. Paradoxically, the translations may have shown their readers what could be done in the future. There is certainly a remarkable improvement in the standard of original English prose after about 1480, but in the meantime, the greater part of that prose remained competent only when organised on a simple level.

It is significant that a writer who was capable of a good deal more could remain satisfied with this simplicity. In John Capgrave's *Chronicle of England*, completed about 1463, and particularly in the early part, the author is content to express himself in very short simple note-like sentences, often without conjunctions and sometimes without verbs. Describing the Book of Ezekiel, he writes:

> He sey a glorious trone in the firmament. He receyved a book, and ete it. He sey many sites, in whech divers kynges and puples for synne schuld be distroyed.[57]

When he wants to be, Capgrave is competent in a variety of preposi-
tional phrases, and can handle apposition, lists, or complex explanations
without losing the thread of his syntax. Not surprisingly, his prose is
then reminiscent of Latin. But never for long. It has been fairly said of
him that though his is not the extremely plain structure observed in the
earliest English chronicles, it never shows hypotaxis over long
sequences.[58]
    It was impossible for this age of linguistic innocence to last if
English prose were written in increasing quantity. Whether from the
influence of Latin or French, or verbatim translation, or mere pro-
ficiency increasing with practice, the prose writers were bound to
develop an awareness of their medium and a control over it. Watching
them feel their way towards this, often apparently unconsciously, is
one of the fascinations of English prose at the end of the middle ages.
    Although the more competent writers were beginning to use English
in patterns like those of Latin, the conscious heightening of English
style was largely achieved through diction, not syntax. In many
writers of the late medieval and early Tudor periods we can see an
awareness of the force of the individual word rather than of patterns of
words. That old-fashioned and rather solemn Tudor statesman, Sir
Thomas Elyot, set about supplying the linguistic deficiencies of the
English administrative class by adding Latin-derived terms to the
vocabulary, one by one.[59] William Dunbar's splendid poem "The
Flyting of Dunbar and Kennedy" is a useful example of the attention
which vocabulary naturally received.[60] It is a *tour de force* of pure
poetry, in the literary sense, a virtuoso display of words used for their
own sake. It is made up of an astonishing range and variety of abusive
nouns and adjectives on a simple argumentative base. Dunbar did have
a sense of poetic structure, as we can see elsewhere in his poetry, and
indeed in most of the best English poets of the middle ages. But such
control as they show over syntax seems to be derived, except in
deliberate rhetorical figures, mainly from their instinctive narrative
skill.
    If poetry got little of this attention, prose was given even less. When
attempts were made to heighten the style of prose, the main resources
were in diction, particularly in alliteration, aureation, and the multiplication of synonyms, not in syntactic patterns or in the tropes and
schemes of rhetoric. These resources of diction, especially alliteration
and the multiplication of synonyms, are among the natural resources of
the language, available to all its users. We find them used at all levels,

most intensively, consistently, and consciously by the most educated, but sporadically and instinctively by others. Few medieval authors were less educated than Margery Kempe, who was unable to read or write at all, and had to dictate her book to others. Unlike the mystical writers proper, she is unaware of the possibilities of rhetoric, and writes a simple prose only assisted by the resources of common speech. Among these we notice alliteration and repetition of terms.[61] Her sentences are short and rather monotonous, with no great variety of conjunctions. But she is fond of using two words to convey one concept, and these sometimes alliterate. This can at times grow into a piling up of words for the sake of emphasis.

Alliteration is likely to be conspicuous in any literature which is read aloud, as medieval literature normally was.[62] Among the most highly educated writers, we find that alliteration is one of the distinguishing marks of the prose of Richard Rolle, both in Latin and English, and Chaucer, for all his dismissal of "rum, ram, ruf", tries to reproduce the alliterative patterns of Boethius.[63] But when alliteration is one of the organising forces of language, redundant expression is always a danger, as we see in this passage from the epistle dedicatory which John Trevisa prefaced to his important translation of Ranulph Higden's *Polychronicon*:

> I, John Trevisa, . . . obedient and buxom to work your will, hold in heart, think in thought, and mean in mind your meedful meaning and speech that ye spake and said. . . . I will fond to take that travail . . . as God granteth me grace, for blame of backbiters will I not blinne; for envy of enemies, for evil spiting and speech of evil speakers will I not leave to do this deed; for travail will I not spare.[64]

Trevisa's wish for alliteration has led him into verbiage. It is difficult to see any difference among the four forms of malice he refers to, or his four assertions of determination, or to feel that all four of either are necessary for emphasis.

In the passage quoted, Trevisa combines alliteration and the multiplication of synonyms, but his vocabulary is English. Latin diction, however, also had its attractions. The associations of Latin-derived words with the learned, exotic, and precise language from which they were taken gave them a decorative as well as a functional use. It is well known that some fifteenth-century English poetry suffered from an

excess of aureate diction, but we can also find this diction in prose.
Lydgate uses it to heighten the style of his little history of Caesar and
Pompey:

> To exclude the false surquedie veyneglory and idill laude this
> forseide wrecche schulde of custome and of consuetude smyte the
> conquerroure ever in the necke and uppon the hed. . . .[65]

Caxton was the first layman to show an awareness of alternative ranges
of vocabulary, and he intermittently achieved a diction distinguished
by what he calls "fayr and straunge termes".[66] But despite his unusual
awareness of "register" in diction, his control of syntax was weak. He
was at least aware that it had possibilities. He wanted to avoid the
simple manner of earlier writers, and often tried to do so by the use of
relative sentences and clauses, sometimes piling them on top of one
another until he forgot to complete the earlier ones.[67] At times he
could control a whole series of phrases in apposition, especially the
formulaic series of titles in a dedication, but at others he used all his
knowledge of Latin syntax, particularly of relative and participial
constructions, to attempt to maintain the continuity of his thought,
only to plunge despite himself into ambiguity and solecism.

Caxton admired and was surpassed by that extraordinary cleric, John
Skelton,[68] who in some ways expresses the quintessence of the middle
ages at the very end of them. Most of Skelton's prose has been lost, but
some passages survive interspersed with his poems. In his last work, the
satirical poem "A Replycacion agaynst Certayne Young Scolers"
(1527) we find a prose passage in which the author outdoes even
Dunbar in spectacular linguistic display:

> Over this, for a more ample processe to be farther delated and
> contynued, and of every true christenman laudably to be enployed,
> justifyed, and constantly mainteyned; as touchyng the tetrycall
> theologisacion of these demy divines, and stoicall studiantes, and
> friscaioly yonkerkyns, moche better bayned than brayned, basked
> and baththed in their wylde burblyng and boyling blode, fervently
> reboyled with the infatuate flames of their rechelesse youthe and
> wytlesse wontonnesse, enbrased and enterlased with a moche
> fantasticall frenesy of their insensate sensualyte, surmysed unsurely
> in their perihermeniall principles, to prate and to preche proudly
> and leudly, and loudly to lye; and yet they were but febly

enformed in maister Porphiris problemes, and have waded but
weakly in his thre maner of clerkly workes, analeticall, topicall,
and logycall: howbeit they were puffed so full of vaynglorious
pompe and surcudant elacyon, that popholy and pevysshe
presumpcion provoked them to publysshe and to preche to people
imprudent perilously, how it was idolatry to offre to ymages of
our blessed lady, or to pray and go on pylgrimages, or to make
oblacions to any ymages of sayntes in churches or els where.
Agaynst whiche erronyous errours, odyous, orgulyous, and
flyblowen opynions, &c.[69]

And he continues in verse. The syntax is firm enough, holding parallel
constructions, antitheses, and subordinate clauses through an inordin-
ately long sentence, but the main and most striking characteristic of
this prose is the vocabulary displayed on this framework. Words a foot
and a half long, of the kind Gervase had recommended to the ambitious
learned writer, mingle with onomatopoeia and forceful popular
coinages from daily life, like "burbling", "popeholy", and "flyblown".
French, Latin, and English words are forced together by the thread of
the argument and the links of alliteration. Like Trevisa, Skelton
duplicates his statements, but unlike Trevisa he usually means something slightly different the second time. "Preaching proudly" is not
quite the same as "prating", and hence adds meaning as well as
emphasis to the argument. Aureation, alliteration, and synonyms are
the characteristic of heightened medieval prose style, and in this
Skelton is medieval. But in his reaching towards a more elaborate and
complex syntax he is more a forerunner of the Elizabethans.
    These are the writers who are significant of the future. With the
spread of printing and lay education, both the elaboration of syntax, as
yet unconscious, and the exploitation of diction came to dominate
sixteenth-century prose. The most important milestone was passed in
1524, when Leonard Cox wrote the first manual of rhetoric in English.
The consciousness of rhetoric came to percolate into some very dark
corners. For instance, in the summer of 1538, the mayor and some of
the citizens of Rye denounced their curate to the royal council. Among
the charges which they thought would tell against the unfortunate man
was the accusation that he could not be understood when he read the
Bishop's Book aloud, "for he cannot rede the rethoryck wordes."[70]
Words were becoming more exciting and more accessible, and ignorance of them was something to be ashamed of. With the spread of

printing, a wider reading public developed, each member of which was more familiar with the written word, and each member of which could respond to the words at his own speed, not at a speed set by a lector. Authors could now profitably exploit the expressive potentialities of writing, and encouraged by the Renaissance belief in the power of rhetoric, the Elizabethans took to language like strong drink. In contrast to this kind of writing, we have what one is tempted to call the "non-tradition" of lay prose. Of course many clerics wrote an extremely primitive prose, just as a few laymen like Chaucer and Usk reached a competent if unexciting standard of expression in it. The example of the learned language could have little influence on clerics like Louis de Beaumont, who, when he was elected bishop of Durham in 1318, knew so little Latin that, despite several days coaching before his consecration he could not even read the prescribed words from a book without scandalous mistakes. The balance was somewhat restored, however, when he was succeeded in his see (1333) by the bibliophile Richard de Bury. But capable laymen were less common than ignorant clerics, and even Chaucer found at times that his prose was not adequate to express his thought.[71] When faced with a difficult sentence of Boethius in his translation of *The Consolations of Philosophy*, he tended to string out its clauses with "and", just as lesser men did. It is quite common to find him repeating a key noun when he translated a pronoun referring back to it, as if he were not sure of his own or his audience's ability to grasp antecedents over a long sentence. This pleonastic habit can make his prose seem clogged and over-earnest. But taken as a whole, Chaucer's translation is sufficiently competent to reproduce the meaning and dignity of a far from simple original. Most of his contemporaries and immediate successors were not up to this standard.

When Gregory the Great, at the beginning of the middle ages, had said:

> Imagines et picturae sanctorum, et precipue crucis Christi, sunt libri laicorum,[72]

he had assumed that the laity would be illiterate. And because he was right, the phrase became a medieval commonplace.[73] Literacy was so closely identified with the clergy that the legal advantages of benefit of clergy were extended to any man who was literate. In the early middle ages, even the kings were often entirely illiterate.[74] And throughout the middle ages, the clergy, by virtue of their ability to write, ran the royal administration. The very words "clerk" and "cleric" had not yet become distinct. In the Paston household, the clergy fulfil both clerical functions. But by the fifteenth century, there was a substantial and apparently increasing number of literate laymen.[75] The number of manuscripts copied for laymen as well as clerics grew, and we can discern the beginnings of a mixed and nation-wide literary public, made up of both clergy and laity. It has been suggested that *Piers Plowman* was designed for and successfully captured this audience.[76] By the end of the century it had become necessary to take steps to restrict benefit of clergy to the clergy proper. The causes of the increase in literacy are too complicated to be traced here, but one of them is clearly that land and litigation and literacy go together. Another is that it is also becoming possible for an ambitious man to rise as a layman through the common law, instead of through the ecclesiastical doctorates in canon law and theology. Lower down the social scale, literacy was required in any trade which needed records, as we can see, for instance, in the Cely Papers. It was possible to obtain elementary instruction even in small towns and villages. By 1533, when printed books had been increasing the demand for two generations, Thomas More was able to make the startling suggestion that only about four-tenths of the population was totally unable to write or read.[77]

But it is a long way from the ability to read and write to the mastery of prose, and the man who runs his estates or trades in wool or acts as a justice of the peace need not be steeped in the written word. Such men write awkward prose. If they are not already common knowledge in his society, a man is only likely to discover the expressive possibilities of prose by continuous reading or writing or both. Reading and writing were still, though to a decreasing degree, the duty and privilege of the clergy. And so laymen, to whom writing was "somewhat tedius and paynefull", can be expected under these conditions to write much as they speak, and to direct their attentions more to the matter than the manner of the message. The laity and a substantial part of the clergy of the fourteenth and fifteenth centuries were made up of men like these. A cultivated and highly literate secular stratum in society is characteristic not of the middle ages but of the Renaissance. Chaucer and Caxton are anomalous in their time, and in Caxton the strain shows.[78]

Some professional lawyers were also anomalous since their work also gave them that familiarity with the written word which we only find otherwise among the clergy. A survey of medieval wills shows

that after about 1400 lawyers join the better endowed clergy, some
regulars, and a few great nobles in owning their own small libraries.[79]
It is appropriate therefore that the best organised piece of English prose
written by a layman during the fifteenth century should come from a
lawyer, the Lord Chief Justice, Sir John Fortescue. He has the ability,
essential to a lawyer, of being able to maintain antecedents and qualify-
ing clauses without ambiguity. We find in his *Governance of England*
sentences like:

> The Romaynes, while thair counsell callid the Senate was gret,
> gate, through the wysdome off that counsell, the lordshippe off
> gret partye of the world.[80]

The main structure of the sentence holds syntactic suspense to the end,
while two major subordinate units interrupt the flow, clearly related to
the noun and verb they qualify. To be able to compose original English
prose with this kind of control at this time was something of an
achievement. Such orderly, complex, competent writing looks forward
to that of another great lawyer in the next century, Sir Thomas
More.

The nobility, for all their possession of libraries, were less capable.
The new humanism was to revolutionize the writing of prose. But it
has been made clear by an authority on Renaissance trends in fifteenth-
century England that only two English peers took enough interest in
humanism even to patronise the efforts of others.[81] Although important
as patrons in diffusing the new learning, both were themselves indifferent scholars.[82] Against these two noblemen, Humphrey, Duke of
Gloucester, and John Tiptoft, Earl of Worcester, we may set the more
representative figure of the second Duke of York (the Aumerle of
Shakespeare's *Richard II*). About 1410, he translated a manual on
hunting by Gaston Phoebus, Count of Foix.[83] The book is representative of English writing of its time in that it is practical, it is closely based
on a French original with some additions, and its subject is the ancient
pastime of the nobility. It is also typical in making no attempt whatever
at the literary graces. On the linguistic level, the body of the work is
told in clauses in the simplest conjunction, and the author is really at
ease only with them. When he tries something more complicated than
telling of the hunter's task piece by piece, he gets into difficulties. Early
in the book the Duke tries to apply to hunting the familiar justification
of a course of conduct that it makes a man eschew idleness:

He [sc. the hunter] ne may not be idel ne hym nedeth thenk no where but for to do his office and whan he hath uncoupled yit is he lasse ydel and lasse shuld thynk in eny synnes for he hath ynowe to doon to ryde or foot wel with his houndes and to be ay ny hem and to hue or rout wel and blow wel and to loke wheraftir he hunteth, and which houndes bene vanchasours and parfiters and redresse and brynge his houndys in to the ryght whan thei han envoised and fallen rascaile and whan the hert is ded or what other chace that he hunteth, for yit is he lasse ydel and lasse shuld thenk to don evel for he hath ynowe to doon to thenke to wel undo his hert in his kynde and wel to reyse that hym perteyneth and wele to doone his cure and to loke how many of his houndes lakketh of hem that he brought to the woode in the mornyngis, and for to seke hem and to couple hem.[84]

There is an engaging *naïveté* in the way in which he is desperately hanging on to his meaning throughout. He clearly lacks the command of language which would enable him to grasp and use the patterns of this long sentence to control the material in it, nor can he distinguish the material into several sentences and relate them to each other. He wants to relate every part of hunting to the justification of the whole, that hunting keeps a man too busy to sin. The more aspects of hunting he mentions, the more convincing the explanation will be: but the more clauses he puts in, the more faintly the later ones will be felt to be controlled by his original proposition. By the time he is half way through, he has nearly lost his syntax. There is no formal subject for "redresse", and the natural one seems to be "vanchasours", the front dogs in the pack. The reader has to fight his way through a tangle of clauses to work out from the context that "redresse" is one of the things the hunter "hath ynowe to doon". In his struggle, Edward has lost the infinitive marker "to" which would reveal this, and which he has been using for this purpose earlier in the sentence. He is only able to regain control by repeating at length the formula with which he has started, that the hunter has too much to do to have time for sin. He then adds the rest of the hunter's daily routine, and stops. We do not need to assess his thinking as moral philosophy: the internal organisation of this piece is enough to reveal the noble author's lack of intellectual sophistication.

All Edward can handle with confidence is a single narrative thread. And, as we might expect, the paragraph suffers from the same deficiency as the sentence. The passage in which this sentence is found is an attempt to demonstrate that hunting conduces to health in this world and salvation in the next. But to achieve this Edward has to fall back on a detailed enumeration of events in the whole twenty-four hours, with interjections: to opt for a basis of narrative rather than argument as such. Narrative provides a writer with its own structure because there is a temporal sequence in the events related, and so it does not make the demands which argument does on a writer's ability himself to give form to inchoate material.

It is interesting to compare with this extract an amusing passage in which a Tudor chronicler ascribed almost the same motive (among others) to one of the characters of his story. In his *Union of Lancastre and York*, Edward Hall is describing the Duke of Orleans of Henry IV's reign:

> Aboute this season Loys Duke of Orliaunce brother to the Frenche Kyng, a man of no lesse pryde than haute courage, wrote letters to Kynge Henry advertysyng hym, that he, for the perfighte love whiche he bare to the noble feates of chyvalrie and marciall actes, in avoidying the slowe worme and deadely Dormouse called Idlenes, the ruine of realmes and confounder of nobilitie, and for the obteignying of laude and renoune by deades of armes and manly enterprises, coulde imagine or invent nothyng eyther more honourable or laudable to them bothe, then to mete in the fielde. . . .[85]

This is only the first third of his sentence. Hall has no difficulty in attaching not one but three motives to his story. The avoidance of idleness is elaborated into a complicated and decorative rhetorical phrase, and slipped expertly into a subordinate clause in an already complex sentence, without depriving the author of the energy to build further patterns of sounds and words, or to follow out his sense.

Hall's chronicle is heavily dependent on Polydore Vergil's Latin *Historia Anglica*, but logical and rhetorical patterning came also to dominate original prose; not only in the expository writing where it was so obviously needed, but also in narrative fiction. In the most famous of the expository writings of Elizabethan England, Hooker's *Ecclesiastical Polity*, we find thought which, though firm and eloquent, is not concise, and which could not have been expressed in English without an elaborate syntax to order and clarify the author's complex material. But a yet more rhetorical control, and one beyond the strict needs of the matter, can be seen exercised for its own sake in Lyly's and Sidney's romances, and above all in Nashe's *Lenten Stuffe* (1599), where a mock-encomium on the red herring provides the author with an occasion for obtaining every variety of effect which organised prose can give. English prose of this time had become something very different from that of the fifteenth century.

Despite a handful of exceptions, nearly all clerics, the Duke of York is all too representative of fifteenth-century prose. The letter-writers and the chroniclers are particularly uncomfortable in explanation, and only at ease with the simpler syntax and given structure which is possible in narrative. They tend to avoid elaborate participial constructions, suspended clauses, and passages in apposition to the main structural units of a sentence. Even Caxton, for all his experience, falls back on parataxis for story-telling, as for instance in the tale of the rich dean and the poor priest with which he ends his version of Æsop, or the well-known anecdote of the Kentishwoman who did not understand the Yorkshire word for eggs.[86] The following passage about Hengist and Vortigern is typical of the dominant parataxis in the early part of *The Brut*, the most popular history of England in the fifteenth century:

> And at that day the kyng come with his conseil, as it was ordeynede; but Engist hade warnede his knyghtes priveliche, and ham commandede that everyche of ham shulde put a longe knyf in his hose; and whan he saide, "faire sires! now is tyme forto speke of love and pees," everyche anone shulde draw his knyf and slee a Britoun. And so thai quellede xxx M and lxj of knyghtes; and with miche sorwe meny of ham ascapede; and Vortyger him-self was taken and lade to Twongecastell, and put into prisoun; and somme of Engistes men wolde that the kyng hade bene brent al quyk. And Vortiger tho, to have his lif, grauntede ham as miche as thai wolde axen, and yaf up all the lande, tounes and castelles, citees, and burghes, to Engist and to his folc.[87]

This simplicity is not without its advantages. It helps to add verisimilitude to even the more improbable fictions of *Mandeville's Travels*, and it can give a dignified pathos to tragic moments in the chronicles. Among fifteenth-century letter-writers, William Lomnor's letter telling John Paston I of the murder of the Duke of Suffolk is justly famous, but it is matched by the anonymous chronicler who records the judicial murder of the Earl of Lancaster.[88] The hasty trial, the buffeting of the brutal soldiers who knocked Lancaster about and snowballed him on his way to execution, and his fear of death are set off by the simplicity of the style in which they are related. There was still a future for this style for some time to come. It finds its last great embodiment at the very end of the seventeenth century, in the *Journal* of George Fox, the founder of the Quakers.[89] Unlike most of his contemporaries, but like the writers of the "non-tradition" we have distinguished, Fox had had little formal education to show him the expressive possibilities of a complicated written prose. He preferred simplicity anyway, and like Margery Kempe, he did not write his book, but dictated it to a succession of amanuenses. We are not surprised therefore, to find a simple paratactic style very like that of the fifteenth-century chronicles, a style which only emphasises the passionate sincerity and indefatigable endurance communicated by the *Journal*.

But nevertheless, the chronicle style is a very limited one, unsuitable for reflecting the movement of a sophisticated mind, for organising complicated material, or delivering ironic judgements, and it is doomed to extinction by the proliferation of the printed word. It was broadly in this "non-tradition", already in his time a little old-fashioned, that Malory wrote.

III

Narration

An author who tells a story will not normally use language uniformly throughout his book. An imitation of an action will demand both narrative and descriptive writing in various proportions, and it will be unusual if it has no place for direct speech or commentary by the narrator. Malory uses all four of these modes, and since each makes different demands on his medium, it will be convenient to consider them separately. The categories have a good deal in common, and something of what we discover of each is likely to be true of the others. There is, for instance, little narration which does not call up some kind of picture in the reader's mind. But the distinctions will serve to bring different sets of problems into focus.

We may well begin by examining the narrative proper, both because it is statistically preponderant in the *Morte Darthur*, and because it is the simplest to deal with. In an examination of the narrative we shall be able to establish certain conclusions which we shall find are partly valid for the other modes, but in which we shall not be confused by the various special circumstances which attend those other modes by their very nature. We closed the last chapter with an assertion that Malory was writing "lay prose", helped only by the traditions of the spoken language, and not by those extra resources which accumulate in a tradition of written prose, and which were to come to dominate Elizabethan English. There is no hint of the future in Malory's prose. If Dunbar is pure literature, Malory is very impure literature indeed. Of all the great English authors, he shows the least interest in words for their own sake. This is not what we expect in a prose romance. From Sidney's *Arcadia* to Mervyn Peake's *Gormenghast*, the English prose romance has cultivated an artificial and decorated expression. In a less extreme form, the romances nearer in time to Malory, including his own French sources and Lord Berners' *Arthur of Little Britain,* display a style discernibly more literary than Malory's.

But Malory is not writing an ordinary romance. He is putting romance material into chronicle form. We can begin to see where the distinction lies if we look at the difference between the very first sentences of the *Morte Darthur* and of that most literary romance, Chaucer's *Knight's Tale.* The two authors have the same problem to solve, but they go about it in different ways. Both are dealing in material which is notoriously fantastic, and both must somehow make the reader or listener suspend his disbelief. Later in the *Canterbury Tales,* the Nun's Priest uses the incredibility of romance subjects to turn upside down his affirmation of the truth of his own tale.

> This storie is al-so trewe, I undertake,
> As is the book of Launcelot de Lake,
> That wommen holde in ful gret reverence.[1]

Chaucer must neutralise this attitude if the first of his tales is to succeed. And so he begins:

> Whylom, as olde stories tellen us,
> Ther was a duk that highte Theseus;
> Of Athenes he was lord and governour,
> And in his tyme swich a conquerour,
> That gretter was ther noon under the sonne.[2]

As we might say, "once upon a time . . . ," and so he charms us into suspending our disbelief, with the familiar disclaiming formula. It was all a long time ago, and things were different then. Malory on the other hand opens with matter-of-fact exactness; he might be continuing a set of annals:

> Hit befel in the dayes of Uther Pendragon, when he was kynge of all Englond and so regned, that there was a myghty duke in Cornewaill that helde warre ageynst hym long tyme, and the duke was called the duke of Tyntagil. [V 7.1]

He does not make us suspend our disbelief: he assumes our belief, and gains it by the very absence of suasions. This is not to suggest that Malory was a fifteenth-century Defoe, deliberately exploiting a matter-of-fact style for the sake of verisimilitude. The occasional inconsistency of his style, of which we must say more later, prohibits such an idea. Rather, we can reasonably trace this chronicle style to a motive shared by the chroniclers and letter-writers of Malory's time, with whom we have already noted his stylistic affinity in one point. They wrote with an interest in their matter and, with rare exceptions, show none of the element of play which is almost always found, however sublimated, detached, or disinterested, in what we call literature. Malory's interest was in King Arthur, and his unselfconscious expression shows many of the characteristics of speech which these other writers share. In the previous chapter we have already looked at one of these characteristics, the element of complex organisation in language. But there are others, and as speech is by no means a uniform thing, we must see which occur in what proportions in the *Morte Darthur,* if we are to recognise the kind of world which the book presents to our imagination.

Some of these characteristics have been identified in recent work on Chaucer. In an article on Chaucer's colloquial English, Professor Margaret Schlauch distinguished three main structure traits in it: repetition, ellipsis, and special syntax.[3] By special syntax she means the use of parataxis to express complex relationships which in consequence must be understood partly from the context. We will consider these three traits as they arise in Malory's work before going on to deal with some points she does not include. Of the three, parataxis is the most pervasive, and we will examine it first.

The basis of all Malory's story-telling is the simple declarative sentence or collocation of co-ordinate main clauses, and the expression by this of a sequence of actions, perceptions, or facts. This is a primitive and fundamental narrative device. Its predominance in Malory establishes a characteristic tone of flat truth which the more accomplished, fluent, and varied subordination of clauses in his French sources cannot convey. His is the chronicle style, and we find extreme examples of it in the Paston Letters and the Cely Papers:

> I met Roger Wyxton a thyssyd Northehamton and he
> desyryd me to do so myche as drynke with hys whyfe at Laysetter
> and after that I met with Wylliam Daulton and he gave me a tokyn
> to hys mother and at Laysetter I met with Rafe Daulton and he
> brahut me to hys mother and ther I delyvyrd my tokyn and sche

prayd me to come to brekefaste on the morrow and so I ded and
Plomton bothe and ther whe had a gret whelfar and ther whos
feyr oste and I pray yow thanke them for me Syr and ye be
remembyrd whe thaulkyd togydyr in hour bed of Dawltonys
syster and ye ferryd the condyscyons of father and brethyrn byt
ye neyd not I saw hyr and sche whos at brekefaste with hyr
mother and ws sche ys as goodly a yeunge whomane as fayr as
whelbodyd and as sad as I se hany thys vii yeyr and a good haythe
I pray God that hyt may be inpryntyd in yur mynd to sette yowr
harte ther. . . . [4]

Two striking similar pieces of narrative are William Cely's account of
a skirmish off Calais in 1480 and Margaret Paston's story of an attack
on her chaplain in 1448.[5] Parataxis is the readiest and easiest narrative
style, making the minimum assertion of relationship between the
juxtaposed clauses. And, as one authority puts it: "many fourteenth-
and fifteenth-century writers would seem from their prose to have
been unaware of any thought relationship which cannot be expressed by
'and'."[6]

It is interesting to notice here that some of those few writers in the
vernacular who show that they were aware of other thought relationships think conjunction normal and sufficient. The author of the
prologue to the second edition of the Wycliffite Bible, a corrected
version made about 1388 and usually attributed to John Purvey,
discusses translation from the Latin, giving detailed equivalents
for Latin constructions like the ablative absolute. Significantly he says:

A relatif . . . mai be resolvid into his antecedent with a con-
junccioun copulatif, as thus, *which renneth, and he renneth*.[7]

Purvey, if it is he, shows a firm if hardly outstanding grasp of words,
and is certainly not afraid of relative clauses. But if he thought the
simplest relationship of clauses sufficient, people with less knowledge
could certainly be expected to feel that it was too. And so, where the
only relationship to be stated is simple succession, as in narrating
an incident without explanations, parataxis naturally tends to be
dominant.

This can have considerable effect. Parataxis, for instance, is said to be
part-cause of the spurious impression of honesty which "Mandeville"
gives.[8] We get a similar impression of honesty from Malory. Malory

is also unobtrusive. Where complicated syntax would draw the reader's attention to a controlling mind, Malory's simplicity of style leaves our attention on the narrative rather than the narrator. The simplicity of narrative technique allows events to make their own impression on the reader, so that they seem to have an objective existence. Two features of style which have attracted many authors would have destroyed this. If the language were strongly patterned or exotic in vocabulary or otherwise the obvious product of art, or if on the larger scale of narrative the author's reflections on the action or his advance knowledge of what was going to happen later were to intrude into the story, this impression of objectivity would be lost. But we do not know what is going to happen and we are almost never shown a character's thoughts, let alone given an analysis of him by an omniscient author. We will examine Malory's function as narrator more fully at a later stage; but here it will suffice to note that the narrator's commentary is so limited and his advance knowledge so fragmentary as we are shown it, that both seem to put the teller of the tale on the same level as its readers and actors, as spectators of something which is happening outside them all. This effect of making the reader a spectator is one of the things which the *Morte Darthur* has in common with the rather different art of the Icelandic sagas. The events in the *Morte Darthur*, with the moral overtones which are built into them, seem simply to happen of themselves. For instance:

> And there he pyght hys pavylyons and sought all the contrey to fynde a towmbe, and in a chirch they founde one was fayre and ryche. And than the kyng lette putte hem bothe in the erthe, and leyde the tombe uppon them, and wrote the namys of hem bothe on the tombe. [V 71.25]

The majority of Malory's narrative sentences and many of his main clauses begin with "and", "but", "then", "for", and "so". This establishes a continuity in the flow of his prose, each sentence taking up from its predecessor. Sentences with "zero starts" are rare. We might expect this at a time before modern grammar and punctuation had trained writers to feel the existence of the sentence as a unit of thought, complete in itself and separate from its context. The development of this feeling was a gradual process, but some would say it was not complete until Milton.[9] Nor was it until well after Malory that the English paragraph became an established structural unit in prose.[10] So it is not surprising that the co-ordination within and between Malory's sentences urges the reader steadily on into the story.

But the continuity of Malory's narrative is occasionally spurious. Sometimes Malory's conjunctions connect things which have no natural connection. He will even use "for" and "so" for this, despite their firmly established causal value in his time.[11] But the continuity is established, whether justified or not, and this device is still common today in the speech of the sub-literate, who use it, at the expense of narrative variety, to prevent others from interrupting their train of thought. The example above is of simple sequential action, but Malory tends to parataxis even when his facts are more complicated:

> In the bedde lay a good man syke, and had a crowne of golde uppon his hede. (*which* had . . .) [V 1028.17]

> Than the kynge and the quene were gretely displeased with sir Gawayne for the sleynge of the lady, and there by ordynaunce of the queene there was sette a queste of ladyes uppon sir Gawayne, and they juged hym for ever whyle he lyved to be with all ladyes and to fyght for hir quarels; and ever that he sholde be curteyse, and never to refuse mercy to hym that askith mercy. [V 108.29]

The internal organisation of the clauses in the second example is unusually varied and complicated for Malory, especially so early, but the basic structure is still paratactic, one fact laid end to end with the next. Though Malory later became more competent in handling clauses, the simple unqualified main clause always remained the staple of his narrative style. This development in the *Morte Darthur* is very similar to that in the main part of *The Brut*.[12]

Just as Malory was normally sparing with adjectives, so he kept to the simplest, most natural, and most unobtrusive syntax. Even in hypotaxis we often find the order of narration is the same as the order of events.[13] So his commonest hypotactic constructions are adverbial clauses of time to open a sentence, and clauses of result to close it, as, for example:

> And as kynge Arthure loked besyde hym he sawe a knyght that was passyngely well horsed. And therewith kynge Arthure ran to hym and smote hym on the helme, that hys swerde wente unto his teeth, and the knyght sanke downe to the erthe dede. [V 34.6]

> And anone as she saw hym there, she sowned thryse, that all

ladyes and jantyllwomen had worke inowghe to hold the quene
frome the erthe. [V 1251.31]

The simple co-ordinate sentence is much better suited to narrative
than to explanation, as we have seen from other late medieval writers.
Matter matches grammar, and the presentation is normally given in the
order in which things happen or are perceived. Malory is content with
this and makes little effort to indicate simultaneity of action. We do
not notice much more than the occasional pluperfect:

> And by than they had getyn a grete fourme oute of the halle,
> and therewith they all russhed at the dore. [V 1167.8]

We may contrast the general simplicity of Malory's narrative with the
conscious virtuosity of an earlier English poet. In a passage in the
Knight's Tale much longer than the passage just quoted from Malory,
Chaucer exploits all the resources of language and rhetoric to produce
an impressionistic picture in which so much is happening so fast that
no one thing can be fully and accurately perceived:

> The heraudes lefte hir priking up and doun;
> Now ringen trompes loude and clarioun;
> Ther is namore to seyn, but west and est
> In goon the speres ful sadly in arest;
> In goth the sharpe spore in-to the syde.
> Ther seen men who can juste, and who can ryde;
> Ther shiveren shaftes up-on sheeldes thikke;
> He feleth thurgh the herte-spoon the prikke.
> Up springen speres twenty foot on highte;
> Out goon the swerdes as the silver brighte.
> The helmes they to-hewen and to-shrede;
> Out brest the blood, with sterne stremes rede.
> With mighty maces the bones they to-breste.
> He thurgh the thikkeste of the throng gan threste.
> Ther stomblen stedes stronge, and doun goth al.
> He rolleth under foot as dooth a bal.
> He foyneth on his feet with his tronchoun,
> And he him hurtleth with his hors adoun.
> He thurgh the body is hurt, and sithen y-take,
> Maugree his heed, and broght un-to the stake,

As forward was, right ther he moste abyde;
Another lad is on that other syde.[14]

From the first emphatic "Now . . . ," the actions break up into brief
flashes seen without their causes or consequences from all over the
field of battle. A sensory immediacy is conveyed, by parallelism and
powerful running alliteration; by onomatopoeia and that kind of near-
onomatopoeic alliteration which Chaucer favoured for sensory effects;[15]
by crowding demonstratives and near-demonstratives, as in the use of
"he" towards the end; and by bringing the tense, for this passage only,
into the historic present. The amount of linguistic resource is surprising.
In "In goth the sharpe spore in-to the syde," Chaucer even anticipates
a favourite technique of the Augustans, employing the generalising
power latent in the definite article.

There is little attempt in the *Morte Darthur* to show things happening
simultaneously or with the intense immediacy of the description from
Chaucer.[16] In the final fight in the tale of Balin, for instance, the reader
has no feeling that there is an audience watching, except when Balin
himself transfers his attention from his opponent to the towers of the
castle (V 89.25). Malory always tends to simplify his narrative line. The
French prose *Tristan* at one point includes the reaction of the audience
in its account of a joust, but Malory leaves this out and keeps to the
participants.[17]

Malory's simpler narrative line is one of the concomitants of his
simpler, more paratactic prose. The hunting of Lanceor is a good
example of the difference between the moderate French hypotaxis and
Malory's parataxis. The French runs:

> Or dist li contes que quant li chevaliers se fu partis de son hostiel
> ensi armés comme il estoit, il chevaucha et issi fors de la ville et
> trouva les esclos dou chevalier qui devant lui s'en aloit. Et nepor-
> quant il ne le connissoit mie trés bien, mais aventure le mist en
> chelui meisme chemin ou il aloit. Tant chevaucha en tel maniere
> le grant aleure qu'il ataint au pié d'une montaingne le chevalier
> qu'il aloit querant. Il li crie de si loins com il cuide qu'il puist
> oir. . . . [L 18]

The English:

> So thys knyght of Irelonde armed hym at all poyntes and dressed

his shylde on hys sholdir and mownted uppon horsebacke and toke hys glayve in hys honde, and rode aftir a grete pace as muche as hys horse myght dryve. And within a litill space on a mowntayne he had a syght of Balyne, and with a lowde voice he cryde.. ..
[V 68.16]

Malory gives one inconspicuous subordinate clause. The main structure of his passage is a relentless "and ... and ... and ..." which fits the tension of the chase very well, and also gives a notably more realistic effect.[18] The French is fluent and various in its subordination. Its most common grammatical forms all occur here: the adverbial clause of time before a main clause ("quant li chevaliers se fu partis ... il chevaucha"); the casual clause with "que" ("tant chevaucha ... qu'il ataint"); and co-ordination not as strong as in the English ("il chevaucha et issi ... et trouva"). But the numerous usages are so readily varied that no particular form is dominant. And it is noticeable that the simple co-ordinate clauses are handled with a sense of stylistic balance: the second is nearly twice as long as the first, and the third is as long as the other two put together, creating a pleasing symmetry. Both writers become more paratactic when relating action, and especially fighting, but the French author still varies his clause types too much to be strongly mannered. It is noticeable that paratactic simplicity characterises the fighting and journeys throughout the Morte Darthur. For instance:

> Than departed sir Percivale frome hys awnte, aythir makyng grete sorow. And so he rode tyll aftir evyosonge, and than he herde a clock smyte. And anone he was ware of an house closed well with wallys and depe dyches, and there he knocke at the gate. And anone he was lette in, and he alyght and was ledde unto a chamber and sone unarmed. And there he had ryght good chere all that nyght.
>
> And on the morne he herde hys masse, and in the monestery he founde a preste redy at the awter, and on the ryght syde he saw a pew closed with iron, and behynde the awter he saw a ryche bedde and a fayre, as of cloth of sylke and golde. Than sir Percivale aspyed that therein was a man or a woman, for the visayge was coverde. Than he leffte of hys lokynge and herd hys servyse.
> [V 907.19]

And part of the power of the "Morte" comes from the prevailing simplicity of the narrative in contrast to the relative complexity of the dialogue.

The simplicity of Malory's narrative style limits its subtlety, but gives it the opposite strengths of verisimilitude, directness, and pathos. We see this in the pursuit of Lanceor quoted above, and at the climax of the story in:

> And syr Launcelot awok, and went and took his hors, and rode al that day and al nyght in a forest, wepyng. And atte last he was ware of an ermytage and a chappel stode betwyxte two clyffes, and than he herde a lytel belle rynge to masse. And thyder he rode and alyght, and teyed his hors to the gate, and herd masse. [V 1254.1]

This is the simplest form of narrative. The descriptive element is confined to "wepyng", "stode betwyxte two clyffes", and "lytel [belle]". These images stand out in the passage because of their rarity, but they are not complex and neither call for close attention to understand them nor draw attention to the author's skill in finding them. The bulk of the passage consists of the statement of actions in unobtrusive clauses, so that we see them in the order in which they happen to or are perceived by or performed by Lancelot. On arrival we see first the two buildings, then their background, then hear the sound coming from them, then close up on the gate and the entrance to the church for the ceremony. We arrive almost as Lancelot does. It is most important to notice that we have no sensation of an author's mind displayed in grammatical gymnastics between us and the facts of the scene. We need no effort to understand the implications or apprehend facts, as we would for instance in a poem by Browning. It is in keeping with this that there is no place in Malory's narration for irony or discriminated levels of preception or knowledge, in author, reader, and characters. Irony in Malory is only to be found in the mouths of his character, and never in that of his narrator. So the story seems to take place very much of itself, to be reality impinging directly on us rather than to be manipulated artifact, and the reader is free to feel undivided sympathy with Lancelot, and to be affected by the pathos of his situation.

This paratactic narrative is one aspect of the colloquial basis of Malory's prose, in narration as well as dialogue. The underlying drive of colloquial expression is to make the necessary communication forcefully in the fewest words in the least complicated relationship. This relationship can often be simpler than it would be in the written language, because the spoken words can be taken in a wider context, including the tones of voice, gestures, expectations, and assumptions of the speakers. In this situation, even silence can at times have one of a variety of meanings. But nevertheless, the basic tendency of speech towards a paratactic simplicity of structure is varied by certain charateristic complications which the written language rarely displays.

Besides parataxis, Professor Schlauch also considers two of these complications, repetition and ellipsis. Malory's use of repetition and ellipsis, of anacolouthon and of sequence of persons and tenses, are among the ways in which his narrative style resembles speech rather than later and more literary written English. Ellipsis, repetition, and anacolouthon are characteristic of speech because composition and delivery are more nearly simultaneous in the spoken language than they are in the written. This encourages the speaker to deal with one clause at a time: a speaker who was to abandon this would lose the advantages of tentativeness and ease of delivery in order to gain a complexity which might be needless, and which his audience might lack the training to understand.

Ellipsis is a natural feature of speech, since in direct person-to-person communication things which may be left out for the sake of brevity can be inserted later if the hearer is seen not to understand. Literary prose has to use more elaborate formal relationships to guide the reader to a complete understanding which the writer cannot see being achieved. It is a characteristic of Malory's narration that he leaves out on occasion nouns and pronouns, subjects and objects, and even verbs. One scholar has found Malory's use of asyndetic clause constructions particularly noticeable.[19] This can produce formal ambiguity, and among the examples was one which might have been taken as accusative and infinitive, asyndetic relative, or noun clause. Significantly, however, the meaning was the same in each case, and more generally, Malory's competence ensures that his uses of ellipsis rarely lead to misunderstanding.

One of the most striking of his elliptical usages is the omission of the pronoun-subject of verbs:

> He clave the hede downe to the chyne, and felle downe to the erthe dede. [V 116.10]

We have to gather from the context that the subject of the first clause is not also the subject of the second.[20] Unambiguous omission of this type is very common, in some cases amounting to no more than a lesser feeling for the integrity of the sentence than in modern literary prose. Medieval punctuation both reflects and reinforces this. It is not until well into the sixteenth century that the period or full stop came to be reserved for the end of a grammatically complete unit only. So we should not infer too much from cases like:

> He was passyng hevy.... And so departed sore wepynge and cursed the tyme that he was borne. [V 895.29]

> They saw an honde shewynge unto the elbow, and was coverde with rede samyte.... [V 943.7]

It is difficult to tell in many cases whether a synthetic verb was felt to be self-sufficient, or whether a previous pronoun was supplied mentally. Certainly, cases as striking as the first of the three examples cited above are very rare in Middle English,[21] and seem to show little feeling for the more patterned meanings of modern prose.

Malory can also leave out the object of a sentence:

> Insomuche ye have enchaced oute of your courte by whom we were up borne and honoured. [V 1052.14]

And cases like this are also rare. Although omission of the object is common in Middle English, as it is later, it is extremely uncommon when another clause depends on the missing member.[22]

In his omission of the verb we find further proof that Malory's style of narration followed a colloquial pattern, one clause at a time, as Workman says is typical of fifteenth-century prose.[23]

> He arose and fledde, and sir Torre afftir hym.... [V 113.7]

Tor was not fleeing, though at first sight we might think so. Here in fact, we simply have the omission of a verb of motion which can be supplied from the context, as in:

> [They] made hir knyghtes alyght to wythdraw hem to a lytyll wood, and so over a litill ryvir.[24] [V 34.23]

Verbs of action are often omitted in the Middle English verse romances when their auxiliaries are expressed, or where an adverb of place or direction is present.[25] We see this with other types of verb:

> Never jantylman more that ever we herde rede of.   (*dyde* more)
> [V 375.17]

> Ye . . . suffird me in perell of deth.   (*to be* in)   [V 969.15]

> They shewed hym the lettyrs of kynge Arthure, and how he was the gastfullyst man that ever they on loked.   (and *seyde*)
> [V 191.19]

> Now leve here sir Launcelot, all that ever he myght walop. . . .
> (*waloping* all)[26]   [V 1137.5]

Occasionally larger elements of the sentence are left out and have to be understood, though this also rarely brings any difficulty.

> And whan hit happed ony of [the Quenys Knyghtes] to be of grete worshyp by hys noble dedis, than at the nexte feste of Pentecoste, gyff there were ony slayne or dede (as there was none yere that there fayled but there were som dede), than was there chosyn in hys stede that was dede the moste men of worshyp that were called the Quenys Knyghtes.   [V 1121.21]

The Round Table is not mentioned anywhere in this sentence or its context, but to give meaning to the sentence, we must understand "ony *of the Table Rounde*" in the third line. Similarly,

> Than sir Percivale aspyed that therein was a man or a woman, for the visayge was coverde.   [V 907.30]

> They had as much fleyssh and fysshe and wyne and ale, and every man and woman he dalt to twelve pence. . . .   [V 1250.25]

In the first case we must supply "a woman, *he knew nat whych*", and in the second "ale *as they wolde*", to make factual sense. These three examples are of course careless writing, but a man's literary vices are as much part of his style as his virtues. It may not be too much special pleading to argue that an occasional touch of the typical defects of speech adds to the verisimilitude of the colloquial style of Malory.

Repetition is as much part of the colloquial style as ellipsis. It elucidates the structure of speech, where the hearer cannot look back to clarify uncertainty, and so it is sometimes useful to recall or anticipate a subject, or to amplify it later, if in mid-sentence the speaker realises that he has not made himself sufficiently clear. It is necessary to point out that Malory occasionally, especially in his early work, presses on amid repetitions to his end while his syntax disintegrates under him. So we find the restarts of:

> Thenne Merlyn wente to the Archebisshop of Caunterbury and counceilled hym for to sende for all the lordes of the reame . . . that they shold to London come by Cristmas upon payne of cursynge, and for this cause, that Jesu, that was borne on that nyghte, that He wold of His grete mercy shewe some myracle, as He was come to be Kynge of mankynde, for to shewe somme myracle who shold be rightwys kynge of this reame.   [V 12.13]

The colloquial is here brought to confusion.[27] And even later on, Malory tends to occasional small needless repetitions, as if to make sure of his syntax. Sophisticated types of repetition can be and later were exploited in styles whose principal effect was to suggest the tentative mind in action. Malory was no Henry James, but the reader feels something of the same tentativeness in him. We see it in the more competent and unobtrusive colloquial touches when Malory repeats or amplifies a previous pronoun-subject:

> So within a whyle sir Tristrames saw hem byfore hym, two lykly knyghtys.   [V 398.9]

> "And that may nat I suffir that she shulde be brente for my sake."
> [V 1171.15]

Or conversely, when a previously stated subject is recalled more briefly:

> Than hit befelle uppon a day that the good knyghte sir Bleoberys de Ganys, brother unto sir Blamore de Ganys and nye cosyne unto the good knyght syr Launcelot de Lake, so this sir Bleoberys cam. . . .   [V 396.17]

For sir Bors and sir Palomydes and sir Saffir overthrew many knyghts, for they were dedely knyghtes, and sir Blamour de Ganys and sir Bleoberys, wyth sir Bellyngere le Bewse, thes six knyghtes. . . . [V 1192.5]

Anacolouthon, though rarer than ellipsis or repetition, is more striking, since it is a break in construction rather than a mere modification of an existing train of thought. Anacolouthon comes from not thinking far enough ahead, and hence it is used by conscious stylists to suggest sudden inspiration: the great master of this in English prose is Richard Hooker. In Malory we see the phenomenon in various stages of prominence. It is not easy to say when the break in continuity becomes sharp enough to be called anacolouthon, but the beginnings can be seen in the habit of thinking only one clause at a time:

With hym rode syr Kaynus, his sone, and yong Arthur that was hys nourisshed broder; and syr Kay was made knyght at Alhalowmas afore. [V 13.21]

And than all maner of knyghtes were adrad of sir Palomydes, and many called hym the Knyght with the Blacke Shylde; so that sir Palomydes had grete worship.[28] [V 386.21]

In both these relatively simple cases, the meaning would be clearer if the third clause were second. In the last example, the reader is driven for a moment to wonder why the name given to Palomides was especially honorific, then to consider if perhaps the very bestowing of a nickname was a sign that a knight was respected, and at last to realise that the final clause results mainly from the first. So he is prepared for the more definitely dislocated example of:

And whan the kynge of that contrey knew that and saw that felyship (whos name was Estorause), he asked them. . . .[29] [V 1033.19]

This corresponds to a trait of speech in which the change in the tone of voice, which we can now conventionally symbolise by parentheses, would make the meaning clear. This method of clarification was not available to Malory. A similar case occurs in the Paston Letters:

The 13s. 4d. which ye sent by a gentleman's man for my board, called Thomas Newton, was delivered. . . .[30]

It is still found in the language of the following century. In his life of Cardinal Wolsey, Cavendish talks of being lodged "in a gentlemans howsse called Master Hall. . . ."[31] These anacoloutha can be surprisingly long and completely separate from the subject of the sentence they interrupt:

> So whan trumpettis blew unto the fylde and kynge Arthur was sette on hyght uppon a chafflet to beholde who ded beste (but, as the Freynshe booke seyth, the kynge wold nat suffir sir Gawayne to go frome hym, for never had sir Gawayne the bettir and sir Launcelot were in the fylde, and many tymes was sir Gawayne rebuked so whan sir Launcelot was in the fylde in ony justis dysgysed), than som of the kyngis, as kynge Angwysh of Irelonde and the Kynge of Scottis, were that tyme turned to be uppon the syde of kynge Arthur.   [V 1069.8]

The interruption is longer than the main sentence, as it is also in the first sentence of the last subsection of the "Tristram" (V 839.1). Such interruptions are especially common in explanations and at the beginning of sections of narrative. The final subsection of the last part of the *Morte Darthur* begins with a sentence containing two anacoloutha, which need the full resources of modern punctuation to clarify them without alteration of the word order. Even in cases like this, the original construction is picked up and completed, however loosely, afterwards. This reinforces the impression of a spontaneous departure. With these interruptions, our attention is drawn to the mind of a narrator behind the story.

Sequence of persons and of tenses present a few problems in the course of the *Morte Darthur*. The main difficulty in sequence of persons is the temptation for the reader to supply the wrong subject to a synthetic verb. The later written language developed forms of repetition and parallelism to avoid these and other ambiguities. One example of these misleading forms has already been quoted (p. 46), and there are others:

> "I woll nat be to over-hasty, and therfore thou and thy felowys shall abyde here seven dayes; and shall calle unto me my counceyle. . . ."   [V 186.17]

Aythir smote other in the myddys of their shyldis, that the paytrels, sursynglys and crowpers braste, and felle to the erthe bothe.... [V 322.25]

For that horne dud never good, but caused stryff and bate, and allway in her dayes she was an enemy to all trew lovers. [V 430.21]

And sir Percivale toke hit and founde therein a wrytte, and so he rad hit, and devysed the maner of the spyndils and of the ship.... [V 994.21]

And on occasion, Malory can be confusing in his use of pronouns of gender:

There he saw a passynge grete birde uppon that olde tre.... so *she* sate above and had birdis whiche were dede for hungir. So at the laste *he* smote hymselffe with *hys* beke which was grete and sherpe, and so the grete birde bledde so faste that *he* dyed.... [V 956.6]

"He" looks like the masculine pronoun, but is presumably the obsolete feminine pronoun which descended from the Old English "heo". By this time the old pronoun had already died out, since its intrinsic ambiguity encouraged the spread of the "she" form. As we can see here, the ambiguous "he" has led Malory into an inaccurate "hys" later in the sentence. It is typical of Malory that he either does not know or does not care about the ambiguity of the pronoun.[32] And it is not surprising to find Edward of York in his company, in the *Master of Game*.[33]

These occasional small obscurities do not in themselves contribute much to Malory's characteristic style, but his use of tenses does. He tends to the simplest verbal forms, both in meaning and in form, although he has at his command the more complex ones, such as the perfect passive infinitive "to have bene accorded [with sir Launcelot]" (V 1190.18). But the clarity of his story is aided by the dominance of simple over periphrastic tenses. The predominant tenses of the *Morte Darthur* are the present and preterite. The clear and distinct impression of one thing at a time comes from the scarcity of periphrastic and continuous tenses as well as from the sequential presentation of parataxis. Everywhere we find forms like:

> And as kynge Arthure loked besyde hym he sawe a knyght
> that was passyngely well horsed. ... [V 34.6]

instead of:

> And as kynge Arthure was lokynge. ...

In his use of the simple tenses, Malory was presumably making a
virtue of necessity. The range of periphrastic forms of the verb was
still being developed during the fifteenth century, partly to replace
lost inflected forms, and partly as a result of a natural urge to make
meaning more accurate and less ambiguous.[34] In a rapidly developing
language, those writers without Latin training often had difficulty
in managing tenses and especially sequence of tenses. They were almost
always tempted to seek the simpler form, even when the meaning
demanded a more complicated one, as in the following typical example,
from *The Ordinance for the Burial of a King* of 1483.

> Then the body must be bamed if it may be goton, and wrapped
> in lawne or raynes, then hosen, shertes, and a pair of shone of
> redde lether, and do over hym his surcote of clothe, his cap of
> estate over his hede, and then laie hym on a faire burde covered
> with clothe of gold, his one hand upon his bely, and a septur in the
> other hand, and on his face a kerchief, and so shewid to his nobles
> by the space of ij dayes and more if the weder will it suffre.[35]

The sentence switches constructions in a way alarming to our modern
sense of symmetry, presumably because the author cannot keep up
the complex of auxiliaries; but the sense is still clear. So too with
Malory's:

> Than was sir Lavayn armed and horsed ... and rode to per-
> fourme hys batayle. And ryght as the herrowdis *shuld cry* "Lechés
> les alere!" ryght so com sir Launcelot dryvyng with all the myght
> of hys horse. [V 1138.1]

Malory has slipped from what would in normal sequence be a condi-
tional perfect into a similar but simpler periphrastic form.

There is one surprising restriction on Malory's range of tenses. We
do not find him using the historic present, although the tense is very

prominent in his sources,[36] and it is an easy and natural colloquial form which gives a story force and immediacy. It appeared more and more in English, apparently under French influence, from the mid-fourteenth century onwards.[37] Other translators of the time preserve it: Caxton does in his version of *The Foure Sonnes of Aymon*.[38] But Malory does not, although his story is made forceful and immediate by other means. We noticed that Chaucer used demonstratives and the historic present among his other resources for making an incident more vivid. Malory uses demonstratives, but not the historic present. Consider his use of demonstratives in "The Poisoned Apple":

> So there was all only at *that* dyner sir Gawayne and his brethern, *that* ys for to sey, sir Aggravayne.... And so *thes* four-and-twenty knyghtes sholde dyne with the quene... and *there* was made a grete feste. ... and *thys* sir Pyonell hated sir Gawayne.... So *thys* was well yet unto the ende of mete... and *there* sir Patryse felle downe suddeynly dede.... And *there* opynly sir Mador appeled the quene of the deth of hys cousyn.... So with *thys* noyse and crye cam to them kynge Arthure, and... he was a passyng hevy man.... (For the custom was such at *that* tyme that all maner of shamefull deth was called treson.)   [V 1048.15–1150.3]

The high points of the structure of the incident are emphasised in this way, so that quoting the demonstratives in their context has given us almost a *précis* of the story. And it seems to me undeniable that this structural use of demonstratives adds to the force and immediacy of the incident, as well as to its colloquial character, for demonstratives imply a demonstrator. Probably the reason Malory did not follow his sources' use of the historic present is contained in the phrase "at that time". In his mind the story of Arthur was set in a distant past from which it could be contrasted with the degenerate present. The act of comparing past and present draws attention to the presence of the narrator, but the nature of these comparisons places the narrator and the story in different eras. So does the use of tenses, which also sets the action firmly in the past. Part of the impression in the *Morte Darthur* of a noble but vanished time is given us because we are never persuaded to imagine ourselves present in the past.

Another of Malory's devices for easy immediate presentation is the use of a large amount of direct instead of reported speech. Occasionally this gives a momentary illusion of the historic present if narrative changes into dialogue without warning, but in most cases a change of pronoun informs the reader that the mode of presentation has changed. This change, which is seen also in the Paston Letters and quite commonly in the Middle English verse romances, is a frequent and deceptive trait of Malory's,[39] and a very competent editor has missed at least one example:

> And also there was faste by a sygamoure tre, and thereon hynge an horne, the grettyst that ever they sye, of an olyvauntes bone, and this Knyght of the Rede Launde hath honged hit up there to this entente, that yf there com ony arraunte knyght he must blowe that horne and than woll he make hym redy and com to hym to do batayle. [V 320.30]

From "and this Knyght. . . ." the passage should be part of the next speech by Lynet. Shorter examples occur where reported speech has just begun to change into direct speech.

> He wold fetche hym oute of the byggest castell that he *hath*. [V 7.34]

> There was comyn into theyre londis people that were lawles. . . . and *have* brente and slayne all the people that they *may* com by withoute mercy, and *have* leyde sege unto the castell. . . . [V 40.14]

> Sir Bleoberys overthrewe hym and sore *hath* wounded hym. [V 397.23]

Narrator's comment or direct speech explains:

> By the kynges advyse hit was provyded that hit sholde be . . . at Kyng Kenadowne . . . for there *is* a plenteuouse contrey. [V 360.14]

Another anomalous present is a mistaken indicative for subjunctive:

> But if he fyght for a lady and hys adversary *fyghtith* for another.[40] [V 109.2]

c

Sporadic cases of present tenses possibly caused by scribal omission of a letter occur throughout the *Morte*, where present and preterite conflict:

> And so they *departe* and rode into a valey, and there they mette with a squyre which rode on an hakeney, and anone they *salew* hym fayre. [V 943.22]

> And anone he was unarmed and resceyve hys Creature.[41] [V 944.26]

The supposition that these are misspellings is encouraged by two facts: the second case cannot be correct as it stands, and both are apparently emended by Caxton.[42] Further examples are the result of being lost in periphrastic auxiliaries, as in the case quoted on page 53, and in:

> So than there was made grete ordynaunce . . . and the quene muste nedis be jouged to the deth. (*Have ben* jouged. . . .) [V 1174.19]

And in several other cases the introductory formula "thus seyth the tale" has apparently affected the tense of the first narrative verb, though not of the subsequent ones:

> Now leve we thes knyghtes presoners, and speke we of sir Launcelot de Lake, that *lyeth* undir the appil-tre slepynge. About the none so there com by hym four queenys. . . . [V 256.17]

> Now *rydith* Galahad yet withouten shylde, and so rode four dayes. . . . [V 877.1]

This last case lacks the introductory formula, but it begins a major subsection of the "Grail", which is heavily signposted with such formulas in such places. This last and very rare type may well be the only example of the historic present in Malory: that is, the only type of case which Malory would not have corrected had it been pointed out to him. The probability is slightly increased by Caxton's not emending these either.[43] These varied examples show that Malory must have been resisting a constant tendency to slip into the easiest and most direct style of narration. For someone who found the finer points of syntax difficult, to do this demands an overbalancing contrary impulse. This was obviously the conviction in his own mind of the "pastness" of the events he was narrating.

Nothing else explains the constant use of the past tense when we consider how little sense of formal virtuosity Malory shows in his use of tenses, how natural the use of the historic present is as a means of expressing immediacy in the everyday speech of the uneducated,[44] and how easily Malory could have been affected by sources which he sometimes followed closely. As some of the examples we have seen show, he can be careless and confused by difficult constructions, but always returns to the simple preterite for the basis of his narrative. This constant use of the preterite sets the scene of the story as firmly in the past in the reader's mind as it seems to have been in its author's.

The world which any story presents to its readers is as constantly affected by the words the author chooses as by the relationships between them. And so, while examining narrative, the most basic of Malory's modes, we must consider his diction as well as his syntax. And when we do this we find that diction as well as syntax tends to colloquial simplicity rather than to literary virtuosity. The elaborate style common in later English prose romances is partly the product of a diction neither colloquial nor simple. Choice words culled from an exotic or archaic vocabulary give an appropriate flavour to tales of far away or long ago, and we particularly notice nouns fortified with colourful or sensory adjectives. Malory's chronicle style is quite the opposite of this. Just as his verbs tend to be without modifying auxiliaries, so his nouns often stand alone, the objects they denote not further defined by adjectives. And most of the adjectives he does have are simple, common, and much repeated. This is the most ubiquitous of the restrictions which his style puts on his power of description, a power we shall have to consider more fully in a later chapter.

But before we move on to examine the other modes, or even consider the consistency of Malory's style, we must establish a little more firmly the kind of vocabulary he used. It would have been natural to consider it first, were it not that extravagant claims have recently been made for it, and it is best to approach these with a firm idea in mind of the kind of syntax Malory used. Diction and syntax are likely to be related in any writer, and particularly in one who shows the signs of unselfconsciousness we find in Malory.

We would therefore expect his diction to be colloquial and normal; to be praised, if at all, rather because it is suitable to its subject, than because it is original. To a reader who previously has only known Malory, even a small amount of reading in the period will show how many of the key phrases of the *Morte Darthur* were in common use at the time. It would be tedious to document the obvious at irrefutable length, but we may notice the following from various writers in the Paston Letters, which are as close as anything which survives to fifteenth-century spoken English:[45]

> Wherefore it is necessarie that my Lord loke wele to hym self and kepe hym amonge his meyne, and departe nat from theym, for it is to drede lest busshementes shuld be leide for hym.
> A news letter (I, 266–267)

> On horssebak in the most goodly wyse. . . .
> William Wayte (I, 151)

> To his shame and grettest rebuke that ever he had in his lyve.
> John I (I, 276)

> A grete felyshyp and strong.   William Botoner (I, 424)

> They shold never depert fro me whyll I leveyd. . . . They ar as good menys bodys as eny leve. . . .   John III (II, 387)

> If they had satte uppon us, they had be distroyed. And . . . my mastre, Sir John . . . hathe gate hym as grete worship for that day as any gentleman myght doo, and so it is reported of the partye and in all Norwiche. . . . viii. of them in harneys, and ther they wold have myscheved me and the Scheryf letted hem. . . .
> Richard Calle (II, 205)

> And whan Sir Gilberd aspyd them comyng, he and his fele-chipp flede and rode ageyn to Seynt Olovys.   Margaret (II, 240)

> All fals noyses and sclaundres. . . .   Justice Yelverton (I, 167)

> That they myght not cary, they have hewen it a sonder in the most dyspytuose wyse.   Margaret (II, 251)

> Thynk verely it may not lenge endur.   Margaret (II, 291)

Remembre the onstabylnesse of thys world.

John Russe (II, 182)

The recurrence of these and many other words and phrases suggests that Malory is putting ordinary words and phrases to powerful use, rather than inventing or adapting words. The same conclusion is suggested by a number of internal features of the *Morte Darthur*. For instance, we are not jolted by surprising and unusual words on every page, as we are in more conscious inventors, from the *Gawain*-poet to Joyce. Nor, among the particular predilections of this period, are we overwhelmed by the Latin-derived polysyllables favoured by one school of writers, or the constant heavy alliteration affected by another. On the contrary, the most emphatic words, in position and meaning, are often familiar stock phrases like the following:

berdles boye [V 17.22]; fyghtynge as a wood lyon [V 33.35]; blood up to the fittlockys [V 36.19]; grete tray and tene [V 85.30]; on the ryght honde and on the lyft honde [V 1071.4]; morys and mares [V 284.16]; wente to have gone the same way [V 1126.26]; both towarde and frowarde [V 890.15]; overthwarte and endelonge [V 893.23]; as beste tylle a bay [V 1216.5]; for fayre speache nother for foule [V 1227.26]; by fayre meanys and foule meanys [V 1228.25]; that myght nat say hym a good worde [V 1229.5].

Instances could be multiplied indefinitely. Some of the phrases above have survived as linguistic commonplaces to the present day; some are recognisably colloquial from the contexts in which they are quoted from works before Malory's own time by the NED and MED; and some have the alliterating mnemonic balance which marks them as the property of all men rather than the creation of one. Any passage of Malory will supply further examples. The frequent use of this type of phrase, the repetitiveness of Malory's vocabulary at large, and the corroboration of his colloquial syntax would seem to confirm a reader's impression that Malory's diction is unobtrusive and transparent, allowing attention to focus on the subject rather than on its manner of expression.

But this view has been challenged, in the only study which has so far been devoted exclusively to Malory's diction.[46] In this essay, Dr Robert Rioux expends considerable industry in demonstrating

that Malory is an innovator with words. He finds in Malory the first
English use of a score of French-derived words, and, on the strength of
this bestows on him the title *"Créateur Verbal"*. Such a suggestion needs
close examination. *A priori*, it seems unlikely that a writer, most of
whose work depends on the effective repetition of very ordinary
words in normal patterns, should be a creator of words in the sense of a
coiner of them. In fact, Dr Rioux's investigation is vitiated by defective
method and insufficient knowledge of Middle English.

His praiseworthy aim was to treat Malory's vocabulary exhaustively.
We are surprised to find him saying that Malory has a vocabulary of
3111 words. This is startlingly small for any major writer, and sus-
piciously exact. It may well have been arrived at by counting the 3241
entries in the glossary of Professor Vinaver's edition, perhaps deleting
some of its 353 cross-references.[47] He apparently did not notice the
statement at the head of the glossary that the only words included in it
were those which differed from present-day usage. It could hardly
have been less suited to his purpose. Though excellent for checking
archaism, such a compilation, if accurate, will only record linguistic
innovation in those cases where the word coined has died out or
substantially changed in form or meaning between its invention and the
compilation of the glossary. And as we shall see in a moment, this led
Dr Rioux substantially to underestimate the number of new words in
Malory.

His next stage was to check his words against the NED, not knowing
the notorious inadequacy of that work for the period, and assuming
that the earliest attestation in the NED was the first use of the word.
Even if he did not know that these assumptions had been questioned
in connection with work on Chaucer's vocabulary,[48] a small acquain-
tance with the development of medieval English would have told him
how little creativity was needed for the first use of a French word in
English during the fifteenth century.[49]

A more rigorous check on passages from the *Morte Darthur* will
reveal the deficiencies of Dr Rioux's method of dependence on an
unsuitable glossary and the NED. No full account will be possible
until the MED is completed, but a spot check on two passages of a
total of 220 pages, one early and one late in the 1260-page Vinaver
edition, reveals thirty-one words not cited before Malory by the NED.[50]
This check on less than a fifth of the book reveals more apparent
neologisms than Dr Rioux was able to find in the whole work. But if
these words are checked against the more exhaustive MED, which so

far has covered the alphabet only to I, we find that of the twenty-one apparent neologisms within its range, eight are cited from works earlier than Malory and one from an author contemporary with him. And "unbecaste", which is not of course cited in it, appears in Edward of York's *Master of Game,* written about 1405. Among Dr Rioux's own examples, the first eight words are within the scope of the MED. Of these, six are cited from texts before Malory and one probably precedes him, leaving only one for Malory to claim as first user. So it is plain that incautious use of the NED is likely to put us about fifty per cent out in our calculations, merely on the basis of what has survived of the written language of the fifteenth century.

But still, as we have seen, Dr Rioux's score of neologisms is likely to be a considerable underestimate. If more than half the apparent coinages which the NED records prove to be illusory, we may still be left with several score words of which Malory preserves the first written record. Even this, however, would not make him a *"créateur verbal".* Texts of the fifteenth and preceding centuries are few, relative to the task of the total recording of a language, and the more so when that language was in as fluid a state as English. At that time, an extraordinary number of French words were being naturalized into English, and many must have been floating, semi-naturalized, in the language of the upper and middle classes, forming a stratum whose linguistic status was between those of present-day *"maître d'hôtel"* and "café". We find the Pastons, for instance, using "plancher", "garcon", "avaunt", "devoir", "glaives", and "gardevians" (travelling trunks) with no sign of awk-wardness.[51] If Malory were the first to write down some of the words in this class, he is more likely to have done so with a sense that they came from a socially acceptable part of his own language than with a feeling that they were linguistic innovations from another.

French-derived words were common in the speech of the upper classes, unremarked and unremarkable. It was only when those who did not naturally use this part of the English vocabulary started to display it that contemporaries took notice. In the fourteenth century, John Trevisa translated from Higden's *Polychronicon* the observation that "oplondysch men wol lykne hamsylf to gentil men, and fondetᵹ with gret bysynes for to speke Freynsh, for to be more ytold of." This particular snobbery became proverbial, and in the following century Caxton in his printed edition on the *Polychronicon* added to Trevisa's words the proverb: "Jack would be a gentleman if he could speak French."[52] The process can be seen in action in Chaucer's Friar, who more than any other of the Canterbury pilgrims is unwittingly condemned out of his own mouth. The Friar thinks the poor unworthy of his attention, and dismisses them as "poraille", just such a French-derived word as might have come naturally to one who was in rank, if not in other ways, a gentleman.[53] The Pastons were of that social rank, and so was Thomas Malory. Malory does use many French-derived words, but his prose is much less gallicized in phrasing than that of some of his contemporaries; less than Caxton and Nicholas Love, and less even than Thomas More after him.[54] His diction may have given a distinctive touch to his style for contemporary readers, but it would not have seemed eccentric or adventurous. He would certainly not have been thought of as a *"créateur verbal"*. The title would be extravagant at any period for one who naturalized words from another language without altering their meanings: to apply it to a writer who did this to a handful of French words in English in the late middle ages shows a startling lack of scholarly judgement.

Any examination of Malory's style must consider if it was merely reproduced from its sources. The anomalous "Lucius" must be taken into account here. A great part of its story is in phrases from the source, the alliterative *Morte Arthure*, and carries the mark in short phrases in which two alliterating words bear the main stresses. Malory incorporated so much of the diction of alliterative poetry that Caxton entirely modernised the story before publication.[55] And there are traces of his sources in other parts of the *Morte Darthur*. The decisive proof that the stanzaic *Le Morte Arthur* is one of the sources of Malory's "Morte" is the use in the prose of certain alliterating phrases from the poem.[56] But Malory's rendering of his French sources is not what Workman calls "stencil translation": word for word and construction for construction.[57] We have already noticed that Malory tends to reproduce the French story in a different type of syntax and with redundant words shorn away.[58] He has equivalents for French phrases at times: "I wille well" corresponds to "Ce vueill ge bien," and "Wyte you well" to "Sachiez veraiement".[59] But these are unusual. What stencil translation from the French is really like is shown by a fifteenth-century translation of the prose *Merlin*.[60] Malory usually uses his own English syntax and diction, but even when his phrases exactly translate French ones, and hence syntax is parallel, the diction is English. The few French words he incorporates into the story with any regularity are the names of characters like Uwayne le Blanche Maynes, Torre le Fyze Aryes, Aries le Vaysshere, and of course Launcelot du Lake. Each of these names should be taken as a unit, the descriptive part of them now no more concerned with meaning than is the name proper, as a sort of testimony to the author's use of the "Freynsshe booke". Lord Berners gave his narrative a similar authenticity when translating Froissart:

> And as for the true namyng of all maner of personages, countreis, cyties, townes, ryvers, or feldes, whereas I coud nat name them properly nor aptely in Englysshe, I have written them acordynge as I founde them in Frenche. . . .[61]

If Malory thinks the meaning of a French name important, he will give both the authoritative French form and a translation:

> Hit was called the Castell Plewre, that is to sey "the wepynge castell". [V 413.4]

So indeed will Berners.[62] Otherwise, Malory does not retell the story of Arthur word for word from the French, and so does not seem to introduce an exceptional number of French-derived words into his story.

We have suggested that Malory's relative independence of his sources was due to his decision to shorten them. Although this may not have been the only cause, we can see from other romances translated at this time how easy it was to be dominated by a French source, in diction, idiom, and syntax. This is apparent in *Valentine and Orson*, in *Oliver of Castile*, and in *Melusine*, to name only three of the romances translated in the generation after the printing of the *Morte Darthur*. Amongst those translated a little earlier, *The Foure Sonnes of Aymon* and the prose *Merlin* are much closer to their originals than the *Morte* to any of its sources, and we find in them substantial numbers of words and phrases which had no place in English, then or later. Every other kind of translation from the French was equally subject to this vice,[63] but the romances are a better illustration of the pitfalls which Malory avoided.

With a small number of words, we might be mistaken as to their status, and their effect on style would in any case be negligible over the length of the book. But when the number is large, and many of them are taken literally from the corresponding passage in their original, statistics can confirm the reader's impression that the language into which the story is being translated is not quite English. In one passage of eight lines from the prose *Merlin*, for instance, we find a noun, a verb, and an adjective which are all taken from the French and unrecorded elsewhere in medieval English:

> Ther-with departed the kynge Ventres and his company, that was a moche man of body, and a gode knyght and yonge, of prime *barbe* . . . , and rode agein Arthur.
>
> Whan Arthur saugh hym come, he dressed a-gein hym his horse hede . . . , than smote the horse with the spores, that it ran so faste and so *briaunt*, that alle hadden merveile that it be-helden. And he *afficched* hym so in the sturopes that the horse bakke bent. . . .[64]

"Briaunt" and "afficched" come straight from the French source,[65] and although "of prime barbe" does not appear in a surviving version, it is most unlikely that such a Gallic phrase, and one unknown elsewhere in English, should be anything but a literal translation from the French. Again, when we find that the source of a phrase like "alle the renges fremysshed" reads "tout li renc en fermisent", we do not allow a single previous dictionary citation to convince us that the verb "fremisshen" had led a lively but unrecorded existence in spoken English.[66] The whole phrase has clearly been rather transliterated than translated.

This begins to affect even thoroughly naturalized words, as in:

> There . . . be-gan the *chaple* so stronge and dured longe tyme. Ther men myght se many feire *chevalries* don on bothe parties. . . .[67]

"Chaple" (a fight), which has come straight from the source and is otherwise unknown in medieval English, contaminates the nearby "chevalries" (deeds of chivalry); the reader has been made sensitive to alien words and is, so to speak, reading the story in a French accent. There is some justification for such a reading here in that although "chevalries" had been known in this sense in English from about 1325, in this passage it also has come straight from the source. We can feel the same influence at work in the last example but one, in the innocuous phrase "than smote the horse with the spores". It is a literal translation of a familiar French formula "lors huerte li cheval d'esperons" which is familiar from all the French prose romances, but which

Malory chose not to use in his armoury of stock phrases. This literal translation is far from a "creative" use of language. Although it introduces previously unknown words into English, there would be more creativity in a simple adherence to the linguistic norms of English.

Malory does not give way to such an overwhelming influence from his French sources. There are, as always with him, a few exceptions, but we can fairly say that he does not put unknown French words into his English text: his "beards" are never "barbes". Nor does he use marginally acceptable French words when there are more normal English ones. This can be illustrated from a passage from the French prose *Merlin* which both Malory and the English prose *Merlin* translate.[68] The French uses "garçon", which we have noticed was acceptable English to the Pastons: the English *Merlin*, as we might expect, has "garcion", but Malory gives the normal English "boye". When we are struck by the French origins of a word, we will usually find reason to suppose that it was part of the English of the time, at least amongst those who had inherited the remnants of language of the Normans. The image many readers retain from the *Morte Darthur* is of a knight riding alone through a forest, "makynge grete dole." Remembering the French "graunt duel", we would be inclined to say that Malory had been overcome by his sources: but "dole" had been widely used in English since the thirteenth century, and although it has itself vanished, has left us modern English "doleful", which has not.

And we can say much the same of Malory's use of French idioms and locutions. He moves towards an English norm while hack writers give us stencil copies of even the most alien formulas. The English prose *Merlin*, for instance, discards the simple and familiar English "kynge X" in favour of "the kynge X", on the pattern of the French "le roy X". We have seen some others of these words and phrases already. It is not any one case, but the frequency and cumulative effect of the whole, which makes us feel that these authors are not writing English. Malory's possible Gallicisms of syntax, on the other hand, like his French-derived words, usually seem to have been acceptable English in his day. He occasionally puts an adjective after a noun as the French do, as Chaucer had done when he was translating from the Latin.[69] This may be an aristocratic quirk: to do it several times a page, as in some passages of the *Merlin*, is only bad English. Again Malory uses a phrase equivalent to the optative French construction of "que" plus the subjunctive:

"If ever I dud thynge that plesed The, Lorde, for Thy pité ne
have me nat in dispite for my synnes done byforetyme, and *that
Thou shew me* somthynge of that I seke." [V 1015.11]

This is not stencil translation. The construction is not in the corresponding passage of his source, and he uses it again elsewhere in a
sentence which must be of his own composition.[70] This formula was
always unusual, but it appears in Anglo-Saxon, and then more
commonly throughout the thirteenth, fourteenth and fifteenth
centuries. No doubt French influence helped it to spread, but it
became in the end sufficiently English to be used without hesitation in
original prose. In Malory's time it was clearly still acceptable, but soon
afterwards writers began to feel naked if this locution was not subordinate to another clause or verb, and it appears with ever-decreasing
frequency, even when preceded by an interjection. The last case I
know of, in which it stands on its own in prose, is in a translation of
Till Eulenspiegel printed in 1528.[71]

Like greater writers, Malory sometimes nodded, and it may well be
that there are a dozen or so real Gallicisms in his writing.[72] His French
sources at such points overcame him, but normally he turned them into
acceptable English. It might have seemed a little different from his
own speech to the average Englishman of the fifteenth century, but
not, like some passages in the worse-translated romances, to be another
language.

Surprising though it seems, it was one of the two English poems
which he used for the *Morte Darthur* which most distorted Malory's
style. He found the alliterative *Morte Arthure* more unmanageable than
any of his French sources. But even in the anomalous "Lucius", at
those times when he is summarizing rather than following his source,
Malory drops into his normal narrative, descriptive, or dialogue
style. We find:

Than quene Gwenyver made grete sorow that the kynge and
all the lordys sholde so be departed, and there she fell doune on a
swone, and hir ladyes bare hir to her chambir. [V 195.11]

He is overcome by his source only while following it closely. And in
the "Morte", except in the one striking passage referred to above, he
avoids being dominated by the diction and rhythm of a source very
similar to that of "Lucius".

In the "Grail", Professor Vinaver points out a passage as being a literal translation of twenty French words from a passage five times as long:[73]

> Lorde, I thanke The, for now I se that that hath be my desire many a day. Now, my Blyssed Lorde, I wold nat lyve in this wrecched worlde no lenger, if hit myght please The, Lorde. [V 1034.24]

This has been made completely English. It is not a passage which is dominated by the diction or syntax of French origin, as the greater part of "Lucius" is dominated by the vocabulary, grammar, and rhythms of alliterative heroic poetry.[74] Because he does not solve the difficulties of composition by remaining as close as possible to his model, as does the translator of the English prose *Merlin*, Malory is free to develop his own style. It is not surprising that we do not find him to be a creator of Anglo-French words. This might well have been a sign more of imprisonment by his sources than of creative originality, and would certainly have been out of keeping with the nature of his style as a whole. He returned to the norms of spoken English in syntax and in diction, and although he was overcome by the alliterative *Morte Arthure* while writing "Lucius", he remained free of his model while dealing with the less marked style of the French prose. By the time he is again using an English poem as his direct source, in the "Morte", he has enough independence in matter and manner to write in his own way.

His diction, like his syntax, was that which his subject demanded and no more. It was not surprising in its time, nor, once the reader makes a small allowance for linguistic change, is it now. This gives it a low rating by a criterion which has been useful in both literary criticism and linguistics. It is a commonplace to students of poetic diction that words are more significant in proportion as they are less clearly demanded by the story or argument; or, in the terminology of another school, insofar as they are "contextually improbable". The more unusual the word, the more information it gives us. The same principle naturally applies to syntax. Thus, if I have described Malory's style accurately, it stands condemned as, albeit in a technical sense, relatively uninformative. It seems to me that this is true as a generalisation, and that this is the very characteristic of Malory's style which gives the marvels in his story their seeming objectivity and verisimilitude.

Some further qualifications must be made. It is Malory's closeness to the norms of the language in his time and later which we should stress more than his deviations from them. There is no flicker of Skelton or Nashe in the *Morte Darthur*. But Malory was not quite an arithmetically average writer. Within the accepted English of his day, he tended a little to the colloquial rather than the formal among the emerging patterns of syntax, and perhaps towards a vocabulary which hinted at the French inheritance of the English upper classes. But even this description—English, colloquial, a little upper-class—is very broad, and we must try to refine upon it further in the next chapter.

IV

The Rhetoric of Narration

If we are to talk of the rhetoric of Malory's narration, we must be on guard not to suggest that his art of dealing with words was explicit, systematic, and traditional. There was such an art in the middle ages, the legacy of late classical education. As we have seen, this had its influence on clerical prose, even on some clerical prose in the vernacular languages. It shows still more clearly in poetry. Classical rhetoric taught that there were different levels of style to suit different subjects, and the more educated poets of Malory's period knew this. But even when Lydgate or Barclay or Neville professes to be using the "low" style, it is a style worlds away from that of the *Morte Darthur*.[1] This is clear even if we consider no more than the extended anaphora and final antithesis of six lines of Barclay's fourth Eclogue:

> Sometime this Codrus did under shadowe lye
> Wide open piping and gaping on the skye,
> Sometime he daunced and hobled as a beare,
> Sometime he pried howe he became his geare,
> He lept, he songe, and ran to prove his might,
> When purse is heavy oftetime the heart is light.[2]

But this did not percolate down either to the subjects or to the style of that "non-tradition" of lay prose in which Malory wrote. In the early days of Arthurian romance, Chrétien de Troyes had said of the classical world:

> Car des Grejois ne des Romains
> Ne dit an mes ne plus ne mains;

> D'aus est la parole remese
> Et estainte la vive brese.[3]

This suggests adequately the lack of classical influence on Malory's prose style as well as on his story. Only vestigial remnants of the classical tradition appear in the *Morte Darthur*, whose style is as little connected with the tropes and schemes of rhetoric as its story of the "Emperor" Lucius is with the history of Rome.[4] Those few of the figures and *topoi* of medieval Latin literature which we find in his work can generally be traced to his sources. There is, for instance, no trace in Malory of the *ordo artificialis*, which begins a story in the middle and recapitulates the beginning of the action in the middle of the narrative; or of the professional modesty of the authorial *persona*.[5] Neither is there any trace of the *ubi sunt* theme, which authors throughout the middle ages learnt from one another as a way of combining exhaustive lists of great men with their ever-present sense of the transience of earthly greatness.[6] A set speech of farewell by a hero to his country is such a *topos*; and we do find one in the *Morte Darthur* when Launcelot leaves England (V 1201.9): but this has a parallel in Malory's source.[7] So, when we find a single rhetorical figure appearing with some frequency in his work, we may conclude that it was either spontaneous or derived from a commonplace of vernacular literature. Such is the "inexpressibility topos".[8] The most striking of the examples occurs in the "Tristram":

> And to telle the joyes that were betwyxte La Beall Isode and sir Trystramys, there ys no maker can make hit, nothir no harte can thynke hit, nother no penne can wryte hit, nother no mowth can speke hit. [V 493.2]

It recalls John Paston III writing from the Duke of Burgundy's wedding:

> I have no wyt nor remembrans to wryte to yow half the worchep that is her.[9]

Among the other figures which the rhetoricians classified and which we find at times in the *Morte Darthur* are chiasmus, as in these examples:

> They were sente frome hevyn as angels other devilles frome helle. [V 76.2]

"Oure oste is destroyed, and slayne is much of oure peple."

[V 128.16]

and exclamatio, as in these:

Alas, he myght nat endure, the whych was grete pité! [V 77.1]

Lorde, the grete chere that sir Launcelot made of sir Gareth and he of hym! [V 360.28]

Than who was cheryshed but sir Trystrames! [V 426.3]

Alas! thys ys a greate defaughte of us Englysshemen, for there may no thynge us please no terme. [V 1229.13]

But this kind of rhetoric is common enough in popular texts like *Sir Orfeo*. These cases of exclamatio, for instance, are the unselfconscious interruptions of popular story-telling, when the narrator momentarily transfers part of his attention from his story to his audience. They are similar to but a little more conspicuous than Malory's frequent but unobtrusive "wyte you welle"s.[10] And again, the most famous passage in the *Morte Darthur*, Ector's threnody over Lancelot, is based on one of the figures of word-repetition: the same words introduce each clause:

"A, Launcelot!" he sayd, "thou were hede of al Crysten knyghtes! And now I dare say," sayd syr Ector, "thou sir Launcelot, there thou lyest, that thou were never matched of erthely knyghtes hande. And thou were the curtest knyght that ever bare shelde! And thou were the truest frende to thy lovar that ever bestrade hors, and thou were the trewest lover, of a synful man, that ever loved woman, and thou were the kyndest man that ever strake wyth swerde. And thou were the godelyest persone that ever cam emonge prees of knyghtes, and thou was the mekest man and the jentyllest that ever ete in halle emonge ladyes, and thou were the sternest knyght to thy mortal foo that ever put spere in the reeste." [V 1259.9]

The manuals of rhetoric call this figure anaphora, but the occasional presence of anaphora, exclamatio, or chiasmus does not imply an author familiar with such manuals.[11] The figures are almost certainly accidental. Rhetoric is a conscious art, and there are no signs that Malory was in any way a conscious stylist, and several indications that he was not. His rhetoric, if we may call it that, is the rhetoric of popular speech, which is the product of an unanalysed feeling for the most effective manner of expression. What we normally call rhetoric is an art developed from popular usage, and here we find a few forms in the state of nature.

The sense of form which a rhetorical training develops would, as we have already noticed (pp. 46–52), lead us to make obvious mistakes in the meaning of Malory's prose. It would make us distort the meaning of expressions like Lyonesse's proud and touching words to her brother:

"... for he is my lorde and I am his. ..." [V 334.11]

We would supply "his *lorde*", if we read it with a highly developed sense of the formal balance of phrases. Malory's lack of rhetorical training is also suggested by "Lucius". A conscious stylist would, one would have thought, have normalized the anomalous passages in that tale. So hasty an editor as Caxton felt this necessary before he printed the *Morte Darthur*.[12] As it is, Malory only returns to his normal narrative, descriptive, or dialogue style in his occasional additions to his source, or in passages where he is summarizing too much for the narrative flow of the alliterative poem to influence him. He moves towards simplification by, for instance, excising the catalogues typical of alliterative poetry, but it is significant that he leaves the process of normalization incomplete.[13] This is the method of the instinctive writer. One early critic drew a parallel between Malory and Herodotus, asserting that both had a rhetoric which was the more effective because it was their art to conceal it.[14] The evidence in fact suggests that he had none of the art which conceals art, that final sophistication so much beloved of critics. But the phrase might be reasonably applied to the restrained but often elegant style of his French sources. The style of the *Mort Artu* has indeed been praised as a triumph of conscious art, and that of the prose *Tristan* has been spoken of in comparable terms.[15]

But although Malory was no rhetorician by the standards of those familiar with the thirteenth-century Latin rhetorics, a rhetoric of a kind does appear in those ways of expression which he seems to feel most emphatic and forceful. These ways come from the uncodified arts of colloquial speech, where there is no time in the to-and-fro to memorize or polish elaborate effects. And so most of Malory's effects are simple. The most unobtrusive and the most continually effective of them is his way of shortening the story. We may again take his tale of Balin as an example. The reduction of events in his story is not as drastic as the reduction in words. In 11,000 instead of the 38,000 words of his source, he leaves out almost nothing of the *action* of Balin's career, of the sequence of events which would fill a summary or paraphrase of his life. Of the events he omits, the most important are the death of Balin's host at Pelles' castle, and the silent escape of the swordmaiden from Arthur's court after she has been denounced by Merlin.[16] Both of these are of minor importance, since they have no effect on Balin, whose adventures form the backbone of the tale. The sheer reduction in verbiage is what accounts for most of Malory's condensation, and it is this which creates the sometimes dignified, sometimes brisk, but always factual impression of his narration. It was not a common virtue: brevity was more praised than practised in medieval literature.[17] So the leisurely verbose, and repetitive:

> Apries chou qu'il ot parlet ne demoura plus Merlins, ains s'en ala d'autre part si soutilment que li rois Mars ne li autre qui la estoient ne sorent que il fu devenus. [L 26]

becomes:

> Therewith Merlion vanysshed away suddeynly. [V 73.4]

Malory's story of Balin, then, is very much the story of his source at an increased tempo.

But a number of more occasional effects must also be taken into account. Alliteration and a certain amount of onomatopoeia give the pleasure of sound to Malory's story, forceful words add to its impact, and repetition binds it together at all levels. Stock phrases and proverbs at times give the narrative impersonal authority, but since most of the proverbs occur in the dialogue, we shall defer consideration of them until we come to deal with that.

Several critics have noticed that Malory was fascinated by sound. The nearer the writer is to speech, the more force the sound of words will have for him. It was therefore not surprising that the pounding rhythms of the alliterative *Morte Arthure* overcame him in what was presumably prentice work. Professor Helen Wroten noticed that Malory was attracted by the sound of several words in the alliterative poem, and used words of similar sound but quite different meaning in the corresponding portions of his own story, in many cases where it would be absurd to suggest a mistake in meaning.[18] Professor Vinaver noticed the same happening with the French sources of the "Grail".[19] Some cases in which Malory seems to misunderstand northern phrases in the alliterative *Morte Arthure* can be shown even more definitely to be illusions, since he interprets the phrases correctly elsewhere.[20] He was clearly attracted by sound into replacing the words in his source by near-homophones of quite different meaning. And so Dr Rioux may well be wrong when he suggests that Malory was making a mistake by putting "stabled their horsis" (V 83.10) where the corresponding French phrase was "La feste estoit par tel maniere establie" (L 74).[21] We simply cannot assume that Malory is trying to render the French into English as closely as possible.

His fascination with sound attracts Malory into creating alliterative passages of his own from non-alliterative sources.[22] Alliteration is a concomitant of imaginatively intense expression of many kinds besides medieval romance. For instance:

> Where o'er the gates, by his fam'd father's hand
> Great Cibber's brazen, brainless brothers stand.[23]

Since the simplicity of Malory's syntax and the normality of his diction allow the meaning of most of his prose to be readily grasped, the elements not concerned with meaning can be given a greater share of the author's and reader's attention. And so it is not surprising that alliteration is both common and important. One striking passage occurs at the beginning of the "Tristram". I quote a rather shortened version at the risk of exaggerating the impression it makes:

> She was delyverde with grete paynes, but she had takyn suche colde for the defaute of helpe that the depe draughtys of deth toke hir, that nedys she muste dye and departe out of thys worlde. . . .
> And when she sye hym she seyde thus: "A, my lytyll son, thou haste murtherd thy modir! And therefore I suppose thou that arte a murtherer so yonge, thou arte full lykly to be a manly man. . . ."
> And therewith the quene gaff up the goste and dyed. Than the jantyllwoman leyde hir under an umbir of a grete tre, and than she lapped the chylde . . . fro colde.
> . . . the barowns . . . sye that she was dede and undirstode none

othir but that the kynge was destroyed, than sertayne of them
wolde have slayne the chylde bycause they wolde have bene
lordys of that countrey of Lyonesse. But than . . . by the meanys
that she made, the moste party of the barowns wolde nat assente. . . .
[V 372.5–373.1]

I quote this because it is a striking extended passage with a steady
alliterative undertone, but it is far from unique. For instance, Professor
Wroten identifies forty-eight phrases or complete alliterative verse-
lines in the first twelve pages of "Lancelot", thirty-two in the first
twelve pages of "Arthur", and twenty-five in the first twelve pages of
"The Vengeance of Sir Gawain".[24] The material Malory is using is
itself in part alliterative: the proverbs, the stock colloquial phrases
treated above, and the alliterative lines incorporated from his sources
when (as in two instances out of eight) those sources are alliterating
poems. But even apart from the effects of these, there is a constant
alliterative background to Malory's narrative throughout the *Morte
Darthur*, and this by cumulative effect becomes one of the major
sources of the imaginative intensity of the "Morte". Many of the
climactic phrases of the "Morte" are alliterative:

"Of a more nobelar man myght I nat be slayne." [V 1231.22]

The noble knyghtes were layde to the colde erthe. [V 1236.7]

"Nothynge but watirs wap and wawys wanne" [V 1239.25]

"And leve me here alone amonge myne enemyes" [V 1240.30]

"That moste noble kynge that made me knyght." [V 1249.18]

"Myne harte woll nat serve now to se the." [V 1252.24]

"I praye you kysse me, and never no more." [V 1253.26]

"Dyed upon a Good Fryday for Goddes sake." [V 1260.15]

Alliteration on emphatic syllables of key words, as with "noble
knyghtes", the most important thematic phrase of the *Morte Darthur*,
serves to make the phrase more forceful and more memorable, and in
the narrative flow, the undertone of subdued alliteration makes a
counterpoint in sound to the pattern of sense. The complexity of this

makes for a total engagement of the reader's mind and his sympathies, and is one of the characteristic pleasures of Malory's prose.

Little need be said of Malory's fondness for violent words. It is a characteristic of romance at large, and is shared by all his sources, even the most verbose of the French romances. Illustrations can be found on any page of Malory or of his sources. Malory reflects this tendency in his constant use of words like:

Laysshed at hym with a grete club   [V 271.14]

Hurled his horse unto hym freysshely   [V 395.28]

Everything in the world of romance is heightened and simplified: horses travel at a gallop, knights fight up to their ankles in blood, and emotions are often "oute of mesure".

But the most varied device of Malory's rhetoric is repetition in its various forms. We can usefully distinguish three types of repetition. The simplest is the use of "doublets" like:

He . . . was allway in hys prayers and orysons. . . .   [V 908.7]

The kynge lat rere and devyse. . . .   [V 130.15]

Than there was lawghynge and japynge at sir Dynadan.
                                                       [V 706.3]

They were on bothe partyes well furnysshed and garnysshed of all . . . thynge.   [V 1186.35]

In Malory's normal usage, the second term adds little or nothing to the meaning of the first. The effect is rather of agglomeration than of discrimination of meanings, even when the terms are not synonymous. When Lancelot has "many resortis of ladyes and damesels" (V 1045.22), it is the similarity rather than the difference between these terms which is important, just as it is with the "sclawndir and noyse" (loc. cit.), which he is determined to avoid.[25] This device doubles the emphasis at the vital place by saying the important thing twice, and momentarily slows the progress of the narration by the repetition, so further attracting attention to the key point. It is a characteristic of English writers throughout the fifteenth and early sixteenth centuries, writers as diverse as Nicholas Love, the Pastons, and Thomas More. We find doublets adding emphasis and variety even to the short monotonous sentences of *Mandeville's Travels*. They are especially strong in some passages of obvious importance, to which they give a slow, solemn pace, and a deliberate tone. In the *Morte Darthur*, we might notice this most emphatic example, from the dialogue:

"I nor none othir knyght, I dare make good, saw never nother herde say that ever he bare tokyn or sygne of no lady, jantill-woman, nor maydyn at no justis nother turnemente." [V 1079.11]

It is very strong in the passionate argument of Lancelot and Guenivere which opens "Lancelot & Guenivere" (V 1045-47). One distinguished critic has suggested that this is Malory as against his sources which elsewhere dominate his style.[26] But we might compare Nicholas Love, developing a thought of some importance from a hint in his source:

Thou that art among many bodily, thou maist be solitairie and alone gostly yif thou will not and love not these worldely thinges that the comunalte loveth; and also yif thou despise and forsake tho thinges that alle men comounly desiren and taken; also yif thou flee stryves and debates. . . .[27]

It seems to me more accurate to say that in each case an author who can write in a way rather like his sources has changed to a more emphatic style to make a special point. When Malory is getting on with the story, we need to consider the cumulative effect of many small changes to distinguish his style from that of the French romances, but when he is being serious, the difference is more apparent. And so it is deceptively easy to assume that one style is his and the other is not.

Doublets could easily be overexploited by a conscious stylist in search of magniloquence. It happened in the middle ages, to Trevisa and others, and still more often in the sixteenth century. Among the sixteenth-century chroniclers, Edward Hall was one of those who periodically succumbed, and left what we have called the "chronicle style" far behind. At times his virtuosity is arrogantly amusing:

. . . insomuche that the fat Abbotes swet, the proude Priors frowned, the poore Friers curssed, the sely Nonnes wept, and al together wer nothyng pleased nor yet content.[28]

But by its deviation from the economical norms of the language, a style dominated by this reduplication makes the narrator more conspicuous than the facts he talks of. Such a style after a time deafens the reader, and almost certainly makes the narrator seem repulsively overbearing or conceited.[29] Even in the heyday of rhetoric, Ascham thought Hall had ruined sound matter by his style, so that:

> Many sentences, of one meaning, be so clowted up together as though *M. Hall* had bene, not writing the storie of England, but varying a sentence in Hitching schole. . . .[30]

Malory's instinct to reserve doublets for occasional narrative or dialogue emphasis served him better.

The second effect of repetition is an occasional impression of mimesis of action in fighting, as in:

> And than thus they fought tyll hit was paste none, and never wolde stynte tyll at the laste they lacked wynde bothe, and than they stoode waggyng, stagerynge, pantynge, blowynge, and bledyng, that all that behelde them for the moste party wepte for pyté. So whan they had rested them a whyle they yode to batayle agayne, trasyng, traversynge, foynynge, and rasynge as two borys. And at som tyme they toke their bere as hit had bene two rammys and horled togydyrs, that somtyme they felle grovelynge to the erthe; and at som tyme they were so amated that aythir toke others swerde in the stede of his owne.   [V 323.7]

The normal syntactical flow is broken by these sequences of repetitive present participle forms of similar but not identical length, to describe an interruption of the normal sequence of action by a series of repetitive and similar but not identical actions by the characters.[31] The first sequence is made up of two pairs of synonyms and one word on its own: the synonyms give the passage the length it needs to be conspicuous. The freer sweep of action after the second sequence is imitated by a return to a freer, more progressing syntax. Mimesis of this type is rare, but is found in some form occasionally in many outstanding writers. We might call to mind the railway journey in *Dombey and Son* (ch. 55), or the lovers' encounter in *For Whom the Bell Tolls* (ch. 13).

The last and most characteristic of Malory's uses of repetition to be considered is his use of formulaic expression, in words, word-groups, and sentence openings. This formulaic expression necessarily restricts

Malory's range of expression and description; and it extends through all aspects of his style. A word or phrase will be repeated from narrative to dialogue, perhaps several times. The place of the key word will not be supplied by synonyms:

> So with that *departed* the damesell and grete sorow she made. And anone afftir Balyn sente for hys horse and armoure, and so wolde *departe* frome the courte, and toke his leve of kynge Arthure. "Nay," seyde the kynge, "I suppose ye woll nat *departe* so lyghtly...." [V 64.20]

A word which catches his imagination will be used with cumulative effect half a dozen times in a short passage and then not be repeated again for pages:

> "They shall *assay* ... whan I have *assayde*." [V 62.11]

> "*Assay* ye all...." [V 62.18]

> All the barownes ... *assayde*.... [V 62.24]

> He ... wolde *assayde* as othir knyghtes ded. [V 63.4]

> "Suffir me as well to *assay*...." [V 63.11]

> "Ye shall *assay*...." [V 63.28]

or:

> "A *passynge* good man of hys hondys...." [V 61.34]

> "*Passyng* good knyghtes...." [V 62.5]

> "A *passynge* good knyght...." [V 64.1]

> "A *passyng* good knyght of proues...." [V 67.26]

Outside this cluster, this last phrase does not appear in the tale of Balin at all, though it is one of Malory's favourite terms of praise over the length of the *Morte* as a whole. Key words come up in clusters too: "worship" and "proues" thirteen and fourteen times respectively in the tale, but with by no means an even distribution.[32] Malory will emphasise the word in a short passage, then drop it entirely:

"Manhode and worship ys hyd within a mannes person;
and many a worshipfull knyght ys nat knowyn unto all peple.
And therefore worship and hardynesse ys nat in araymente."
[V 63.25]

It may also happen with a complex of associated words:

"Withoute velony other trechory and withoute treson."
[V 62.1]

"Nat defoyled with shame, trechory, nother gyle, . . . a clene
knyght withoute vylony."   [V 62.20]

Withoute vylony or trechory.   [V 63.18]

"Withoute treson, trechory, or felony."   [V 64.3]

There is a last reminiscence of this in:

"Withoute trechery or vylany."   [V 91.31]

Only the first occurrence has a parallel in the French (L 15). This
repetition happens not only with key words in the action, with emphatic
words of value, and with phrases describing similar actions, but to
some extent everywhere. The number of possible alternative openings
for a sentence of narrative seems to be less for Malory than for the
French authors. Taking the tale of Balin as an example, we find that he
has a complex of clauses centred on a norm: one set begins with the
illative particle "so" and a temporal clause or phrase, which occur in
the first half of "Balin" as follows:

So hit befelle on a tyme. . . .   [V 61.6]

So whan the kynge was com. . . .   [V 61.21]

Than hit befelle so that tyme. . . .   [V 62.33]

So the meanewhyle . . . there com into the courte. . . .   [V 65.10]

So at that tyme there was a knyght. . . .   [V 67.7]

So in the meanewhyle com Merlyon unto the courte. . . .
[V 67.19]

The meanwhyle as they talked there com a dwarff. . . .

[V 70.33]

The meanewhyle as thys was adoynge, in com Merlion. . . .

[V 72.3]

So anone aftir com. . . . [V 74.27]

So at that tyme com in. . . . [V 75.34]

So in the meanewhyle com one. . . . [V 76.6]

His other ways of opening sentences fall into comparable complexes.[33] This density of use in narrative in a few pages establishes certain expectations in the reader: the unassertive simplicity has an almost hypnotic effect.

This use of repetition creates patterns in meaning as alliteration does in sound, and gathers force cumulatively towards the "Morte", where many of the most striking and important phrases recall and gather meaning from previous uses. This is most important in dialogue, which will be treated later, but its use is also striking in Malory's narration. The iterative basis is provided by the introduction into the story by Malory of proper names from previous books,[34] and by an unavoidable similarity of phrase in the description of similar actions. But Malory's tendency to formulate expression in groups of associated words goes beyond any necessary minimum of similarity, and recalls earlier books.

1. furnysshed and garnysshed . . . drew hym unto hys stronge castell. . . . [V 1186.35, 1187.5] stuffed and furnysshed and garnysshed all his . . . castellis.
[V 1204.23]
toke the Towre of London, and . . . stuffed hit . . . and well garnysshed hit. . . . [V 1227.18]

stuffe hym and garnysshe hym, for . . . he wold fetche hym oute of the . . . castell. . . . [V 7.33] furnysshed and garnysshed two stronge castels. . . . [V 7.36]

2. their horsis wente in blood paste the fyttlockes. . . .
[V 1193.33]

hir horses wente in blood up to the fittlockys. [V 36.19]

3. and he laye as he had smyled.   And she laye as she had smyled.
... [V 1258.16]   [V 1096.16]

The most interesting example of this usage is the word "depart", which fascinated Malory so much that his constant use of it in tragic contexts gave it its own special overtones. We have just seen this at work at the beginning of "Arthur", after which it gathers cumulative effect until a climactic passage in the "Morte":

> Than sir Launcelot toke hys leve and departed. ... There was sobbyng and wepyng for ... hys departynge. And thus departed sir Launcelot frome the courte for ever.
> "I muste departe. ... And now I shall departe, hit grevyth me sore, for I shall departe with no worship; for a fleymed man departith never ... with no worship. ... and I had nat drad shame, my lady quene Gwenyvere and I shulde never have departed. ...
> "... suche lyvelode as I am borne unto I shall departe with you ... I shall departe all my lyvelode ... frely amonge you."
> And so they were accorded to departe wyth sir Launcelot ... and holé an hondred knyghtes departed with sir Launcelot at onys. ... And thus he departed hys londis and avaunced all hys noble knyghtes. [V 1202.23–1205.1]

There are of course two senses of "depart" here: another sign of Malory's fascination by sound. This is an example of a constant thematic use of words. Another is his use of "noble knyghtes", which occurs throughout all the books, but especially here, emphasising the tragedy of the destruction.[35] An allied effect is given by the description of Lancelot as the "moste nobelyst knyght of the world" (V 1194.13 and 1255.12). This has been one of the thematic phrases of the book since Lancelot's first adventures, though most commonly found in dialogue, where other characters praise Lancelot. This kind of repetition of phrases, like Malory's syntax and diction, is colloquial in basis. The motive for it is no doubt economy of effort: the speaker does not have to think of a new phrase each time he mentions a familiar object. Its effect is simplicity and emphasis as against complexity and discrimination; and it gives unparalleled effectiveness to the final tragedy of the *Morte Darthur*.

V

Description

Description is related to narration in literature much as decoration is related to structure in architecture; it is impossible entirely to separate one from the other. There is little description which does not add to narrative, and few words in the baldest narration which have no pictorial content. This is particularly important to a study of the *Morte Darthur* since the book contains little elaborate or set-piece description. Most of what we see, hear, and so forth in the story comes from sentences which function primarily by forwarding the action. Description slows the pace of a story and tends to make each incident more self-sufficient, while narrative invites the question "And what then?"

These simple categories are less inadequate than they would be for a piece of twentieth-century literary impressionism because, by a modern reader's expectations, the pictorial element in the *Morte Darthur* is limited both in amount and in complexity.[1] Medieval romance is less descriptive than the average modern novel, and the *Morte Darthur* in turn is less descriptive than most medieval prose romances. As a modern poet has said:

> Malory eschews realistic detail. All villages and cities are fair, all towers strong, all abbeys white-stoned, all chapels little. . . . Though certain ladies may be "passing fair", their faces, figures, and colouring cannot be guessed.[2]

Robert Graves's opinion has not commanded universal assent. C. S. Lewis, for instance, praised the pictorial vividness of "the sheer foreground fact, the 'close-up'," in medieval literature, in a perceptive critical essay in which he explicitly exemplified his contention from Malory.[3] Both statements contain part of the truth, though the statistical advantage lay rather with Professor Graves than Professor Lewis. As I have tried to show in the previous chapters, Malory wrote with no sign of self-consciousness or of explicit literary theory. So the greater part of his story is naturally written in the readiest and easiest way, in stock phrases, interrupted by flashes of vision and insight at climactic moments. Such high points are the more striking against the low tension of the mass of his work, and this has persuaded more than one sensitive critic to think of him as a colourful and descriptive writer.[4] This use of stock words and phrases stylises what little pictorial content his work provides. His ladies are all fair, as Robert Graves remarks (unless we take it by default that those of them who are merely "rychely besene" are not), and they are not distinguished into degrees and types of beauty. Malory's work is full of the anomalies of an unselfconscious writer, and he has one solitary young lady with "fayre yalow here" (V 119.15).[5] This only points up the fact that we do not know the colour of Arthur's or Lancelot's or Guenivere's. Again, exceptionally, we know the colour of Arthur's eyes, Gareth's height, and Gawain's taste in fruit,[6] but we do not know these things about anyone else in the story, and we finish the *Morte Darthur* with no idea of what either Lancelot or Guenivere looks like, except that the former has a scar on his cheek (V 1075.36). And this, like the scar on Bors's forehead and Gawain's taste in fruit, is necessary to the action.[7]

This sort of occurrence of physical detail in small memorable incidents of the "man-bites-dog" type is a characteristic of chronicles concerned more with the matter than the manner of their story. For instance, in the most famous of all chronicles, we find a similar unique reference to physical height:

> And behold, there was a man named Zacheus, which was the cheefe among the Publicanes, and he was rich. And he sought to see Jesus who he was, and could not for the prease, because he was litle of stature. And he ranne before, and climed up into a sycomore tree to see him, for he was to passe that way.   [Luke xix 2–4(A.V.)]

And so with the hairy hands of Esau (Gen. xxvii 22–23) and the linen cloth worn by the young man in the Garden of Gesthemane (Mark xiv 51). In a chronicle, incidents like these either explain some turn in the action, or catch the attention because they are strikingly odd.[8]

They all interrupt with unusual descriptive detail a story which normally has no place for it in the progress of psychology, morality, and action.

This description, like the narrative, is nearly all in stock phrases rather than new-minted epithets. Since stock phrases are common both in the *Morte Darthur* and in its sources, it might at first sight be thought that Malory is merely taking his stock phrases from his sources, particularly from his French sources. This is further suggested by the fact that some of the phrases in the English are literal translations of phrases common in the French. "The best . . . of the worlde" corresponds to "le plus . . . del monde", and "Ce veuille ge bien" to "I wille well."[9] But further consideration suggests that the causes are more complicated. Some of Malory's phrases are taken directly from the corresponding point in his source, but a good many of the French phrases do not appear in his work at all. "Lors huerte li cheval d'esperons" is one phrase common in all the French romances which Malory does not adopt.[10] Some of the phrases are found in original composition in Malory's time and seem to be part of the English language. And others are replaced by English ones which are not even inspired by the French, let alone translated from it. When a French knight charges his enemies, he normally "les fait voler a terre," where the most common phrase in Malory is "smote them over their horses' tails." This habit of description in stock phrases would seem to have been drawn not so much from the texts in front of him as from the combination of a chronicler's attitude to his story with the composition habits of spoken rather than written prose. C. S. Lewis finds something similar in primitive epic, and attributes it to the necessities of oral delivery.[11] Although we have no reason to doubt that Malory wrote out his story, we have seen that he did not develop those special potentialities of language which written communication encourages and rewards. And this is as true of his description as it is of his narration.

But though the habits of speech may explain why Malory's descriptions tend to be stock, and the chronicler's urge to press on with the story helps to explain why his description is limited in quantity, this is not the whole explanation. To some writers, the physical realities which description conveys are an essential part of a story. Malory's book is very different.

A recent critic has shown that the strong moral tone of Malory's martial chivalry cannot be traced to the amatory psychological romances which were his sources, but depends on the complex of factors, religious, ethical, psychological and physical, which go to make up "worship" and "chivalry".[12] Some of the best work on Malory has been put into the elucidation of precisely what those terms mean in the *Morte Darthur*, and the investigators have not been unanimous in their conclusions, although there have been considerable areas of agreement. But fortunately for our investigation of style, we can agree that Malory's style was morally emphatic, without having to say precisely what his morality was.[13]

In keeping with the importance of chivalry to his book, Malory's descriptions of people are normally not physical but moral and emotive ones. They force a certain response on us: such are descriptions of Lancelot as "the best knight in the world", and of Arthur as "the most noble king that made me knight".[14] A comparison of the parallel texts edited by Helen Wroten of the *Morte Darthur* and the alliterative *Morte Arthure* shows that one of Malory's most frequent changes is to substitute "noble knights" for the plain "knights" of the alliterative text. He even on one occasion makes the enemy "noble Romaynes".[15] This is his view of his characters and theirs of each other. So we as readers have to create a physical appearance to fit our idea of a noble knight, instead of having some idea of the appearance of the man who plays out his part before us, and deciding for ourselves that he is noble.

A story can range between a montage effect like a film, presenting the facts and leaving the emotional response to us, and prescribing our response to some degree. The first technique is used by the traditional border ballads and Swift's *Modest Proposal*; by Ivy Compton-Burnett and Albert Camus. It is significant that stories using a technique like that of montage usually deal with subjects such as death, sex, and family relationships, which can be counted on to produce a strong and similar reaction in nearly all readers. The alternative is to try to control the reader's response directly, and this is the norm of most authors at most times, some more strongly than others. If, of course, the reader refuses the prescribed response, he will reject the story with a violence proportionate to the emotion it has been forcing on him. This is why many people dislike *Mansfield Park*: they feel the story is forcing them into approval of things they abhor. Malory calls forth the strongest degree of evoked emotional response to be found in any English author of major literary status, and this response is largely produced by the cumulative effect of description in moral and emotive terms. His characters cannot be separated from the response he builds into them.

In the action, the reader apprehends the indivisible unit of the "*noble king*" or the "*good* knight". This is the basis of a story whose structure and substance are seen in the same terms: of good and bad, shame and honour, God and conscience.

The overwhelming effect of the *Morte Darthur* comes from the unification of all levels of the story, but in an examination of the style, it is the more immediately verbal elements which concern us. A detailed comparison of a passage of Malory's story with its source will show us how his visual imagination worked.

Quasi-statistical measurements can only act as pointers to literary judgements, and not as substitutes for them. But it is a strong pointer that in the whole tale of Balin, Malory originates no piece of description more striking than "hir mantell ... that was rychely furred" (V 61.26). Almost all his description is inspired by the French and incorporates words and sometimes translates whole sentences from it. In the later parts of the *Morte Darthur*, however, he does add occasional physical details to the story. But Malory is not only unwilling to increase the descriptive element in this story; he also ruthlessly cuts out a great deal of it from his sources. In the tale of Balin, this starts in the first paragraph, where the wounded messenger on his foundered horse is replaced by "ther com a knyght". He does the same in the two major descriptive passages of the French: the scene of Balin's adventure with the *pensif chevalier*, and the scene where he and his brother attack Royens and his knights.[16] I propose to examine the second of these in detail.

The French is a tense, lucid, and relatively naturalistic account of a particular ambush. It is a much more convincing military incident than any fight in the *Morte Darthur*. A mind which delighted in the immediate details of the chivalric life shows us the knights waiting in the moonshadows at the roadside, the anxious half-suspicious conversation with their unrecognised guide, a narrow road which makes it possible to attack Royens's knights all at once, and the physical appearance of the wounded Royens regaining consciousness, giving parole at the point of the sword, and finding himself unable to ride. The delight in the practical details of the chivalric life overflows into ironic comment on cowardice and its results:

> Si tornerent erramment en fuies. Et ne voient comment il se puissent eschaper, si se laissent cheoir a val la montagne, car ensi cuident il bien fuir et eschaper; mais l'avalee estoit si roste et si

D

haute qui'il laissent la doutouse mort et emprendent la certainne: car nus qui a val se laisse cheoir ne la puet eskiver qu'il ne muire erraument. [L 34]

The French incident is a little wordy, but it is competent narration by any standards.

Malory is not at his narrative best, but shows indications of where his later strength will lie. The skilful description which gives a clearly visualised, coherent, and probable course of events is discarded except for a few lines. Not one of the points of detail listed above is retained.

We notice several characteristic kinds of omission. The first is of merely connective detail. The French author puts his characters in the wood to wait for nightfall. "Ensi parloient entre eus trois ensamble de moult de choses." This purely connective detail of little visual or causal value serves in the French to make the progress of the story more solid, but Malory removes it. Such things recur continuously in the French romance from the beginning, and in the English are always drastically reduced and usually cut out, so that the sequence of actions in Malory tends to be abrupt and even disconnected. Similarly in the French prose *Tristan*, two knights prepare to fight one another, and the author describes the process in some detail. The knights exchange their challenges through a squire, and "L'escuier s'empart, et vient a Persides et lui dit les paroles que Palamedes lui mandoit."[17] Malory reports the words of the challenge as they are given to the squire, but gives nothing corresponding to the sentence quoted. We must infer from the resulting actions that the squire has done as he was told. All the French authors give a good deal of this civilised background of behaviour. The details of Lancelot's rising in the prose *Lancelot* are one example:

> Et Lancelot est vestus et appareillies, et orent oy messe entre lui et les .iij. chevaliers qui avec lui estoient. Il envoierent querre lor armes au chastel. . . .[18]

Again, at the end of a day in the *Mort Artu*:

> Au soir quant il fu tens de couchier, Lancelos se parti de leanz a grant compaignie de chevaliers, et quant il furent a lor ostel, Lancelos dist a Boort. . . .[19]

Or a passing phrase earlier in the same book:

Quant les napes furent levees. . . .[20]

None of the phrases appears in Malory, who is disinclined to be circumstantial at any time, and who shows us next to nothing of the refinements of manner or the details of daily life among his noble knights. Phrases such as these do naturally appear in those English romances which are translated closely from the French. We may instance the following, from Caxton's translation of one of Charlemagne romances:

> Fayr was the courte, and the daye was full fayr and bryght, and fayr was the company, as of xv. kynges, xxx dukes and lx erles. They wente to the chirche for to here the fayr messe that was song; and moche riche was the offeryng. And whan they had herde the messe, they cam ayen to the palays, and asked after water for to wasse their handes; and the dyner was redy, so they wasshed and set theym doun to dyner.[21]

Malory steadily reduces this kind of description in the *Morte Darthur*. He can use flat summary statement similar to "ensi parloient entre eus trois ensemble de moult de choses;" indeed, one of his most characteristic traits of style is to have someone neither visualised nor individualized making great cheer or great dole in a totally formulaic way.[22] But this is rarely filling in time or space. It is almost always the beginning or end of something, establishing the grief for a suicide, the compassion for a burial, or the curiosity for a quest: a structural part of the action.

Secondly, within the action itself, the descriptive detail is cut down, even though it may contribute to the progress as well as to the mood of the story. The French ambush of Balin convinces us because we see the moon rising as the mounted squire thunders past the lurking ambushers, and we see the trees whose shadows conceal them on the side of the road away from the steep slope. The physical circumstances cause and explain much of the action: they are a large part of the reality which the French story gives us. The main structure of Malory's incident is less the physical circumstances of the act and more its central significance, that the two have defeated the forty. This is the kind of story which Malory always tells.

And something is lost as well as gained by this. This shows in Lord Berners' translation of *Arthur of Little Britain*. As with many of the English romances translated from the French about this time, a short passage might be mistaken for Malory, but the small differences of style have a cumulative effect which is quite different over a period. One difference is a consistently more pictorial narrative, as in:

> Whan he saw one of hys knyghtes slayne . . . , he snuffed in the nose, and bette togyder his teth, and bended his browes as though he had ben wode, and called for his helme and for his horse. . . .[23]

Arthur's long fight with the monster of Brosse, although it is very much romance and has nothing of the military incident about it, is a clearly visualised and tense piece of narrative.[24] We are given the right imaginative touch in the final struggle; the monster has torn Arthur's helmet off, and in his death agony his teeth go right through it and meet in the middle. This detail brings a physically consistent world vividly to life. And in this romance the description is a constant fact throughout, not confined to big set-pieces. It imperceptibly creates a world more lively than Malory's, in which the scene is commonly blurred except for a single significant detail or so.

A much later ambush of even greater importance to the plot of the *Morte Darthur* is even less circumstantial than the one in the tale of Balin:

> But so, to make shorte tale, they were all condiscended that, for bettir othir for wars, if so were that the quene were brought on that morne to the fyre, shortely they all wolde rescow her. And so by the advyce of sir Launcelot they put hem all in a wood as nyghe Carlyle as they myght, and there they abode stylle to wyte what the kynge wold do. [V 1173.26]

The incident concentrates on the personal relations: who holds the initiative? who counters him? not on physical facts.

In the French tale of Balin, Merlin appears "desghisés . . . d'une roube d'un conviers toute blanche," but in English only "disgysed so that they knew hym nought."[25] Similarly, Malory does not often bother to recount the particular blows which win a fight. He omits the more brutal facts of the fight between Lancelot and the knights who set on Kay. In his source, Lancelot flays the face off one of his opponents.[26] And this holds generally throughout the *Morte Darthur*. There are, as always with Malory, exceptions; there is no sign that he did not add to the French of his own initiative:

Arthurs swerde braste at the crosse and felle on the grasse amonge
the bloode, and the pomell and the sure handyls he helde in his
honde. [V 143.29]

But such clear and detailed description is very exceptional, even at
climactic moments. He reduces a two-stage fight in the French prose
Tristan to "by forse".[27] In proportion, the pictorial element of the
French sources is cut much more than the dialogue.When Malory keeps
or adds descriptions, they are usually connected clearly with meaning.
So when he adds "no speare in hys reste" to a fight, it is to justify the
good knight Sir Tristram taking a fall.[28] The most striking piece of
description in Malory's tale of Balin is Merlin's statuary (V 78), which
serves to emphasise the central theme of the triumphant knightliness of
Arthur. It also provides a clear foreshadowing of the Grail story: a
persuasive motive for preserving it, since Malory is particularly
interested in the early books of the *Morte Darthur* in establishing
forward links with the later ones. One suspects that it is these reasons,
and not a desire to visualise, which have persuaded Malory to preserve
this notable descriptive passage.

Elsewhere his real interest shows when he makes Tristram overcome
Palomides through "clene knyghthod" where the French made him
win by brute strength.[29] We must dismiss any idea that this concern
with chivalrousness was forced on him by an age which had not learnt
to see or to describe. Many fifteenth-century soldiers had a shrewd
tactical eye for ground. Agincourt and Castillon, to name no more,
were battles partly decided by the choice of the battlefield. And this
sense can be embodied in writing, as it is in a little book which makes
an illuminating contrast with Malory. In the *Historie of the Arrivall of
Edward IV*, written just after Malory died, an anonymous "servant" of
King Edward shows all the instincts of a sound military historian.[30] In
his account of the second battle of Barnet, and the campaign which
followed it and led up to the battle of Tewkesbury, he sketches in the
political background and personal motives, brings in details of the
stratagems and intelligence work on each side, notices supply lines and
recruiting areas, and describes the weather and the lie of the land. Here
is his account of the last stage of the race between the Lancastrians and
Yorkists for the Severn fords:

They (sc. the Lancastrian army) shortly toke theyr conclusyon
for to go the next way to Tewkesbery, whithar they came the

same day, about four aftar none. By whiche tyme they hadd so
travaylled theyr hoaste that nyght and daye that they were ryght
wery for travaylynge; for by that tyme they had travaylyd xxxvj
longe myles, in a fowle contrye, all in lanes and stonny wayes,
betwyxt woodes, without any good refresshynge. . . . So, whethar
it were of theyr election and good will, or no, but that they were
veryly compelled to byde by two cawses; one was, for werines of
theyr people, which they supposed nat theyr people woulde have
eny longer endured; an other, for they knew well that the Kynge
ever approchyd towards them, nere and nere, evar redy . . . to
have pursuyd and fallen uppon them . . . and, paradventure, to
theyr moste dyssavantage. . . . And, for that entent, the same
nyght they pight them in a fielde, in a close even at the townes
ende; the towne, and the abbey, at theyr backs; afore them, and
upon every hand of them, fowle lanes, and depe dikes, and many
hedges, with hylls, and valleys, a ryght evill place to approche, as
cowlde well have bene devysed.

The Kynge, the same mornynge . . . devyded his hole hoost in
three battayles, and sent afore hym his forrydars, and scorars, on
every syde hym, and so, in fayre arraye and ordinaunce, he toke
his way thrwghe the champain contrye, callyd Cotteswolde . . .
that Fryday, which was right-an-hot day, xxx myle and more;
whiche his people might nat finde, in all the way, horse-mete, ne
mans-meate, ne so moche as drynke for theyr horses, save in one
litle broke, where was full letle relefe, it was so sone trowbled
with the cariages that had passed it. And all that day was evarmore
the Kyngs hoste within v or vj myles of his enemyes; he in playne
contry and they amongst woods; havynge allway good espialls
upon them. So . . . he came . . . to a village callyd Chiltenham . . .
where the Kynge had certayn knolege that, but a litle afore his
comynge thethar, his enemyes were comen to Tewkesbury, . . .
wherein they purposed to abyde, and delyver hym battayle.
Whereupon the Kynge . . . incontinent, set forthe towards his
enemyes, and toke the fielde, and lodgyd hym selfe, and all his
hooste, within three myle of them.[31]

This is certainly a chronicle style, in which narrative is dominant. But
description has its place, and a larger place than in Malory. This feature
of style corresponds to a world with a large proportion of existential,
morally indifferent facts. The nature of the ground to be covered, as

well as the driving force of King Edward's will, helps to decide whether or not the Lancastrians will escape into South Wales. None of Malory's battles is decided by the physical circumstances in which it takes place. And no two of Malory's battles have the different physical presences which the *Arrivall* shows us in Second Barnet and Tewkesbury.

This distinction must not be pressed too far. The *Arrivall* shows the importance of leadership, determination, and physical courage in the nobles on both sides, and for Malory the ideal of knighthood was a complex one which included a strong arm as well as a generous heart. But in his battles, ambushes, and fights against odds, it is always the moral aspect which interests him more. When he has one of his characters praise others for keeping together and supporting one another in a mêlée, we feel that the praise is given more to chivalrous unselfishness than to sound cavalry tactics.[32] To the anonymous author of the *Arrivall*, the kind of wood and the exact distance to Carlisle in Malory's ambush would have been sharply realised, because they would have been both interesting and important: to Malory they are not.

A striking exception to the general lack of description in the *Morte Darthur* is "Lucius", which is much more vivid and colourful than the parts of the book derived from the French. Malory is always affected by his sources, and just as he preserves whole lines of alliterative poetry in his narrative, so he keeps Arthur's dream of the dragon. And part of the description of the giant of the mountain is also preserved.[33] All the physical details in Malory come from the alliterative poem, and he only adds:

> He was the foulyst wyghte that ever man sye, and there was never suche one fourmed on erthe, for there was never devil in helle more horryblyer made. [V 202.27]

This is typical of Malory's description; a non-visual negative and superlative. The reader's imagination must respond to its own image. There is a similar image in a fifteenth-century condensation of Mandeville's *Travels*. The redactor of this version tended to omit the facts and keep the marvels from the full version, so producing a tale of wonders.[34] But for once his imagination runs dry and he is left to try to stimulate an image rather than presenting his reader with one of his own:

> In the myddis of that vale undyr a roche shewith opynly the hed of a devyl orible and foul, that no man dar lokyn theron. Ther is

no man in al this world that ne shulde have dred to loke upon his visage, so oryble and foul it is, and forsothe no man dar aprochyn it thedyrward. [35]

A considerable amount of colourful positive description in "Lucius" remains. But when we compare Malory's tale with its source in detail, we can see that Malory has in fact drastically excised the descriptive. Clear, rich, set-piece descriptions are among the most striking beauties of English alliterative poetry, and the *Morte Arthure* contains some outstanding ones. Malory makes a clean sweep of them all. The vivid picture of the embarkation for France has vanished without trace. The seventy-line description of the feast for the Roman ambassadors is reduced to three lines, and its descriptive content to one word:

> So they were led into chambyrs and served as rychely of *deyntés* that myght be gotyn. So the Romaynes had thereof grete mervayle. [36]

Malory has reduced all the overwhelming catalogue of culinary achievement to a single evocative phrase. Had he had an explicit theory of style, he would presumably have "normalized" the prose of "Lucius", in imagery, rhythm, and syntax. As it is, we can see in the enormous incomplete change which has taken place, a confirmation that his reshaping of the French was not accidental. In the *Morte Darthur*, physical detail is not the ultimate reality: we are not given a phenomenological view of life.

Once again Chaucer shows us that Malory's is not the only method of telling a story open to a medieval narrator. His fabliaux are masterly in their realisations of a concrete physical world. In this world the size and position and movement of people and things are immensely important. For instance, in his *Reeve's Tale* the miller and his family go to bed in the same room as the two Cambridge students they have tricked and humiliated. We know where each one is, and then John sets his revenge in train.

> And up he roos and softely he wente
> Un-to the cradel, and in his hand it hente,
> And baar it softe un-to his beddes feet. [37]

The whole of the rest of the story, including its bitter, uproarious climax, and the twist at the end, depends on this insignificant physical alteration of the scene.

The first instinct of a twentieth-century reader is to praise Chaucer's method and condemn Malory for not following it. But a little reflection will show that Malory's way emphasises the values of his story by underplaying its physical embodiment. John Bunyan, who also writes literature from outside the literary world and its traditions and dis-coveries, resembles him in this. Consider this scene from the story of Mr Fearing:

> At last he came in, and I will say that for my Lord, he carried it wonderful lovingly to him. There were but a few good bits at the Table, but some of it was laid upon his Trencher. Then he presented the *Note*, and my Lord looked thereon and said, His desire should be granted. So when he had bin there a good while, he seemed to get some Heart, and to be a little more Comfortable. For my Master, you must know, is one of very tender Bowels, especially to them that are afraid, wherefore he carried it so towards him, as might tend most to his Incouragement. Well, when he had had a sight of the things of the place, and was ready to take his Journey to go to the City, my Lord . . . gave him a Bottle of Spirits, and some comfortable things to eat.[38]

The action of the story is related to us with no more of the physical surroundings than are needed to explain the action. We cannot picture the food on the table, nor see what those actions were which gave heart to Mr Fearing, unless our own imagination supplies them. The narration is swift, summary, and external, and the moral concern quite as inseparably integrated with the action as in Malory. Consonant with this, the prose is paratactic, though not exclusively so, and its distance from literary tradition is shown not only by this simplicity of syntax, but also by the numerous phrases from common speech. We have noticed some touches of carelessness in Malory's grammar, and we may put down to the same colloquial influence the slight confusion of grammatical number in Bunyan's "few good *bits*, but some of *it*. . . ."

In this world, the exact duration of the "good while" before Mr Fearing takes heart matters no more than just what were the "com-fortable things" he was given to eat. Bunyan is concerned with the moral economy of his world even more directly than Malory is; and physical causality, and chronological time, which is an essential part of the working of cause and effect, are often very vaguely realised. The same trend is seen in Malory. In the French romances, there is a strong interest in times, dates, and ages. We are told that Le Morholt was sixty when he fought Tristan, who was only twenty-eight; and that in the battle at Benwick, Arthur was ninety-two, Gawain seventy-six, and Lancelot fifty-five.[39] Malory ignores the ages of his characters, and time itself is less important to him than it is to the authors of his French sources. The author of the French story of Balin tells the tale carefully marking the days and sometimes their canonical hours as well, and tells of the distances in "English leagues". The French Balin meets the *pensif chevalier* on the ninth day of his quest, just before midday. He speaks to him and is rebuffed, watches and hears him sigh at None, resolves to wait until evening if need be to discover why the knyght is sad, and at Vesper-time stops him from committing suicide (L 84–6). Even though we could work out a probable time scheme for Malory's story of Balin, its times are never as clearly defined as this, and seem to serve an entirely different purpose. The moonrise which times the French ambush marks a certain point in one more day and helps to explain the mechanics of its success, but the "nyghe mydnyght" of the English ambush does not. There is nothing in the English skirmish to indicate that it is not taking place under daylight conditions. We are not here in a world where mechanics has much to do with success. The time relates itself to the major fact of the passage, intrepidity against odds. Balin is being established as someone who will fight anything anywhere and at any time.

Malory's third sort of omission gives his style a certain abruptness. He leaves out connective facts and reminders such as we expect from any narrative. The French gives a brief scene where Royens explains that he is too badly wounded to ride, so the brothers

font errament une biere chevaucherece et metent le roi dedans.

[L 37]

In Malory, immediately after agreeing not to kill him, they

leyde hym on an horse littur   [V 74.18]

If the fact of his wounding is important enough to the action to give rise to this unexpected and unexplained object, the reader normally expects some form of connective or reminder of the wounding or a statement of the brothers' noticing he needed transport: even something as short as "seeing his wounds, they. . . ." This transition would conceal the fact that this mysterious object has appeared from nowhere. But we are given nothing and so have to infer several minor actions and decisions here beyond what is given in the narrative, from our previous knowledge. Similarly, we have to assume the death of the knight Malory calls Peryne de Mounte Belyarde from the preceding words and the subsequent action, where the French gives:

> Et si tost comme il a cest parole dite, il s'estent maintenant et lors li part l'ame dou cors. [L 45, V 81.12]

The French writer has a sharp eye for significant actions reflecting character, whereas Malory does not often use his talent for this. The French shows Royens regaining consciousness, and later struggling out of his litter though severely wounded to walk over to Arthur and kneel to him unaided, the futile half-flight of the girl Balin kills, the uproar in Pelles's court with cries of "Take him" (yet no one doing anything to bring this about), and most striking of all, the gruesome account of why Balin did not recognise his brother after their savage fight:[40]

> Il le regarde assés longement, mais onques ne le pot reconnoistre, car il avoit le viaire taint de sanc et de suour et le ieus clos et enflés et la bouce plainne de limon et d'escume toute ensanglentee. Et quant il revint de pasmisons. . . . [L 107]

Malory reduces this last passage and rephrases the incident to emphasise the brothers' relationship and the tragedy rather than the physical horrors. He adds, for instance, "that *unhappy* sword" to the passage (V 89.22). He can when he wishes invent details which show considerable insight into character, even this early in the book.

> And so for sorow he myght no lenger beholde them, but turned hys horse and loked towarde a fayre foreste. [V 70.1]

> But for he was poore and poorly arayde, he put hymselff nat far in prees. [V 63.5]

> Balyn went a litill frome hym and loked on hys horse. . . .
> [V 86.18]

None of these is in the French.[41] However, this sort of presentation of character and significance through described or stated action is much more rare in Malory than in the French *Merlin*. Throughout the *Morte Darthur*, the general lack of sustenance for the visual imagination gives his infrequent *aperçus* a startling force: as in the picture of Guenivere standing rigid and silent while Lancelot excuses himself (V 1046.32), or "And ever sir Launcelote wepte, as he had bene a chylde that had bene beatyn" (V 1152.35). It is noteworthy that all these examples are from moments of some moral as well as emotional significance, and are at critical points in the lives of the major characters on the scene. It is at such moments as these that Malory's imagination is at its most intense and penetrating.

Most of Malory's images are stock ones which recur throughout a passage, sometimes throughout the whole book. To rise to acute sensory perception or to a formal simile is rare with Malory, and he repeats the figures which he does use, often several times.

They twenty knyghtes hylde them ever togydir as wylde swyne, and none wolde fayle other. [V 526.14]

A company of good knyghtes, and they holde them togydirs as borys that were chaced with doggis. [V 1070.19]

Smote hym to the colde erth. [V 254.9]

The noble knyghtes were layde to the colde erthe. [V 1236.7]

And than they fought togiders, that the noyse and the sowne range by the watir and woode. [V 30.17]

They com in so fersely that the strokis redounded agayne fro the woode and the watir. [V 33.4]

Ever he wepte as he had bene a chylde. [V 358.19]

Ever sir Launcelote wepte, as he had bene a chylde that had bene beatyn.[42] [V 1152.35]

Some are separated by only a few pages, some by the major part of the *Morte Darthur*. But as one of the few striking elements in a style generally unobtrusive, they serve to bind the whole work together, like the stock phrases dealt with in the previous chapter .But they do not draw attention to the narrator as an individual, for, however appropriate their use, the comparisons are those of the ordinary man:

A grete steede blacker than ony beré. [V910.5]

Sylke more blacker than ony beré. [V 915.35]

Horse and man all black as a beré. [V 934.30]

A stronge blacke horse, blacker than a byry. [V 962.28]

These elements of the common speech do not attract attention: we focus on the facts they represent and not on the manner of their expression. They give little hint of physical sensitivity in their author. Even when strikingly just, and the description of Lancelot weeping is of unsurpassed insight, it is not the physical resemblance which impresses the reader, but the psychological and moral comparison.

Linked with this description is a type of action of which the French author is very fond, and which Malory retains to a large degree: the chivalric ritual statement. It has been said that the chivalric romances were "a self-portrayal by feudal knighthood of its mores and ideals".[43] Though this was no doubt more conscious in the sophisticated Chrétien de Troyes who provoked it than in our present author, it may well explain the prevalence of the sort of statement in which "Balin left" becomes "Balyn sente for hys horse and armoure, and so wolde departe frome the courte, and toke his leve of kynge Arthure" (V 64.21). The chivalric ritual statement is an expression of a sense of the proper, the feeling that the acts which are the outward signs of the knightly way of life should have a place in expressing knighthood. Everyone *goes*, but only a knight sends for his horse and armour and takes his leave of the king. When Lancelot says:

"Now woll I do by your counceyle *and take myne horse and myne harneyse* and ryde to the ermyte sir Brastias. . . ." [V 1047.32]

the function of these apparently superfluous words is not to inform Bors of the obvious, nor, as it might be in a different mode of writing, to prepare for some twist in the action for which Lancelot needed to be mounted and armed, but to stress again the knighthood of Lancelot,

62624

which is the thesis to be set against the antithesis of his sin, in the dialectic of Malory's story. In the French story of Balin, the author describes the first meeting of the brothers in a formula which Malory gives in very similar words:

> And whan they were mette they put of hyr helmys and kyssed togydirs and wepte for joy and pité. [V 70.4, L 21]

This is the proper, the admirable, the knightly thing. So is Lanceor's pursuit of Balin, quoted on pages 43-4. So it is generally that heads should be smitten off lightly, that horses should be ridden a great pace, and that knights should thrust and foin, trace and traverse, in statements with a minimum of descriptive content.

This neglect of physical detail is matched by something of a disregard for human limitations. Malory's knights share with their French originals an intensification of activity above the human norm but rarely quite impossible. The fights are therefore not *quite* realistic, since it is improbable that any man could, for instance, fight all day in armour without resting. The reader blinks when he finds Lancelot *en queste* cleaving one adversary "unto the throte", a second "unto the pappys", and a third "to the navyll".⁴⁴ Similarly with the small details of life: squires appear from nowhere when needed and are forgotten when not. But reality is almost the rule. Pumpkins rarely turn into stage-coaches, and when they do, it is not by a knight's contrivance. The problems which King Arthur's knights have to face remain analogous to our own: the final tragedy is simplified but still real.

Perhaps the climax of "Gareth" reaches the ultimate in chivalric ritual statement:

> Than com in the Grene Knyght . . . with thirty knyghtes; and there he dud omage and feauté to sir Gareth. . . . Than com in the Rede Knyght wyth three score knyghtes with hym, and dud to sir Gareth omage and feauté. . . . Than com in sir Persaunte of Inde wyth an hondred knyghtes with hym, and there he dud omage and feauté. . . . Than com in the deuke de la Rouse with an hondred knyghtes with hym; and there he dud omage and feauté to sir Gareth. . . . Than cam the Rede Knyght of the Rede Laundis that hyght sir Ironsyde, and he brought with hym three hondred knyghtes; and there he dud omage and feauté. . . .
> [V 361.12]

This is artistically appropriate not because it saves effort in constructing
a long story (it would save even more effort to construct a shorter
story), but because what is being emphasised here is not the difference
of individual persons but the similarity of all knights. Mark Twain,
who did not sympathise, was provoked to fury by this:

> "The truth is, Alisande, these archaics are a little *too* simple; the
> vocabulary is too limited, and so, by consequence, descriptions
> suffer in the matter of variety; they run too much to level Saharas
> of fact, and not enough to picturesque detail; this throws about
> them a certain air of the monotonous.... They come together
> with great random, and a spear is brast, and one party break his
> shield and the other one goes down, horse and man, over his
> horse-tail and brake his neck, and then the next candidate comes
> randoming in, and brast *his* spear, and the other man brast his
> shield, and down *he* goes, horse and man, over his horse-tail, and
> brake *his* neck, and then there's another elected, and another and
> another and still another, till the material is all used up; and when
> you come to figure up results, you can't tell one fight from
> another ... and ... its [sic] pale and noiseless—just ghosts scuffling
> in a fog."[45]

Twain's world is the individualist, competitive society of the United
States in the nineteenth century, as his political and industrial vocabulary
demonstrates. He is a hostile witness but a fascinated one: so fascinated
that he wrote a wish-fulfilment fantasy to burlesque Malory, and to
him the primary facts of Malory's prose style were the similarity of
incident and the lack of pictorial effect.

But if one is not looking for any stick with which one can belabour a
feudal Roman Catholic, these traits of style may not be seen so readily
as faults. The omission of connective statement, pictorial description,
and inferable fact, the reduction in the number of small incidents
revealing character, and the pruning even of the formulaic chivalric
statement contribute to a style of unified effect. These fit in with the
increase in pace given by reducing the story to a quarter of its length,
with the unobtrusive stock words and phrases, the simple co-ordination
of clauses, and the constant tone produced by the repetition of moral
and emotive terms of praise. All these factors combine to increase
verisimilitude, and to ensure that the reader's attention is given to the
facts of the narrative, and not to the narrator or his manner of narration.

Insofar as we are aware of the narrator whose *persona* comes off the page to us, our impression is of a somewhat naive man, who cares only for the essential facts, who tells a plain blunt tale, despising all mannered writing which might interfere with the truth. The relation of this *persona* to Sir Thomas Malory is a matter of biographical interest only, but the verisimilitude which it conveys forces the reader to suspend his disbelief in the rather crudely narrated ambush which we have examined. It is this pictorial asceticism which emphasises those moral implications of the story which in the end dominate its effect. Malory's style is the result of a complex of elements too heterogeneous and irregular in their combination to be the results of conscious art; but the careless yet subtle amalgam into which its elements have been fused will bear comparison with the greatest and most distinctive styles in English prose.

VI

Dialogue

Much of Malory's story takes place in direct speech, and through it his characters mainly reveal themselves. He never in his own person analyses characters with the subtlety of understanding shown in the speeches he gives them, and so most of our grasp of their natures must come from action and dialogue.[1] It has been said that transcribing thoughts was then unknown, so that the characters could only live through speech.[2] This is not true, but Malory so rarely chooses to give a character's thoughts that the effect is much as if it were.[3] Certainly Malory reaches the highest peaks of his style in dialogue; and critics who have exemplified that style have almost to a man given quotations from the speech of his characters at crucial moments in the story. And since, as will become apparent later, Malory's rendering of speech differs considerably from the techniques of modern authors, we must examine his methods if we are to give a true account of his book.

If we are looking for range and variety in Malory's speech, an interesting passage in the "Tristram" suggests that class distinction might give us some provisional categories:

> Wherefore, as me semyth, all jantyllmen that beryth olde armys ought of ryght to honoure sir Trystrams for the goodly tearmys that jantylmen have and use and shall do unto the Day of Dome, that thereby in a maner all men of worshyp may discever a jantylman frome a yoman and a yoman from a vylayne. For he that jantyll is woll drawe hym to jantyll tacchis and to folow the noble customs of jantylmen. [V 375.23]

This suggests at first sight that there may have been an accepted upper-class speech in the fifteenth century, recognisably different from that of the rest of the population; and if so, that this, like other aspects of fifteenth-century life, may be reflected in Malory. Chaucer seems to have given the speech of his nobles and commons some of the marks which distinguished their counterparts in real life.[4] As far as Malory's book is concerned, such a distinction would of course be a matter of upper and lower classes only. The middle class had ridden into English literature in the unobtrusive shapes of Chaucer's five guildsmen, but the ever-rising bourgeoisie have no place in the *Morte Darthur*. The quotation above refers specifically to the vocabulary of hunting, and we see several times in the *Morte Darthur* passages where the author has "drawn him to jantyll tacchis" and described hunting in the technical terms of an enthusiastic sportsman.[5] He at least could readily have been discovered from a yeoman by his own criterion.

The appearances of yeomen and the like in the *Morte Darthur* are generally brief, even if we are solemn and exhaustive enough to include dwarves in the count.[6] Labourers, cowherds, carters, sailors, fishermen, and villagers appear briefly in knightly adventures, give directions or information, and are never seen again. We find that collectively they show no special obsequiousness to the upper classes: they can be as firm and defiant and brusque as any knight. They occasionally use French-derived words and the contemptuous "thou" just as knights do. The labourer who directs Pellinor on his quest uses terms common in knightly speech: "grete dole", "ryde a pace", "waged batayle" (V 114). The "peple" who condemn Balin use "dolerous" and "vengeaunce" (V 86). The sailors who take Tristram to the Red City and the archers who stop Lancelot even use the most common emphatic formula from knightly speech: "Wyte you well".[7] The only linguistic class barrier seems to lie in the use of "ye" and "thou". And even there, the barrier is not rigid. Perceval in his quest for the Grail is very courteous to a yeoman and calls him "fayre frende", "you", and "sir", and only "thou" in a moment of exasperation (V 910).

The distinction between "ye" and "thou" as alternative forms of the singular pronoun of address is an important marker in speech which modern English has lost. Malory uses these pronouns for several different purposes. "Ye" is the more distant and respectful: "thou" marks intimacy, or contempt, or difference of rank. The first of these uses of "thou" is the least common, both in the *Morte Darthur* and among Malory's contemporaries. Even in Chaucer's time people were apparently being more polite to their families and, under French influence, were using the courteous pronoun instead of the intimate one in the family circle.[8] By Malory's time, the "thou" of intimacy was probably rather old-fashioned. We find it in the *Morte Darthur* when the dying Balin uses the pronoun to Balan; Arthur uses it again to the dying Gawain, and Ector uses it in his lament over the dead body of his brother Lancelot.[9] For the bereaved and the dying, emotion is too strong for etiquette, and the closeness of the pronoun is an attempt to deny the separation of death. And, oddly enough, it must be this use which Lancelot employs when he uses "thou" several times in an agonised prayer to the Trinity (V 1152). Three Persons in one Nature does not put his pronouns into the plural (and respectful and distant) form. We may notice in passing that the "thou" of intimacy has apparently begun to spread again in those languages in which it has survived.[10]

The most notable use of "thou" as marking the difference of degree comes on Gareth's first appearance at Arthur's court (V 294). Arthur is very favourably impressed by the young man, and says "Nowe aske ye . . . and ye shall have your askynge." Gareth's request for food and drink for a year seems to brand him, as Kay suggests, as a runaway from some hungry monastery, and the king instantly changes to "thou", which he continues to use until Gareth is revealed as his nephew.[11] Yet the knight's affection for this striking young man appears in every word he speaks. There can be no question of contempt or intimacy, yet the suspicion of a social barrier causes an instant shift in the pronoun of address. It is incidentally noticeable that Arthur generally addresses his knights by the courteous "you", whereas his irascible father had insisted on his royal dignity by calling everyone but his wife "thou". To use "thou" and be addressed as "you" is a mark of accepted distinction in social rank, as is apparent in the majority of cases where a knight is talking to someone of lower social status. That this reflected contemporary conditions is shown by the Cely Papers, in which Richard Cely calls his son George "thou", and George calls his father "you".[12] The Pastons, on the other hand, are more modern. They never use the intimate "thou" at all. For them the pronoun is always a sign of contempt, and usually a deliberate insult.[13] John III wryly reports a quarrel he had with Sir James Gloys:

> "We fyll owght be for my modyr, wyth 'thou prowd prest' and 'thow prowd sqwyer'."[14]

The exceptional cases in Malory go to substantiate yet further this use as a mark of different social levels. Tristram, like Dr Johnson's Rasselas, apparently oscillates between manners and affection for his mentor Governayle, sometimes calling him "you" and sometimes "thou". When Perceval calls a yeoman "you" and "fayre frende", it is a sign of his overflowing courtesy at a moment when his knightliness is being tempted to robbery by force, as much as of his desperate need for a horse. Conversely, when the "passing foul carl" and the forester call Lancelot and Ector respectively "thou", they are taunting them as a knight would, disregarding social position. So it seems that even in the use of the pronoun which divides the social classes, the classes have the same usage. Levels in the social hierarchy are not marked by any linguistic distinction in the *Morte Darthur*.

The contemptuous use of "thou" had developed out of the others. In the fourteenth century, the use of "thou" had not been an insult, even among people of high rank, but rather the sign of a plain man.[15] But the use of "ye" spread until in the fifteenth century it had become an insult *not* to use it to one's equals, although "thou" was still, as we have seen, acceptable to one's inferiors and in certain cases within the family. The contemptuous use of "thou" implied an unwarranted assumption of superiority by an equal or inferior. This insulting usage is commonplace throughout the *Morte*. Whenever two knights are about to fight, they slip into thou-ing one another. When Balin and Garlon are on the point of coming to blows, they cram as many "thou"s into their speeches to each other as possible, and let fly (V 84). A revealing case comes from Lancelot's meeting with Sir Phelot (V 282–284). Phelot has had his wife persuade Lancelot to climb a tree to catch her hawk, so that Phelot can trap him unarmed. When Lancelot discovers this, he not unnaturally starts thou-ing Phelot, until Phelot has no further need of pronouns of address. But though Phelot's wife is deeply involved in this treachery, Lancelot calls her "you" with painful courtesy, even in the face of her uncomprehending stupefaction at her husband's death.

This use of "thou" is found even when Lancelot is fighting in disguise against a friend. He says to Sir Raynolde:

"I know thou arte a good knyght, and lothe I were to sle the."
[V 276.29]

So the remarkable contrast between Gawain and Lancelot in the

"Morte" becomes yet more striking. Until he is dying, Gawain always addresses Lancelot contemptuously as "thou", which reinforces the effect of his provocative and intemperate words. But apart from a few slips in the heat of their arguments, Lancelot continually calls Gawain "you". Even in mortal combat he says:

> "Now I fele ye have done youre warste! And now, my lorde sir Gawayn, I muste do my parte, for many a grete and grevous strokis I have endured you thys day with greate payne."
>
> [V 1217.26]

This courtesy is apparently unique, and reinforces both Lancelot's dilemma and his knighthood. Similarly, the fluctuations of Lancelot's and Guenivere's relationship are marked by this device. Lancelot, even when driven to sarcasm (V 1066), does not abandon the courteous pronoun, but she is always slipping into the contemptuous one. Her behaviour is an index of the torment which loneliness, jealousy, and fear inflict upon her, and of her attempt to work up enough scorn to kill her love.

Although there are no purely linguistic distinctions between classes in the *Morte Darthur*, Malory's knights have certain psychological traits in common, and these, which tend to distinguish them from the other characters, are revealed in the style of their speeches. Three particularly revealing points of style are found in the use of stock phrases, ironic humour, and taciturnity.

We have seen that Malory often writes in repetitive phrases which have echoes throughout his work. This applies to dialogue as well as narrative. It therefore seems worthwhile to examine certain particular phrases which seem to show unusually little variation in tense, order of words, and person of pronoun, though occasionally susceptible of minor alterations like intensifying adverbs. These phrases rarely have closely related negative or interrogative forms, and often stand alone, or are separated by "X said" from the other words spoken. These are the formal characteristics of stock phrases. I have dealt with: "That/Hit is trouthe"; "I take no force"; "I woll that you/thou wete"; "Kepe thyself"; "I woll welle"; and "Wyte you/thou welle". It is impossible to be exhaustive in this, since particular groups of words have these characteristics in varying degrees, and there is and can be no sharp boundary separating the least settled stock phrases from the most firmly defined "free" phrase. And therefore, since the survey had to be typical rather than exhaustive, I omitted several phrases with as good claim to inclusion as those examined: "I require you"; "Fie upon you"; "Ye say sothe"; and "Ye say welle". I also left out of consideration the last two-thirds of the "Tristram", which is reasonably consistent in style throughout, and took the first third as representative. The overall distribution of phrases showed a general but irregular tendency for the phrases to increase in the later books, that is, as Malory's style matures.[16] The phrases were not confined to knights, but they were predominantly used by knights, and examination of each occurrence shows that the more knightly the character, the more often these brief formulaic statements and intensitives will occur in his speech. "Kepe thyself" was revealed as a marginal case, for of its twelve appearances, five were irregular.[17] Some of the phrases are intrinsically unlikely to be used by anyone but knights, and others are unlikely to appear in negative or interrogative forms. But though it may have been partly produced by accident, the result is a body of speech which seems special, fixed, and proper to a knight, even though others may use it. And so, whenever a knight uses a typical phrase, he is affirming his knighthood, and enforcing a comparison between his actions and the standards of knightliness which permeate the whole of the *Morte Darthur*.

The contrast in style in every aspect between "Lucius" and the rest of Malory's work forces itself on the reader's attention. It is typical of the stylistic oddity of "Lucius" that none of the phrases examined occurs in it at all. We have noticed earlier that the narrative part of the tale is strongly affected by the style of the alliterative poem which was its source. And the dialogue, no doubt because it is often less severely shortened than most of the narrative, is even more affected by the *Morte Arthure*. The sentences abound in short clauses with two stressed alliterating words, which give "Lucius" an abrupt dominating rhythm quite different from Malory's norm.[18] This norm does however emerge in many places, especially at the end, where Malory is inventing a link-passage, and even at the beginning where he proses two speeches from the alliterative poem.[19] In the latter, occasional phrases in the style of the poem stand out, like "call unto me my counceyle". But on the other hand, we also find the phrase "myne harte wolde nat serve . . . ," which occurs throughout the *Morte Darthur* at a number of crucial points.[20] And generally, where he invents, the style of the *Morte Arthure* disappears. This is naturally most common in the speeches of Lancelot, except those which are transferred from other speakers, and in the speeches about him, since Lancelot's part in "Lucius" is almost wholly Malory's invention.[21] For instance:

> "Sir," seyde sir Launcelot, "meve you nat to sore, but take your spear in your honde and we shall you not fayle." [V 215.13]

> "Sir," seyde sir Cador, "there was none of us that fayled othir, but of the knyghthode of sir Launcelot hit were mervayle to telle. And of his bolde cosyns are proved full noble knyghtes, but of wyse wytte and of grete strengthe of his ayge sir Launcelot hath no felowe." [V 217.10]

All the key words here are such as occur throughout the *Morte*: "fayle", "knyghthode", "felowe", "mervayle to telle", "noble knyghtes". Where the *Morte Arthure* gives "knyghtes", Malory consistently gives "noble knyghtes" on many occasions throughout the tale.

The structure of these sentences is Malory's norm, even to the slight confusion which seems to overtake the second sentence of Sir Cador. This movement away from the style of his source towards that which he uses elsewhere in the *Morte* confutes C. S. Lewis's plausible observation that Malory has "no style of his own, no characteristic manner."[22] It seems to me that it could more convincingly be argued that Malory's style was characteristic to the point of monotony, and I shall attempt later to forestall such a charge in so far as it might be levelled at his dialogue.

The second aspect of Malory's speeches which I should like to consider is his sense of humour. The strong and simple emotional responses which romance educes demand that humour be carefully controlled if introduced at all, or it may deflate the reader's whole reaction. Malory is without the sure control and discrimination of tones which the *Gawain*-poet possessed, and there can be few readers who have not at one time or another found his book unintentionally hilarious. He normally takes no risks with his audience's laughter. His humorous situations are few, and though they can be complicated, a few main trends stand out. Firstly, the explicitly humorous passages are almost all in dialogue, and those few narrated are jokes by the characters, not the author being amusing at his characters' expense. The only incident in which this dangerous laughter at a character's expense has been deliberately courted comes when Sir Belleus climbs into bed with Lancelot in mistake for his mistress:

and toke hym in his armys and began to kysse hym. And whan sir Launcelot felte a rough berde kyssyng hym he sterte oute of the bedde lyghtly, and the othir knyght after hym. [V 259.30]

This scene is described with gusto, in much the same mood as that in which the damsel beats Alexander the Orphan on the helm with a sword to wake him from a love-trance "that hym thought the fyre flowe oute of hys yghen" (V 647.17). And this latter event the characters all find very funny indeed. Perhaps in the case of Sir Belleus, Malory felt that Lancelot was so firmly established as hero that no farce could make him ridiculous. Certainly he does not deliberately risk satirising other heroic characters elsewhere. Occasionally his literary tact deserts him, as in Lamorak's complaint, which Malory and king Mark and Lamorak himself find "a grete piteuos complaynte":

"O, thou fayre quene of Orkeney, kynge Lottys wyff and modir unto sir Gawayne and to sir Gaherys, and modir to many other, for thy love I am in grete paynys!" [V 579.23]

That fatal "many other" is the product of Malory's tendency to heighten everything. We should in any case find the complaint bathetic; the genealogy does not at the time seem relevant, though it becomes so later, when the queen of Orkney's family kills her for sleeping with Lamorak. But everyone on the spot agrees that it is "the dolefullyst complaynte of love that ever man herde". Since Malory does not mean to ridicule his Number Three knight, the mistake is his.[23]

Lancelot's escapade with Belleus typifies the first sort of humour: that of active horseplay. We find other examples when Lancelot dresses as a woman to joust with Dinadan, when Tristram pretends to be a coward, when Merlin deceives Arthur as to his identity, and when Gawain, after a noble fight, pretends to be a mere yeoman of Arthur's wardrobe.[24] There is a comparable case in *Arthur of Little Britain*, where Jaket finds his master Governar with a present of money which a lady has given him, and in a broadly comic passage, flatly assumes that Governar has robbed a church.[25] The incidents are exuberant and dramatic, depending on the bewilderment or incomprehension of a victim, and although the result may be that "whan quene Gwenyver sawe sir Dynadan ibrought in so amonge them all, than she lowghe, that she fell downe" (V 669.36), it is unlikely that the reader will share her plight. Malory tells these simple practical jokes without any remarkable suspense, subtlety of tone, complexity of action, or justice of outcome.

The second type of humour, the verbal play on unknightliness, is confined, except for one instance, to Dinadan. The exception is Kay's remark "I rode in Goddys pece" (V 287.2), after he had journeyed in Lancelot's armour. It resembles Dinadan's characteristic humour, which depends on verbal dexterity and a pretence of unknightliness in one who has been established as a good knight. The last condition is essential: Kay has recently fought gallantly alone against three knights, and Dinadan, albeit under protest, takes his part with Tristram in fighting the thirty knights who ambush Lancelot.[26] Dinadan's function in the French romance is as a scoffer against the ideals of knighthood; Malory tones down his words and bolsters him up with comment until he is a jester *within* the knightly system. His sting is drawn, and there is scope for laughter in his performance as a proto-Jacques:

> "And there he lay lyke a fole grennynge and wolde nat speke. . . .
> And well I wote he was a lovear." [V 688.33]

These two types of humour, however, though striking, are rare, comprising less than twenty instances in all, and though some of them are extensive passages, so many of them are associated with one character that they cannot be typical of knightliness as Malory presents it. All the knights find Dinadan funny, but none attempts to imitate him.

The third type of humour, which has a tenuous connection with the second through verbal dexterity, derives from the fundamental knightly quality of self-possession as an aspect of courage. Irony and understatement are its principal manifestations, and both typically emerge in the face of danger. It is typical of Malory, and rare, though not unknown, in his sources and contemporaries.[27] The courage and courtesy stemming from self-control are evident in the comment of Ban and Bors that those who had attacked Arthur "were our good frendes", Arthur's references to the Giant of Mt St Michael as a "saint" to whom he will make a "pilgrimage" alone, and to the corpses of his enemies as a "tribute", Lancelot's "Ye sey well" to the woman who had tried to kill him, and Gareth's and La Cote's remarks to their sharp-tongued damsels, especially Gareth's "Damsell, your charge is to me a plesure".[28] Understatement is even more common, and it is impossible to set limits to it. Right at the beginning of "Arthur", Uther's remark that he "wold *fetche hym oute* of the byggest castell that he hath" (V 7.34) is understated. The speaker and his audience, the author and his readers, all realise the violent implications in the matter-of-fact phrase.

Irony and understatement do not often come near to provoking laughter, but we, and presumably Malory, recognise the exhilaration of humour in "Som of the beste of hem woll telle no talys" and "Now art thou of a syse . . . lyke unto oure ferys," though not in such a degree of intensity as to interrupt the flow of the story. This type of humour is not out of place in "Grail", for it does not disturb the mood of the tale, where farce or mockery of Dinadan's sort would have done. The self-possession of Lionel is in marked and effective contrast to the agitation of everyone else as he single-mindedly sets about murdering his brother. He cares not at all when a priest intervenes, saying that Lionel will have to kill him first:

> "Well," seyd sir Leonell, "I am agreed," and sette his honde to his swerde, and smote hym so harde that hys hede yode off bacwarde. [V 971.3]

The casual phrasing of the speech emphasises the horror of the action. The level of humour in this presumably does not rise above a certain grim self-satisfaction, expressed in Lionel's terse determination. And we find the same ominous irony in two muted threats elsewhere in the Grail story: " 'No?' seyde one of them. 'Hit shall be assayde',," and " 'and ye woll abyde by that ye shall have inowghe to do'."[29] The two instances show the same mood we can find in ironic knightly speech elsewhere in the *Morte Darthur*. We recognise it in the undoubtedly humorous "we shall so handyll the . . . that thou shalt wysshe that thou haddyst be crystynde" and "thou arte full large of my horse and harneyse!"[30] The mood is one which is fundamental to knightly behaviour as it is seen in the *Morte Darthur*.

It is noticeable that the amount of irony and understatement decreases towards the end of the *Morte Darthur*, and I could find no striking examples at all in the "Morte" itself. All the characters are kept from any real mental equilibrium by the violence of events; and fear, pain, sadness, and troubled consciences make their mood too serious for the verbal play of litotes. From the writer's point of view we may suggest that the verbal energy which was earlier being directed into this sort of humour is now all being channelled into tragic statement.

The third characteristic of knightly speech is terseness of an entirely serious nature. Brevity of speech is not exclusively the property of knights. We do not find in the appearance at court of Aries the Cowherd (V 99–101) a contrast between the loquacity of the plebeian and the taciturn competence of the knight. Aries is quite garrulous and circumstantial with his "For I shall telle you . . ." and "my wyff and I", but a mere page before, King Leodegreaunce of Camelarde has outstripped him in loquacity. And if the newly knighted Tor is suddenly comically heroic with his laconic "Dishonoure nat my modir," the cowherd can be just as brusque: "I suppose nat," and "Hit ys the lesse gryff unto me." Malory does not rigorously distinguish social class by amount of vocabulary any more than by its type.

But in situations of pain or danger, terseness and even silence can become virtues, and at these times, the good knights tend to show them. The extreme of silence under pain is praised by Malory in Lionel:

> But he seyde never a worde as he whych was grete of herte.
> [V 960.28]

Or again:

> "Alas, that he wolde nat complayne hym, for hys harte was so sette to helpe me." [V 1238.24]

But to use few words rather than many, or cautious words rather than boastful, is to display the same virtue in a lesser degree. And there is a reference to this in "Arthur", when the king praises Tor:

> "He seyth but lytil, but he doth much more. . . ." [V 131.28]

This may refer to Tor's modesty rather than to his laconic speech. Although his recent adventures have displayed his taciturnity rather than his modesty,[31] the more general characteristic would better fit the antithesis of Malory's statement. But it is possible that Malory did not clearly distinguish here between few words and modest ones. We have a more complete picture of the virtue behind the statements above if we take into consideration Guenivere's praise of Kay after the war against the five kings:

> "And amonge all ladyes," seyde the quene, "I shall bere your

noble fame, for ye spake a grete worde and fulfylled hit worship-
fully." [V 129.20]

This is the traditional Germanic courage and prudence. A man who
behaved according to this ideal would be cautious and close-mouthed
for the most part, but before a great endeavour would speak his boast,
and go out to fulfil it or die in the attempt. This is the virtue of the
sagas and Old English heroic poetry: the converse of it is found in
Malory's arch-villain:

> Many in the courte spake of hit, and in especiall sir Aggravayne,
> . . . for he was ever opynne-mowthed. [V 1045.21]

It is not surprising then that brevity of speech is one of the most
striking differences between Malory's knights and those of his French
sources, especially in situations of tension and danger. The French ideal
of behaviour was a more eloquent one, and one whose effect we can
see in Chaucer and the *Gawain*-poet, as well as in Malory's sources.
But whether by tradition or temperament or mere accident, Malory
gave us a very different society. Paradoxically, his characters seem,
because of their apparent inability with words, to be more dignified
and direct, more capable of suffering and courage and human incoherence, than those they were derived from. The brief, slightly
repetitive, perhaps overemphatic speech in which Malory's Gawain
refuses to attend Guenivere's execution seems more that of a man under
pressure from powerfully conflicting feelings than does the logical,
elegant, and courteous speech of the Gawain of the *Mort Artu*.[32] And
on the rare occasions when one of Malory's characters rises to an
extended and orderly exposition, as in Lancelot's great speeches in his
own defence in the "Morte", the contrast with the rest of the book
makes the long speech seem to be the product of intolerable emotion.[33]
On the other side, the stock phrase *je cuic* (I think), which recurs
throughout the French prose *Merlin*, would serve, in its modesty and
frequent superfluity, as a symbol of the delicate pathos which is the
commonest mood of the French romance. The French Balin is asked
by his squire, after his banishment from Camelot, where he will be
found. Balin replies, "Je cuic . . . que tu me troveras en la court le roi
Artus," but Malory's Balin says with confident brevity, "In kynge
Arthurs courte."[34] Similarly the French swordmaiden's "dont je ne
cuic ja mais estre delivré" becomes "I may nat be delyverde". The

characters of the French *Merlin* are given speeches which often show considerable insight into personality, but they are always complicated polite, and devious, and somtimes wordy and sentimental. This is partly the product of linguistic skills shared by all the French romances and many of the closely translated English ones; an ability with casual phrases, skill with pronouns and particles, the use of more complex verbal parallels, and the constant sequence of a considerable range of tenses and moods, which Malory perhaps could not and certainly did not use. This in turn affected Malory's characters, who rarely make long speeches, and if they do seem unable to use words in complex symmetry. This makes his characters seem much more abrupt, terse, even elemental. Each model produces good work: Malory's Uther is portrayed as a naturally violent man, which his original in the French *Merlin* is not; and the French Ygerne seems continually circumstantial and dismayed, where Malory's can be as terse and capable as any of the king's knights.

Typical of the taciturnity of Malory's knights, expressing a certain self-restraint and fortitude, is the fight at the end of the "Lamorak" subsection of the "Tristram". Bellyaunce fights with fury until he is exhausted:

> And at the laste sir Bellyaunce withdrew hym abacke and sette hym downe a lytyll uppon an hylle, for he was faynte for bledynge, that he myght nat stonde.
> Than sir Lameroke threw his shylde uppon his backe and cam unto hym and asked hym what chere.
> "Well," seyde sir Bellyaunce. [V 451.10]

This single pregnant syllable condenses a message of courage and defiance until it has tremendous force. This same syllable is made to convey an equally great but very different meaning when it finally becomes clear that Gawain means to evade serious repentance even in the Grail quest:

> "Nay," seyd sir Gawayne, "I may do no penaunce, for we knyghtes adventures many tymes suffir grete woo and payne."
> "Well," seyde the good man, and than he hylde hys pece.
> [V 892.19]

This expression is untypical of the wordy hermits of the "Grail". Here it expresses a last effort, checked in mid-utterance by a resigned realisation of its hopelessness. It characterises both the hermit and Gawain, and shows that the priest understands the knight. Tristram's treacherous cousin Andred shares at least this knightly quality of brevity:

> "A, Andrete, Andrete!" seyde sir Trystrames, "thou sholdyst be my kynnysman, and now arte to me full unfrendely. But and there were no more but thou and I, thou woldyst nat put me to deth."
> "No?" seyde sir Andred, and therewith he drew his swerde and wolde have slayne hym.   [V 431.26]

Here again the compression of meaning gives the monosyllable tremendous force.

These are in some ways typical knightly speeches. It is one of Malory's favourite devices to set a curt reaction against a relatively long speech as the final element in an incident or exchange of words. This leaves the final pithy reply fast in the reader's memory, especially when the two speeches contrast significantly in tone or content. This device is one of the fundamental resources of effective writing. And because Malory normally does not comment on his characters' states of mind except to set the scene at the beginning, the final terse remark produced by the swing of the emotions in the conversation stands out with extra finality. We see this when Palomides knocks Tristram off his horse.[35] Tristram had not had time to prepare to receive the charge and was furious: Malory tells us so three times. Dinadan tries to comfort him with proverbs, but Tristram's unmollified anger breaks out in "I woll revenge me!" In his rage he is impervious to Dinadan's folk wisdom. Malory no doubt realised, though he does not say so, that a man in that situation would hardly hear it. There is a complex emotional state packed into these five syllables, which stand conspicuously at the end of the incident before an obvious transitional passage. The climax has been left in Tristram's words rather than in any summarizing comment by the narrator, and it stands dramatically independent of Malory.

Malory normally has the tact to remain in the background. And from the background, he rings the changes on his technique of ending a section of dialogue with a short and striking line. This normally demands at least one character with relative self-control. But the same device can be used in the middle of an incident to give a slight check to its flow; it can come with or without explanation of the emotions

beforehand, and the final curt words, packed with meaning, may ever
be separated at some distance, both in words and in narrative time
from the rest of the dialogue they contrast with. This last variation
distanced and without explanation, provides one of the most striking
remarks in the *Morte Darthur*. Before the final conflict, Malory described nothing of Arthur's feelings after saying:

> Kynge Arthur was passyng glad that he myght be avenged
> uppon sir Mordred.   [V 1233.3]

Then there is a mass of active preparations for the battle, which has to
be put off after Arthur's dream has given him ominous warning of the
consequences of fighting. The preparations for the truce are described
in some little detail, central to which are the warnings against treachery
which Arthur and Mordred give to their armies, in very similar terms.
Even apart from the repetition involved in this, the warnings are
loaded with intensitives. The fatal accident happens, and we and
Arthur know more or less what the result is to be. Arthur's reported
words (and hence, we take it, his only words) are

> "Alas, this unhappy day!"   [V 1235.28]

and he rides to his army. Unlike the previous speeches, there are no
repetitions ("that traytoure, sir Mordred"), no intensitives ("Ony
maner", "in no wyse", "well"), and no explanation ("for I in no wyse
truste hym"), just the simplest possible expression of sorrow, implying
realisation of the inevitable disaster and acceptance of it. "Unhappy"
has the older and stronger sense of "ominous", "doomed to miscarry".
The simplicity of this gives a "moment of truth" after the fever of the
dreams and the complexity of the negotiation. This is a narrative climax
created by a natural story-teller, and allowed to stand on its own,
impressively without comment.

This technique is omnipresent in Malory, and is found in both his
major and minor characters. Thus Mador de la Porte's "I am answerde"
both marks the end of one incident with a minute check derived from
the contrast of its laconic force with the preceding agitated argument,
and also characterises Mador with a grim competence which makes
him a force to be reckoned with. These moments gain most of their
variety from the circumstances which lead up to them. We may
compare, for instance, two moments when a defeated knight is

pleading for his life. In "Gareth", the hero in two curt words gives the
Red Knight of the Red Lands permission to live long enough to
explain himself: "Sey on!"[36] In "Arthur", Accolon is slowly realising
what he has been involved in and cries out:

> "Wo worthe this swerde! for by hit I have gotyn my dethe."
> "Hit may well be," seyde the kynge.   [V 145.26]

In each case the words of the victor indicate primarily an act of self-
restraint which he would not have received from the vanquished. But
in the first case it is an exercise in magnanimity in a young knight who
is external to the Red Knight's situation, an inexperienced but impartial
judge. In the second, Arthur is caught in the centre of a web of treachery
which primarily concerns him, and which he is only slowly discovering.
Therefore there is an additional horror in Arthur's feelings at this point
which Gareth does not have, and which makes the less confident form
of words more appropriate.

In many cases, the stock phrases treated above are part of the laconic
habit of speech of Malory's knights. So Segwarides, having frightened
out of his wife the story of her infidelity with Tristram, compliments
her ironically with "ye sey well," and reaches for his armour.[37] By its
blunt irony, the stock formula emphasises the bottled-up fury of
Segwarides; it also marks the end of one part of that incident. However,
a certain amount of brevity is a characteristic of many of Malory's
people: his villeins, messengers, ladies, and churls do not waste words.
Typical of innumerable other laconic meetings is Lancelot's encounter
with the "jantilwoman" he meets towards the end of his part of the
Grail quest,[38] although it does not show the curt crucial remark noticed
above as one of Malory's favourite devices. Guenivere, and to some
extent Elaine of Astolat, can on occasion be as terse and competent in
their speech as any knight. When the Orkney knights spring the trap
on Lancelot and the queen:

> "Alas!" seyde quene Gwenyver, "now ar we myscheved
> bothe!"   [V 1165.22]

This swift, brief, and fearless recognition of the facts is the product of a
self-control which gives great dignity to the scene which follows. When
we see this quality in others, can we say there is a specifically knightly
quality of speech in the *Morte Darthur*?

It seems to me that we can, in trends if not in absolute terms, and few generalisations about Malory are not subject to exceptions. What Malory himself praises as knightly speech is the expression of courage under stress.[39] The speeches which he specifically praises in this way do not noticeably display our three characteristics of understatement, brevity, and stock formulas. But, nevertheless, it is these which impress the reader as the particular expressions of that courage in difficulties which Malory admires.

Because they are especially appropriate to knighthood and are found in many of its most impressive displays, we associate them with knights. Ironic understatement is confined to knights, and strikingly laconic statements, as against brief competence, are rare from other speakers. And although the characters who are not knights are given a substantial number of stock expressions in proportion to the number of lines of dialogue they speak, several contrary factors combine to persuade us that these formulaic expressions are knightly. The knights have all the biggest parts, which means that they will use these phrases more often than anyone else; and they also have the most important parts, which ensures that they will use them more memorably. The action and the ideas behind the story, as well as its style, serve to give the knights a unity and a corporate importance which cannot be matched by any single character outside their number, and this is reinforced by the fact that some of the phrases are, by their nature, almost confined to knightly use. The only body of characters who can be compared with the knights are the hermits in the "Grail", and they have no corporate characteristics, and, apart from a few small exceptions, no individual characters. Their speeches, despite their length and importance, are mere disguised narrative, almost without distinguishing marks.[40] And this itself tends to set the speech of the knights off from that of the other characters in that part of Malory's book; marked out by its stock formulas, brevity, and understatement as possessing those qualities which a knight should have. Some of the other characters seem to possess the knightly qualities and their embodiments to a lesser degree than the outstanding knights, but are compensated for this by a greater share of individuality. This is something we shall have to look at more closely in the next chapter. It has been the purpose of this chapter to show that we complete the book with a sense of the appropriate knightliness of the dialogue of Malory's knights; and that this sense is the product of the style as well as the content of what is expressed.

E

VII

The Rhetoric of Dialogue

For a modern reader, the most striking characteristic of Malory's dialogue is the lack of individualization. The same diction and syntax, the same proverbs and images, are used by one person as are used by another. Lamorak notices on one occasion that Mark is a Cornish knight by his speech (presumably by his accent), and at another time, accent may discover Tristram to Palomides.[1] But Malory makes no discoverable attempt to imitate either accent or dialect. Although one character is not distinguished from another by his speech except on the rarest occasions, Malory is still capable of delineating mood with a masterly hand. His characters speak with considerable range and variety of expression. It is the purpose of this chapter to examine some of the means by which this is done.

Malory is an author whose writing shows no signs of being governed by a theory of style, and so we cannot expect consistency from him. It is probable that many of the characteristics of his style are unconsciously colloquial, because that was the easiest way of telling his story. Though his devices have literary effects, it would be ludicrous to maintain that he consciously chose parataxis as the basis of his narration, or that he was impressed by the thematic possibilities of patterning at all levels. Less effort was needed for parataxis and repetition than for complex subordination and continual variety.

In the dialogue as well as the narrative of the *Morte Darthur*, Malory's strength lies in the powerful use of familiar phrases rather than in the ingenious coinage of new ones. Once again, it would be tedious to document this to the point of irrefutability, but the following phrases may suggest the similarities of expression and sentiment which exist between Malory and the writers of the Paston Letters.[2]

I pray God make you as good a man as ever was any of your kynne.

Margaret (Supplement, 104); cf. Elaine of Corbenic, V 832.12

Here dare no man seyn a gode wurd for yu in this cuntre, Godde amend it.   Margaret (I, 113); cf. the narrator, V 1229.5

I ... send you Goddis blissyng and myn. ...
Margaret (Supp., 106); cf. Uther Pendragon, V 12.6

Which were to us a gret shame, and a rebuke.
Margaret (Supp., 129)

If ye refuse they all wyll do the uttirmest.   John Russe (II, 182)

I haf hir promisse to be my good lady, and that she shall help me by the feith of hir body.   Thomas Denyes (I, 129)

Gret costs and charges that we have, and may growe here after.
Margaret (II, 252)

Ther sche was receyvyd as worchepfully as all the world cowd devyse ... best beseyn of eny pepyll, that ever I sye or herd of.
John III (II, 317)

They are the goodlyest felawshep th[at] ever I cam among, and best can behave them, and the most lyek gentylmen.
John III (II, 319)

In the which matier I reporte me to William Worcestre ... and most specially to my maisters awun remembraunce.
Henry Windesore (I, 431)

He moste a voyde.   Edmund (I, 71)

In that his saying he is fals, that knowith God, &c. And for my playn acquitayll, yf he or any substancyall gentylman wyll say it, and avow it, I say to it contrari, and by lisens of the Kyng to make it good as a gentylman.   John Berney (II, 27)

And, sir, I suppose I shall never see you no more, nor non of myn frendes, whiche is to me the grettest lamentacion that myght come un to myn herte; for, sir, by the grace of God, I shall go to

Rome, and into oder holy places, to spende myn dayes of this present liff in the servise of God. For I hadde lever liffe in gret tribulacion in the service of God in this present liff, than for to folowe the wretchedness of this worlde.   Roger Tavernham (II, 66)

These passages and the ones in the *Morte Darthur* which resemble them are clearly drawn from the reservoir of popular speech. And therefore, as we would expect, there are some very close resemblances, especially in set phrases, and some vaguer ones, forming a penumbra around them. In this situation, we must be more than usually sceptical of any suggestions of literary influence. One or two critics, for instance, have suggested that the *Morte Arthure* provides the source for Ector's threnody over Lancelot, and another critic has suggested that the threnody in turn shows its influence in one of John Paston III's letters.[3] But the similarities do not seem to me to be close enough to demand any other explanation than coincidence, when we consider that both parties in both cases were drawing on a common fund of colloquial speech, and had, as far as we know, the same unwritten arts to teach them how to use it.

But although we can distinguish a number of uniform central trends in the use of this material, presumably the product of Malory's instinct for the most effective way of telling a story, we also find great variety, uncramped by theories of literary decorum. This is especially apparent in the dialogue of his book, which modulates between the equally impersonal extremes of the knightly speeches which we have examined in the previous chapter, and a more colloquial type marked by the rhythm and diction of popular speech. The whole range of expression is characterised more by force and colour than exactness and discrimination, and is fortified by the intensitives of ordinary speech, by the use of oaths and proverbs and vocatives, and by various forms of repetition and reduplication.

We find the more popular level of dialogue in use by all classes and all persons in the *Morte Darthur*. Malory clearly had no such theory of poetic decorum as emerges early in the next century in the prologue to Book Nine of Gavin Douglas's *Eneados*:

> Full litill it wald delite
> To write of scroggis, broym, haddir, or rammale:
> The lawrer, cedir, or the palm triumphale,
> Ar mayr ganand for nobillis of estait.[4]

Malory has no objection to associating "low" vegetation with his
"nobillis of estait". He has a very memorable heath-bush at the climax
of his story (V 1235.21), and there is no sign that he feels any compulsion
to excise imagery in conformity with a theory of high style. Nor is
there any sign that he wishes to censor the behaviour or speech of his
characters in pursuit of an idea of decorum. If most readers finish the
Morte Darthur with a memory of striking dignity of speech, this is because Malory's characters speak as they feel, and are often considerate,
capable, and courageous. It is not because certain types of speech or
action have been ruled out before the start. There is, as I have tried to
show above, a manner of speaking which is especially proper to
knights at critical moments, as the natural expression of knightly
character, but there is a great range of other styles and subjects open to
them. Unlike Milton's angels, Malory's knights are not condemned to
perpetual dignity. Gavin Douglas said of Caxton's version of the
Aeneid: "His febill prois bene mank and mutilait."[5] He might well
have said the same of Malory's style, but the modern reader finds
Malory more natural and convincing.

The range of the Morte Darthur is a little obscured to our eyes, because
Malory does not individualize his characters by traits of speech to the
extent to which the modern novel has accustomed us, and because his
language is uniformly and inevitably distanced from us by five hundred
years of linguistic change. But close reading shows us that all his
characters can be strikingly colloquial, however heroic, good, aristocratic, or womanly they may be. Gentilesse is not yet the genteel, and
for Malory there seem to be no prohibited subjects or phrases which are
lower class or indelicate.[6] When Alexander the Orphan, who is the
hero of his tale, discovers from the damsel that Morgan le Fay wants
him as her paramour, his response is:

> "I had levir kut away my hangers than I wolde do her ony
> suche pleasure!"   [V 643.24]

Alexander Pope did not feel that a hero's genitals should be the subject
of polite conversation. The subject does come up in conversation once
in his poetry; in his scurrilous little "Imitation of Chaucer".[7] Pope
allows himself this liberty in order to characterise what he sees as a
distinctive side of medieval poetry. But his normal opinion can be seen
when he lists The Prurient among the principal subdivisions of bad
style, and describes it as "everywhere known by . . . Images of the

Genital Parts of Men and Women. It consists wholly of Metaphors drawn from [these] two most fruitful Sources. . . ."[8] And he advises the bad poet with an ironic analogy:

> The Physician, by the Study and Inspection of Urine and Ordure, approves himself in the Science; and in like sort should our Author accustom and exercise his Imagination upon the Dregs of Nature.[9]

In Malory the matter is accepted, without the excitement which attaches itself to a prohibited subject.

A related freedom is seen when the most abusive language in the *Morte Darthur* is used by a lady in rank, Linette. "In the devyls name, thou bawdy kychyn knave!" is a chorus to her speeches to Gareth.[10] She later confesses that her abuse was "foule", and that Gareth showed a high degree of courtesy in enduring it; but the wrong lay in the falsity of her accusations, not in any abandonment of good manners.[11] There is no sign that, had Gareth really been a fraud, she or Malory would have felt it improper for a lady to abuse the impostor in violent terms.

In the speech of all Malory's characters, we find the recognisable accent of popular speech, in many particular phrases and in a general stress on forcefulness rather than precision. At one point Guenivere protests to Mellyagaunce: "I had levir kut myne owne throte in twayne rather than thou sholde dishonoure me!" Lancelot says (and to a lady): "The devyll made you a shoter!" And Arthur produces an obvious colloquial phrase to Gawain with: "What, nevew? . . . is the wynde in that dore?"[12] And these are the three most important characters in the story and the highest in rank. Phrases from common speech are found even in speeches of dignity. Before enlarging on Tor's future, Merlin says: "Nay, nay . . . thys ys but japis that he hath do. . . ." And Bors interrupts important speeches with "howsomever the game goth" and the colloquial "by youre good will".[13] In comparison with this, the style of the nineteenth-century Arthurian romances seems emasculated.

We may also pause to notice three additional ways common to ordinary speech by which Malory chose frequently to intensify the effect of his dialogue: oaths, proverbs, and vocatives. Preachers in the middle ages complained that:

> No man now-a-daies unnethis canne speke ony word but if an ooth be at the other eende.[14]

and with due allowance for overstatement, this is also true of Malory's dialogue at every social level. The oaths make the colloquial speeches the more forceful and the dignified ones the more elevated.

The extreme of the impersonal colloquial is found in the aphorisms, *sententiae*, catchphrases, and proverbs scattered throughout the dialogue of the *Morte Darthur*. All of them testify to a common experience shared by the narrator, characters, and the readers, who have formed the language in which these expressions have become accepted as authoritatively true.[15] The proverb proper, which has been defined as a generalisation not completely separated from a specific example, has a history of varied acceptability in literature. Most medieval and Renaissance writers found it a pleasing and persuasive way of expressing truth. One of the improvements in Speight's second edition of Chaucer (1602) was the marking out of Chaucer's proverbs by tiny pointing hands along the margin of the text. The Augustans began a reaction against the proverb, banishing it first from polite conversation and then from polite literature. As inhabitants of the Age of Reason, they preferred their generalisations pure rather than applied. Lord Chesterfield expressed their common opinion in a letter to his son:

> Old sayings, and common proverbs . . . are so many proofs of having kept bad and low company. For example: if, instead of saying that tastes are different, and that every man has his own peculiar one, you should let off a proverb, and say, that what is one man's meat is another man's poison . . . ; everybody would be persuaded that you had never kept company with anybody above footmen and housemaids.[16]

And after this time, proverbs came to have associations with the uneducated, which continue, though to a lesser degree, to our own day. The twentieth-century preference for the concrete rather than the abstract, or at least for the symbol rather than the unadorned concept, has allowed us a renewed sympathy with proverbs.

In late medieval and Renaissance high society, there was no aversion to proverbs, rather the reverse. In Malory's time, the king's brother-in-law, Earl Rivers, could translate a work based on proverbs, the *Dicts and Sayings of the Philosophers*. This was the first book which Caxton is known to have printed in England, and he twice reprinted it.[17] Other writers less exalted also used proverbs and proverbial sayings, some more, some less. In the Paston Letters, the family and their servants

seem to use them equally: Margaret Paston is especially fond of
bringing an argument to a climax with a proverb.[18] Richard Cely the
Younger clinches a letter to his brother with:

> Be well ware how that ye do hyt ys better to pyttye than be
> pyttyd.[19]

Among the writers patronised by the court, the moral Gower found
proverbs a useful source of *sententiae*, and Chaucer put them to varied
uses in his different kinds of writing. He finds them telling, not only
for instruction and for humorous effect, but also for characterisation,
matching the kind of proverb with the character who uses it. Proverbs
are particularly frequent in the speech of five of his characters: the
Wife of Bath, John in the *Reve's Tale*, the falcon in the *Squire's Tale*,
and Pandarus and Criseyde.[20] The last two are the most sophisticated
and self-possessed aristocrats he ever drew. Both delight in resorting to
the authority or consolation of proverbial wisdom.

With this in mind, we should be able to banish any lingering
eighteenth-century suspicion that proverbs are the resort of stupid
or uneducated minds, and we will not be surprised to find Malory, like
most of his contemporaries, using them. A few stand out because they
are explicitly called proverbs:

> Hit is an olde sawe, "Gyeff a chorle rule and thereby he woll nat
> be suffysed."   [V 712.23]

> Hyt ys an olde-seyde saw: "A good man ys never in daungere
> but whan he ys in the daungere of a cowhard."   [V 1126.5]

> Hit ys an olde-seyde sawe, "there ys harde batayle thereas kynne
> and frendys doth batayle ayther ayenste other."   [V 1084.5]

This formal setting-off makes them more conspicuous than the many
others which occur unobtrusively throughout the book. It is consistent
with the nature of the *Morte Darthur* that so high a proportion of the
few explicit judgements on life which punctuate the action should be
spoken by the characters rather than the narrator, and delivered in a
traditional form. When Elaine says to Lancelot:

> "I have gyvyn the the grettyst ryches and the fayryst floure that
> ever I had, and that is my maydynhode. . . ."   [V 796.21]

the phrase is striking not because it is original but because it is right. We may note at this point that with some few exceptions, the proverbs in Malory's book impress in conveying not an individual personality but a common humanity and shared attitudes. In loss or defeat, Malory's characters frequently find dignity and some resignation in those proverbs which, by their very existence as proverbs, testify that others have also faced the insuperable and have not been able to overcome it. Thus we find Merlin accepting his own inability to persuade Arthur at the beginning of the story:

"But thereas mannes herte is sette he woll be loth to returne."

[V 97.26]

And we see the same in Lancelot at the end:

"That shall repente me whyle I lyve, but ayenste deth may no man rebell." [V 1251.13]

One great authority has said that the use of this kind of proverb is characteristic of the late middle ages, and indeed, has gone on to say that proverbs never preach resistance.[21] Their accent, he tells us, is always of resignation. This is misleading if applied to Malory's characters. The proverbs and proverbial phrases they use help them towards the acceptance of a common idea, but the idea may be one which spurs them to action. Such phrases help to confirm Arthur's resolution to fight on in hopeless straits, to encourage Mellyagaunce to take on a formidable opponent, and to give Lancelot understanding to lift him out of despair.[22] One group which does try to instil resignation has an unusual individual quality, demonstrating that Dinadan's common sense is the sense of the common man:

"Lo, sir Trystram, here may a man preve, be he never so good yet may he have a falle; and he was never so wyse but he myght be oversayne, and he rydyth well that never felle." [V 516.3]

But whether they urge the characters to action or passivity, the proverbs add a resonance to their lives. They become more rather than less frequent in the later books, and help to give an air of universality and impersonal authority to much of what is said in the final tragedy.

We are given an important but very different effect by Malory's use of the vocative. Vocatives serve to vary pace and emphasis, especially by doubling up the name and title together. Apart from any dignity in the title itself, and the emphasis put on it by its interruption of the plain-sense flow of the meaning, it divides the speech into significant portions, and often implies a deliberateness in the speaker which has a dignity of its own. The speaker is aware both of what he has to say, and to whom he is saying it. In this at least, Lord Chesterfield would have approved of Malory, as much as he would have disapproved of the casual practice of the twentieth century.[23] The vocatives are part of the ineluctable courtesy of Malory's high moments. For instance:

> "My kynge, my lorde, and myne uncle," seyde sir Gawayne, "wyte you well, now I shall make you a promyse whych I shall holde by my knyghthode. . . ." [V 1186.1]

> "My moste redoubted kynge, ye shall undirstonde, by the Popis commaundemente and youres I have brought to you my lady the quene, as ryght requyryth. And if there by ony knyght, of what degré that ever he be off, except your person, that woll sey or dare say but that she ys trew and clene to you, I here myselff, sir Launcelot du Lake, woll make hit good uppon hys body that she ys a trew lady unto you.
> "But, sir, lyars ye have lystened, and that hath caused grete debate betwyxte you and me. For tyme hath bene, my lorde Arthur, that ye were gretly pleased with me whan I ded batayle for my lady, youre quene; and full well ye know, my moste noble kynge, that she hathe be put to grete wronge or thys tyme. And sytthyn hyt pleased you at many tymys that I shulde feyght for her, therefore mesemyth, my good lorde, I had more cause to rescow her from the fyer whan she sholde have ben brente for my sake." [V 1197.4]

The changes are rung: "my most redoubted king", "my lord Arthur", "my most noble king", "my good lord"; and each emphasises Arthur's dignity, Lancelot's self-control, and his awareness that he is not merely justifying himself *in vacuo*, but speaking to King Arthur. The vocatives also recall their past and irrecoverable relationship. A rather similar effect is achieved in Galahad's last brief speech, and it is the more impressive that so much of so short and crucial a speech should be taken up by it:

"My fayre lorde, salew me unto my lorde sir Launcelot, my fadir, and as sone as ye se hym bydde hym remembir of this worlde unstable." [V 1035.10]

The same effect is found everywhere in Malory, even in polite conversation like that of Pellinor and Meliot de Logres.[24] And our casualness in everyday life probably makes it more effective for us than it was for our forebears.

The speech of the hermits in the "Grail" provides a contrast with the rest of Malory's dialogue. Much of the longer speeches is mere narrative in disguise. The syntax is simple: interjections, vocatives, and oaths are few; and direct speech is found within what is formally direct speech. This last is not found anywhere else.[25] And we even find here a unique instance of the *incipit* of a tale within a passage of direct speech (V 993.27). Malory often had difficulty with the algebraic shifts of tense between direct and indirect speech, shifts which are second nature to even moderately educated writers of the twentieth century. We have seen something of his weaknesses in maintaining sequence of tenses, and his ever-present tendency to lapse without warning from indirect into direct speech.[26] His narrative instinct was for the easiest manner of telling, and he seems only to have been able to find the extra energy needed for keeping a long speech authentic and personal where the issues were abnormally grave, as in the climactic speeches by Lancelot in the "Morte". But whatever the reason, the longer speeches by the hermits in the "Grail" display none of the formal signs of direct speech once they are under way. We cannot think that this near-narrative dialogue is to be regarded as the special speech of the hermits as a class, since their shorter speeches, and the speeches of the hermit in "Lancelot & Guenivere" and the bishop in the "Morte" are without this simplicity.

Interjections, vocatives, and oaths, which are necessarily absent from any normal fictional narrative, are not the only factors which make Malory's dialogue more complicated than his narration. When he is imitating a speaking voice, his syntax is capable of greater grammatical feats. So we more often find a competent use of apposition like:

"Thys ys a grete hurte unto kynge Arthurs courte, the losse of suche a man!" [V 1020.13]

But the modification of one clause by others can be more complex than this simple pronoun in apposition to a suspended noun phrase:

"If ever I dud thynge that plesed The, Lorde, for Thy pité ne
have me nat in dispite for my synnes done byforetyme, and that
Thou shew me somthynge of that I seke." [V 1015.11]

Malory begins to think more than one clause at a time:

"I besech you, as ye have ben ever my speciall good lady, and I
at all tymes your poure knyght and trew unto my power, and as I
never fayled you in ryght nor in wronge sytthyn the firste day
kynge Arthur made me knyght, that ye woll pray for my soule
if that I be slayne." [V 1166.13]

The firm structure of moderately complex syntax is here evident. The
end of the sentence must have been in mind at the beginning, and the
writer had enough syntactic grasp to insert two parallel subordinate
units into the main structure of his sentence without losing control of
it. This was never typical of Malory, but in the later books, and especially in dialogue, he can sometimes produce a sentence like this, whose
tautness is emphasised by the simplicity which prevails elsewhere.[27]
This gives by contrast a special force and dignity to the speeches in
which such control is shown.

The dialogue is also strengthened by a feature we have already noticed
in his narrative, a ready doubling-up of parts of speech, which gives
control of pace and often adds dignity by selective deliberateness and
emphasis:

"And now, sir knyght, at thy requeste I woll that thou wete
and know that I am sir Launcelot du Lake." [V 267.4]

"Sir Percyvale, my lorde salewith the and sendeth the worde
thou aray the and make the redy." [V 913.21]

"I wolde nat for all the londys I welde to knowe and wyte hit
were so. . . ." [V 1076.36]

These doublets too are a growth rooted in common speech. When
John Paston II is trying to placate a very angry father, he asks that he
will:

remember and consider the pain and heaviness that it hath
been to me syn your departing. . . . [I] am not of power to do any-

thing in this country for worship and profit of you ... which
might or should be to your pleasing. ... I shall out of doubt
hereafter do that shall please you to the uttermost of my power
and labour.[28]

This trick of speech can become a habit, especially to a mind with
legal training. The formation laid against Walter Aslak bulges with
emphatic doublets of this kind. The anonymous writer, who may well
have been a notary, complains that the victim was:

> felonowsely slowen and mordered in the most orrible wyse that
> ever was herd spoken of in that cuntre.[29]

And the rest of the letter is similarly overwritten.

The lack of differentiation of individual characters often obscures
from us the potential range of Malory's dialogue, unrestricted as it
was by theories of high style. Though differences in mood are reflected
in speech, sometimes with a masterly hand, there is little difference
between different knights in the same mood. Defiance, affection, and
defeat are expressed in very similar words by different people. Dinadan,
who is conceived by both Malory and his source as an anomalous character, is to some extent an exception to this. But with this
exception excepted, our impression is of the similarity of all knights,
not of the difference between individual men. So with this repeated
challenge:

> Than anone sir Blamour ... bade sir Trystrames, "alyght, for
> thoughe my horse hath fayled, I truste to God the erthe woll nat
> fayle me!" [V 409.8]

> (Lamorak) "Thoughe a marys sonne hath fayled me now, yette
> a quenys sonne shall nat fayle the!" [V 429.15]

> (Gawain) "Gyff a marys sonne hath fayled me, wyte thou well
> a kyngis sonne and a quenys sonne shall nat fayle the!"
> [V 1219.35]

This technique can lead to episodes of impersonal magnificence like
the death of Uwayne le Avoutres.[30] It adds to the intrinsically striking

situation that nearly every phrase of the dying knight's speeches has
been used by other knights previously, which reinforces the jar this
killing will give to the sworn and knightly unity of the Round Table.
For instance, Uwayne says to Gawain:

> "Of a much more worshipfuller manneshande myght I nat dye."
> [V 945.8]

Palomides has said to Tristram:

> "Of a bettir knyghtes hondys myght I never be slayne."
> [V 781.32]

And Gawain himself is to say to Lancelot:

> "Of a more nobelar man myght I nat be slayne." [V 1231.22]

It is not the differences but the similarities which are striking, in the
generous tribute of one noble man *in extremis* to another. Both
Palomides and Gawain are to some extent effectively realised as
characters, yet they express themselves in nearly identical words. The
difference between the effects of these similar phrases is caused by the
difference in the situation and character of the speakers. Love madness
has made Palomides nearly indifferent to death, whereas Gawain has
just been shocked out of an obsessional hatred, and Uwayne has received
his death-wound from his cousin almost by accident. But each thinks
of the man who has killed him as well as of himself. The similarity of
their speeches tends to make this a knightly characteristic and to
emphasise what they have in common, as well as providing a cumulative effect as we read on.[31]

It is significant that both the phrases exemplified recur in the "Morte",
which is full of echoes in phrases and situations recapitulated from
earlier books. The waking of the Archbishop from his dream is
described in terms which recall Lancelot waking in the Grail-castle.[32]
In the "Morte", where Malory's imagination is most active, he is
constantly recalling the earlier books.

This recurrence, which is characteristic of Malory's prose style at all
levels, naturally has a cumulative effect. In dialogue, the cumulative
effect is felt in the stock phrases and the subjects of common interest
which bind the knightly class together. These we have touched on

already. We also find recurrence in a more restricted context. Many of the phrases in the *Morte Darthur* echo across short distances, within or between speeches. This is common in dialogue and narrative and between the two.[33] Repetition within a speech gives us:

> "I slewe sir Marhalte and delyverde Cornwayle frome the trewage of Irelonde. And I am he that delyverde the kynge of Irelonde frome sir Blamoure de Ganys, and I am he that bete sir Palomydes, and wete you welle that I am sir Trystrames de Lyones that by the grace of God shall delyver this wofull Ile of Servage."
>
> [V 442.18]

> "Nevyr shall I se you agayne holé togydirs, therefore ones shall I se you togydir in the medow, all holé togydirs! Therefore I woll se you all holé togydir in the medow of Camelot, to juste and to turney, that aftir youre dethe men may speke of hit that such good knyghtes were here, such a day, holé togydirs."
>
> [V 864.7]

By repetition the first passage stresses the youthful confidence of Tristram, and the second Arthur's prophetic but helpless sadness. Malory's characters frequently echo one another's words between speeches:

> (Guenivere) "And if ye se that as to-morne they woll putte me unto dethe, than may ye rescowe me as ye thynke beste."
> "I woll well," seyde sir Launcelot, "for have ye no doute, whyle I am a man lyvyng I shall rescow you."   [V 1168.32]

A common variation is to find a speech ended with a key word or phrase from earlier within it:

> "Swete Fadir, Jesu Cryste! I wote natt what joy I am in, for thys passith all erthely joyes that ever I was in."
>
> [V 1011.17]

> "That ys trouth," seyde som knyghtes, "but they were slayne in the hurlynge, as sir Launcelot thrange in the thyckyst of the prees. . . . He . . . wyst nat whom that he smote, and so unhappely they were slayne."   [V 1183.22]

And cumulative effect is obviously important in Malory over the whole length of the *Morte Darthur*. Words like "fellowship", "departed", "noble knights" acquire strong overtones peculiar to this book through their insistent use in situations of nostalgia, praise, or sorrow. But words are also patterned on a smaller scale, in dialogue and narrative. This is a feature of the spoken language, where repetition ensures comprehension. If the formulas are similar enough, they call up the past and create expectations of the future. For instance:

> "Sir, us thynkis beste that ye knyghtly rescow the quene. Insomuch as she shall be brente, hit ys for youre sake; and hit ys to suppose, and ye myght be handeled, ye shulde have the same dethe, othir ellis a more shamefuller dethe. And, sir, we say all that ye have rescowed her frome her deth many tymys for other mennes quarels; therefore us semyth hit ys more youre worshyp that ye rescow the quene from thys quarell, insomuch that she hath hit for your sake." [V 1172.14]

The passage is dominated by its patterns of words, many of them drawn from the preceding events, which create and fulfil expectations. The words of the last clause are drawn from the two clauses which launched this piece of reasoning, and give us a sort of climax. The verbal structure is much more complete than the logical one, which is to a large degree assumed. We cannot be sure whether we should supply after the second sentence: "and so you can imagine what she feels like and must in pity rescue her," or "and so you need feel no scruples about killing King Arthur's men who are trying to kill you;" whether there is an undefined feeling that they are both in the same plight; or whether perhaps the second half of the second sentence is interrupting the progress of the argument with a thrill of horror at the thought of a shameful death for the best knight in the world. We do not quite know what Malory's motives were: as so often, a colloquial ellipsis has shortened them. With some motives, we can only tell that they were there though blurred, and strongly felt, and strongly stated. Malory's patterns of words at times give us meaningfulness without settling on an unambiguous meaning.

These devices of stock phrases, of repetition across short distances, of ending speeches with an earlier key word, and of using striking phrases at intervals throughout the whole *Morte*, phrases like "the best knight in the world", create a pattern which suggests meaning and suits an action which itself is full of parallels. For instance, Tristram's situation and character are parallel to those of Lancelot, and the early career of La Cote Mal Tayle closely resembles that of Gareth. This adds universality to the action and certainty to the sentiments, and gives extra force to the idea of the workings of a moral, though mysterious, universe behind the story.

In this world, Malory gives us a style of dialogue which stresses the similarity of all knights, not the difference between individuals. There is small place in it for the verbal minutiae with which the modern novelist discriminates his characters. Neither Malory nor his *dramatis personae* are given to introspection and self-analysis. And yet, when we examine the suitability of his speeches to his speakers, we often find that past events have deeply affected a person's feelings, or an habitual trait of character has created an individual response. Though similar feelings may find similar expression in different characters, the feeling ascribed often does striking justice to the situation. When Balin, pursued by a series of disasters, is told that he must fight a battle as soon as he arrives at a castle after a long journey, he says:

> "Wel," sayd Balyn, "syn I shalle, thereto I am redy; but traveillynge men are ofte wery and their horses to, but though my hors be wery, my hert is not wery. I wold be fayne ther my deth shold be." [V 88.25]

To the external fate which drives Balin to his destruction, Malory's insight has added a weariness at heart which makes him both welcome and fight his doom. His emotion is individual in the sense that it is the product of his own circumstances and no other, but it would be difficult to maintain that the style of the speech is different from Malory's norm. Balin's laconic courage makes us respect him: but many other characters can be brief too.

Even in the "Tristram", in which no critic has found much to praise, Malory shows flashes of insight into character. We see Kay being refused a quest he had boastfully assumed:

> "Sir knyght, " seyde the damesell, "what is your name?"
> "Wete you well my name is sir Kay the Senesciall that wyde-where is knowyn."
> "Sir," seyde the damesell, "lay downe that shylde, for wyte thou well hit fallyth nat for you, for he muste be a bettir knyght

than ye that shall welde this chylde."

"Damesell," seyd sir Kay, "I toke youre shylde nat to that
entente. But go whoso go woll, for I woll nat go with you."

[V 461.24]

It is Malory who makes Kay tell an obvious lie in a confused attempt
to justify himself in his humiliation.[34] Yet there is nothing in Malory's
originality here which is stylistically distinctive. We could not ascribe
the speeches to Balin or Kay by their style.

But although Malory's style is one more suited to expressing what
his characters have in common than the ways in which they differ, he
can occasionally show a fine ear for distinctive traits of speech, in
addition to that knowledge of the human heart which we come to
expect from him as a matter of course. This extra talent seems to be
called into activity by a sudden total intuition of how the characters
feel and how they would act in a certain time and place. It does not
necessarily reappear when the character appears again. There is something very medieval about the characterisation suddenly catching fire
in a particular situation, as when, in the Towneley Plays, Pilate and
Herod are seen as unjust territorial magnates and the Jewish priests as
medieval prelates, so that Anna can rebuke Cayphas for vindictive
hysteria against a helpless prisoner with:

Sir, thynk ye that ye ar a man of holy kyrk. . . .[35]

This could hardly happen partially or intermittently when the ruling
literary theory put a high value on individual psychology. We should
either have more characterisation or none at all. But whatever the
prevailing theory, the best writers always give more than they know.

To Malory, these individualizing insights come most often into the
thoughts and words of those of his characters who are not knights.
None of Malory's knights shows as much individuality as Chaucer's
knight reveals while telling his tale to the Canterbury pilgrims. The
facts must be assessed with a decent caution: one would not like to
assert, when Chaucer's knight uses the lions of Benmarin in a simile
illustrative of fierceness, that he is thinking of his spell of military
service there.[36] Pleasing as such a fantasy might be, literary critical
judgements need to depend on more than a single piece of evidence.

With Malory's insights we have a sufficient quantity. When Tor's
mother brings out the long-concealed secret of his birth, we find:

Whan she was a mayde and wente to mylke hir kyne, "there mette with me a sterne knyght, and *half be force* he had my maydynhode." [V 101.12]

The "half" tells us a good deal about the incident, as does "sterne" in which the older sense of "fierce", "violent" is primary.

Again, in "Gareth", when Morgause of Orkney comes to court (V 338–340), no theory of royal etiquette prevents Malory from faithfully reflecting the accents of the anxious resentful mother, and the uneasy brother who tries to calm her. The syntax of their speeches has a part in conveying this. The slight inconsequence common to Malory's arguments is here turned to advantage in the sudden starts of the thought, and the repetitions serve a structural purpose. Morgause asks first what they have done with Gareth, answers her own question, and asks it again, so no one can evade her meaning. She is slightly incoherent, distracted between two grievances, "What have you done with him," and "Where is he now," but as her lucidity suffers, her character gains. Arthur, all in one sentence, says he is sorry, praises her son, and lays a red herring: "Where is he now?" But she is not to be pacified, and repeats her first charge with added force, echoing Kay's insults to Gareth.[37] Whereon Arthur starts another excuse and again tries to distract her with the same question of where Gareth is now. Then suddenly he realises that some of the blame can be shifted to Morgause herself, so he jumps back to the subject of his previous sentence and develops it at length.

"Fayre sistir," seyde kynge Arthure, "ye shall ryght well wete that I knew hym nat, nother no more dud sir Gawayne, nothir his brethrene. But sytthe hit is so," seyde the kynge, "that he thus is gone frome us all, we muste shape a remedy to fynde hym. Also, sistir, mesemyth ye myght have done me to wete of his commynge, and than, if I had nat done well to hym, ye myght have blamed me." [V 339.19]

It is a true picture of the interaction of two minds at cross purposes reacting on one another and driven by their own impulses and feelings, and the truth of it is in Malory's style.

The end of the "Lancelot" shows several incidents whose tone is high comedy of an excellence surprising in a writer who presented the farce of Lancelot and Sir Belleus. The striking truth to life of the incidents in the "Lancelot" is mostly psychological and difficult to distinguish on stylistic grounds. One speech, however, stands out because of its style, and particularly its diction:

> "Hit is not so," seyde the lady, "truly, he seyth wronge on me. And for bycause I love and cherysshe my cousyn jarmayne, he is jolowse betwyxte me and hym; and as I mutte answere to God there was never sene betwyxte us none suche thynges. But, sir," seyde the lady, "as thou arte called the worshypfullyest knyght of the worlde, I requyre the of trewe knyghthode, kepe me and save me. . . ." [V 284.30]

The lady is completely characterised by this, her only speech. The euphemism "none suche thynges" catches her coyness, and her shallow flirtatious nature is exposed by her voluble, slightly redundant speech ("love and cherysshe", "and for bycause"), and the approach as near as is ladylike to swearing ("truly", "as I mutte answer to God"). It is so true to life that the reader is convinced that there is a purpose to the two "thou"s of the next sentence. Can it be that she is trying to force a slightly jarring intimacy on Lancelot to make sure he will defend her? We feel her to be the kind of person who would quickly drop into the second person singular with a strange man, and sympathise with her taciturn realistic husband. If she has been trying to do this, Lancelot puts her in her place when he answers her courteously with the respectful pronoun.

A passage quite unique in Malory results from his transformation of the meeting of Gawain and Ettard in his sources.[38] The diction is remarkable here too, but this time for deliberate ambiguity by a character, rather than euphemism. What in the source was a slow courtship by the lady has turned into a seduction by the knight, of amazing speed and dexterity. Almost as soon as Gawain has met Ettard and told her he has killed Pelleas, she moves towards a better understanding:

> "Truly," seyde she, "that is grete pyté for he was a passynge good knyght of his body. But of all men on lyve I hated hym moste, for I coude never be quytte of hym. And for ye have slayne hym I shall be your woman and to do onythynge that may please you."
> So she made sir Gawayne good chere. Than sir Gawayne sayde that he loved a lady and by no meane she wolde love hym.

"Sche is to blame," seyde Ettarde, "and she woll nat love you, for ye that be so well-borne a man and suche a man of prouesse, there is no lady in this worlde to good for you."

"Woll ye," seyde sir Gawayne, "promyse me to do what that ye may do be the fayth of your body to gete me the love of my lady?"

"Yee, sir, and that I promyse you be my fayth."

"Now," seyde sir Gawayne, "hit is yourself that I love so well; therefore holde your promyse."

"I may nat chese," seyde the lady Ettarde, "but if I sholde be forsworne."

And so she graunted hym to fulfylle all his desyre.   [V 169.11]

The ambiguous hints of Ettard's "your woman" and "onythynge" is the double talk current among the sophisticates of any period, and the speed of Gawain's expert verbal manoeuvres and her response to them reveal their characters completely. Once again we seem to have a little-portrayed side of fifteenth-century life truly rendered by Malory. The tacit understanding in the ambiguous use of words, and the picture of lechery in action, are not found in the source of this passage, nor anywhere else in Malory. And if Malory felt this to be an integral part of his Gawain's character, as it was in the Gawain traditional in English literature,[39] it does not show clearly in any of his Gawain's other appearances in the *Morte Darthur*. The converse is true at one point. Where the French Gawain had had dishonourable designs on Elaine of Astolat, Malory cuts all suggestion of this from his version of the incident.[40] It might have been because Malory disliked portraying love *paramours*. But whatever the motives for his changes, these incidents show Malory as an author of tantalisingly great potential in the portrayal of individual character through dramatic dialogue.

There are a few other cases of diction individualizing a character. King Arthur refers to himself in the royal phrase as "my person": the Roman Emperor does the same.[41] Later on, we find the Bishop of Rochester making a smooth distinction in passing between the Pope's "worshyp" and his own "poure honesté" (V 1195.24). The clerical unction of this is exceptional. The only passage resembling it is the hermit's speech:

"I have seyne the day ... I wolde have loved hym the worse bycause he was ayenste my lorde kynge Arthure, for sometyme

I was one of the felyship, but now I thanke God I am othirwyse disposed." [V 1075.20]

There is a confessional overtone to "disposed", of a world concerned with "the dispositions at the hour of our death." But Malory does not begin to create a whole ecclesiastical class of speech, as he had created a knightly one. We would expect clerics to be more familiar with the Bible than most people, but the echoes of the Bible in the "Grail" are evenly distributed among knights, hermits, and narrator. And if it is difficult to find distinguishing marks for groups of people in the *Morte Darthur*, it is hardly easier to find distinguishing marks for individuals. Lancelot's hermit is a competent self-controlled man, but although there is a touching justice of feeling to his masterly terseness when Lancelot's folly has undone his work and reduced Elaine to hysterics, and to his outburst when he first recognises Lancelot, neither speech has a personal touch which would identify him and only him as its speaker by its style.[42] But if Malory's characters were more particularized, they would lose a good deal of their universality and of their symbolic suggestiveness.

Some of Malory's most successful effects in portraying emotion through speech come from traits of style which at times appear as weaknesses. Both Palomides and Mark, for instance, love Isode and hate Tristram, and both seem to have obsessional characteristics which reveal themselves in the simple repetitive content and form of their speeches, and which suit their compulsive, passionate, and arbitrary actions.[43] Repetition again is used to reflect a static situation in the determined and resentful fury of Lamorak when Tristram unfairly unhorses him (V 428.31 ff.). Lamorak challenges Tristram three times and is three times refused. Each time Tristram enlarges on his motives, and each time Lamorak produces a new reason for fighting, dismissing Tristram's previous statement with a contemptuous "As for that. . . ." Each echoes his own words and the other's. But where Tristram wants reconciliation, Lamorak wants blood. The repetitions bring out their determination and reflect the unsatisfactory stasis of the situation. These characteristics are added to the scene by Malory, but whether with this intention or not, we cannot say.[44] For part of the power of his dialogue resides in its dramatic presentation without comment: comment which he might well have been unable to express.

In his speakers, we find repetition which displays constancy or obsession, an impression of courtesy from the vocatives, humour and terse speech which show competence and self-control, and a slight awkwardness in explanation which seems the product of impulsive speech or overwhelming emotion in natures more at ease with action than with words. All these may be the work of a man who wrote better than he knew. They would certainly seem to have come from a writer who would have had the same difficulty as his characters in explaining the mastery he felt.

The Narrator

It is the nature of words to communicate, and our first pre-literary response to language is to someone communicating something. Behind every set of words we read or hear is someone writing or saying them to us, with whom we enter into a relationship created by the words. In the case of reading, it is a unilateral relationship. Because he knows every book must have an author, the reader instinctively forms an impression of the kind of person the author is. Thus the way in which an author presents his text and himself is of the first importance in the total literary impression which his book makes. Authors both before and after Malory exploited the possibilities of this with deliberate art. Many very run-of-the-mill medieval poems were clearly written for lively dramatic delivery; readers and listeners were encouraged to visualise exciting moments, and the narrator swore to the truth of the tale, appealed for silence, thanked his audience, and passed round the hat.[1] Better authors used the same relationship with more discrimination. Chaucer, reading his poems before a court most of whose members knew him personally, had to learn to exploit his relationship with them as narrator, and his early poems show him learning to vary this always subordinate position with comedy and to defeat expectation with surprise.[2] Sir Thomas Wyatt can be seen exploiting the same arts of surprise in some of his songs. But it is the nineteenth century, the Romantic century in which writer and audience alike idolized the creative genius of the author, which provides us with the most instructive contrasts. Three of the narrator's traits as we see them in *Vanity Fair*, power, knowledge, and intimacy, will provide us a yardstick for comparisons. Thackeray flaunts his control of his subject, as this passage shows:

... the heroine of this work, Miss Sedley (whom we have
selected for the very reason that she was the best-natured of all,
otherwise what on earth was to have prevented us from putting up
Miss Swartz, or Miss Crump, or Miss Hopkins, as heroine in her
place?). . . .[3]

He also boasts of his omniscience:

I wonder whether she knew that it was not only Becky who
wrote the letters, but that Mrs. Rawdon actually took and sent
home the trophies—which she bought for a few francs, from one
of the innumerable pedlars. . . . The novelist, who knows everything knows this also.[4]

And he deliberately exploits his relationship with his reader:

All which details, I have no doubt, JONES, who reads this
book at his Club, will pronounce to be excessively foolish,
trivial, twaddling, and ultra-sentimental. Yes; I can see Jones at
this minute (rather flushed with his joint of mutton and half-pint
of wine), taking out his pencil and scoring under the words
"foolish, twaddling," &c., and adding to them his own remark
of "*quite true*".[5]

It is revealing to compare Malory with Thackeray in these three
respects. Thackeray is deliberately creating a vigorous, abusive, and
individual relationship with the reader which subdues the world he
observes to his own remorseless, observant, and contemptuous view
of life. He can therefore afford to stand aside at crucial moments and
present the story in crisp sentences of brutal dramatic immediacy.[6]
Malory's situation as story-teller is the antithesis of this. He did not
choose between the brusque independence of a Hemingway and the
clinging stinging intimacy of a Thackeray. He wrote in a strong
tradition which settled the relationship between author and audience,
and even provided many of the phrases which expressed or implied
that relationship.[7] Although this tradition left him some freedom of
emphasis, he did not exploit it to the full as Chaucer did. Rather, he
seems to have accepted it unselfconsciously, and let the story stand on
its own. His structural technique was simple: to begin at the beginning,
to go on until he came to the end, and then to stop.[8] He makes no

effort to indicate simultaneity of events, and his method of narration is, in comparison with Thackeray's, unobtrusive, scenic, and impersonal. It rarely gives complicated judgements, panoramic views, or intrusions into the action. Yet it is as important in our apprehension of events as is Thackeray's.

Unlike Thackeray, Malory claims no power over the events he relates, and little over his manner of telling them. His interruptions of the narrative flow are fewer and less important than those in his French and his English sources. In both kinds of romance, stock phrases which bring both author and audience to mind are common. There are two main types, the first of which marks and emphasises transitions in the story. Such is the frequent "Ore dist li contes" in the French romances. The second kind is make up of assurances of the truth of the story, varying from a mere "vos poïssiez veoir" to calling on God as a witness.[9] These phrases are conventional and hence unobtrusive, but even so, Malory reduces their number. He does not, for instance, reproduce a single "ore dist li contes" by the corresponding formula "now turne we" in his tale of Balin. But though his appearances are fewer than those of the narrators in his sources, they still have a definite effect in revealing to us the kind of person who is telling the story.

Certain of his intrusions into the flow of narrative in his own person fall into a special class. They are not nearly as numerous as the ones we have just mentioned, but they are not conventional, and so they are especially conspicuous. They serve to set the story in the far historical past, and to lament the subsequent decline.[10] Dress, hermitry, love, justice, and funeral rites had all changed since King Arthur's times, and only fickleness had remained constant. Malory begins his story by locating it in time: "Hit befel in the dayes of Uther Pendragon, when he was kynge of all Englond . . . ;" he dates the Grail 454 years after the time of the Passion of Christ; he corroborates his story with the historical evidence of Gawain's skull, still in Dover castle; and he ends his book deciding which version of the story of Lancelot's kinsmen is nearest the truth, dismissing the rejected case with "—but that was but favour of makers!"[11] He breaks into his story to lament the death of a brave man:

All his oste was borne up by his hondys, for he abode all knyghtes. Alas, he myght nat endure, the whych was grete pité! [V 76.33]

He expects prayers for a character much as he asks them for himself:

All maner jantylmen hath cause to the worldes ende to prayse sir Trystram and to pray for his soule. AMEN, SAYDE SIR THOMAS MALLEORRÉ. [V 683.2]

He laments that no man's skill is adequate to relate the facts of the meeting of Tristram and Isode:

> And to telle the joyes that were betwyxte La Beall Isode and sir Trystramys, there ys no maker can make hit, nothir no harte can thynke hit, nother no penne can wryte hit, nother no mowth can speke hit.[12] [V 493.2]

He cites the authority of the "French book" for events seventy times in the course of the *Morte Darthur*.[13] And his other references to his story treat it, as the points above suggest, as unalterable historical fact, in which he has some small freedom of presentation. Such is the effect of phrases like "here levyth of the tale ... ," "now turne we to ... ," "so to shortyn thys tale ... ," "as ye have herde toforehande ... ," "as ye shall hyre or the booke be ended ... ," and "shorte tale to make ... ," which recur throughout the tales, and of the *explicits* and *incipits* which set them off. Such above all is the effect of Malory's unwearying factual style in chronicling the adventures of the Round Table. We are given a definite sense of history, which is *ipso facto* unalterable, by the author or anyone else.

We have seen previously how much Malory's expression shares with phrases in the common speech of his time. It is interesting and significant to notice the coincidences between Malory's epitaph on Sir Tristram and an epitaph on a real hunter, which John Shirley, the early fifteenth-century scribe, inserted into a doggerel list of contents for a manuscript of his. The subject of this epitaph is the very Duke of York whose prose style we have already noticed as illustrating the "nontradition" of secular prose.[14] Shirley writes:

> I prey to god feyre mot him falle
> Duk of York, the last *Edwarde*
> That dyed in the vauntwarde
> Of the bataylle in Picardye
> At Agincourt, this is no lye,
> For as of huntyng, here to fore

> Was never taught so truwe lore
> To alle that beon gentyl of kynde,
> Beon bounde, to have his soule in mynde
> And namelych, of this oure regyoun
> Whiche was cleped Albyoun. . . .[15]

Malory takes up the same points and urges the same obligation on his readers for his fictitious hero:

> For, as bookis reporte, of sir Trystram cam all the good termys of venery and of huntynge, and all the syses and mesures of all blowyng wyth an horne; and of hym we had fyrst all the termys of hawkynge, and whyche were bestis of chace and bestis of venery, and whyche were vermyns; and all the blastis that longed to all maner of game . . . and many other blastis and termys, that all maner jantylmen hath cause to the worldes ende to prayse sir Trystram and to pray for his soule.   [V 682.28]

Without external factual knowledge, it would be hard to tell which epitaph was real and which fictitious. The similarities confirm our feeling of the verisimilitude of the *Morte Darthur*.

Much of our impression of how far the mind behind the story is controlling it comes not from Malory's relatively few appearances as narrator, but from the ever-present effects of the narrative itself. The narration is simple and unobtrusive, tending always to a single narrative line, interrupted by a little prophecy, recapitulation, and commentary. The predominantly paratactic prose in which it is related gives the story a remarkable objectivity, and the simple past tense of the verbs puts the story firmly in a distant and unalterable past. The description of action, such as tournaments, meals, and travelling, is generally brief, factual, and formulaic, not in any way imaginative; so the attention remains on the subject, not on a controlling mind behind it:

> Sir Launcelot seyd all the worship that myght be spokyn by sir Trystram.   [V 535.28]

> So, aftir that, thoughe there were fayre speche, love was there none.   [V 396.9]

The second of these reflections has moved away from the personal towards the authoritative ring of a proverb. These things ensure that the story itself claims the reader's attention, and that the narrator, far from being in control, often seems to be entirely absent.

Our sense of the objectivity of the facts of the story is yet further increased by the treatment of the commentary. Many of the judgements passed are put in the mouths of trustworthy interpreters rather than the narrator. Sometimes these interpreters are ordinary people like Dinadan:

> To hymself he seyde thus: "And sir Trystram knew for whos love [syr Palomides] doth all this dedys of armys, sone he wolde abate his corrage.   [V 738.19]

Sometimes they are spoken by authoritative figures like Merlin. The prophecies which unify the story are often brought about within it, and are heard from the mouths of the characters. The damsel who gives Balin his sword prophesies his death, and Merlin spends most of the tale of Balin in prophecy, yet he is an individual character, not a mere author's mouthpiece.[16] The body of doctrine and judgement and prophecy in the "Grail" is put into the mouths of various hermits. These are conventionally reliable figures, and the device prevents the author from being obtrusive. It is the opinions of others, not the narrator, which establish Lancelot as the best knight in the world.[17] This apparent lack of control over material seemingly independent and existing in its own right is appropriate to a story in which men, although the most important factor in their world, are not the controlling one. God or fate or their sins, human treachery or the chance of war, are likely to bring the best to a sudden end.

Unlike Thackeray, Malory does not claim to be omniscient in the world of his book. The most subtle and pervasive type of omniscience is that of irony from a superior level of consciousness. This is most effective when it reveals a mind which is not only better informed but also more sophisticated and more introspective than the minds of the characters. This it does in Thackeray, who knows more of the way of the world than his characters, knows more particular facts, and especially knows himself and his readers.

In contrast, Malory seems to be very much on the same level as his characters, in knowledge as he is in power. The irony which comes from an author's superior knowledge of the world was of course as available to a medieval author as to a modern one, and perhaps more conspicuously so if the author visualised himself reading aloud to a circle of patrons. It may have been in such readings that Chaucer discovered the effectiveness of assuming the (intermittently transparent) *persona* of a henpecked onlooker, which he uses so successfully in the *House of Fame* and the General Prologue to the *Canterbury Tales*. The reader shares or seems to share the secret thoughts and feelings of the narrator in a way the characters in the story do not. This intimacy makes the narrator very important, even if the characters are clearly in some way better than he is, even if the narrator only knows his own weaknesses.

Among Arthurian writers, Wolfram von Eschenbach uses a self-mockery like Chaucer's to bring his local small beer and personal cowardice into contrast with the great events at the centre of his *Parzival*. And the author of *Sir Gawain and the Green Knight*, when he describes Gawain's winter journey from Arthur's court to Bercilak's, uses his superior knowledge of the world to gain the audience's affection and understanding for his idealistic young hero. It is clear to us that that excellent young man is about to gain knowledge and self-knowledge the hard way. The variations of this technique can set up a delicate balance between the real and fictional worlds, between knowledge and action, which can imply judgements on each from the standpoint of the other. But although his characters are occasionally ironic at one another's expense, Malory does not allow himself as narrator an ironic superiority over them. Because he is not set above his subject by irony, the narrator's comment "X was a hardy knight" seems more the reportage of a person caught up in events independent of him than the activity of a controlling mind.

This impression is further strengthened by the narrator's psychological insight, which is apparently limited. Malory's commentary on his characters rarely goes beyond what could be provided in a few words by any observer without special insight. As with every other generalisation about Malory, there are a few minor exceptions to this. The most important of these few is the narrator's observations on the attempt by Gareth and Lyonesse to anticipate their wedding:

> This counceyle was nat so prevyly kepte but hit was undirstonde, for they were but yonge bothe and tendir of ayge and had nat used suche craufftis toforne. [V 333.5]

For once, the narrator is coming close to that omniscience which puts him on one level and the characters below him on another. Even a little of that would destroy the impression of objective fact which the *Morte Darthur* achieves. And the example of commentary above, sympathetic and endearing though it is, suggests that we should certainly lose by the exchange. It is trivial enough when compared with the unexpressed intuitions latent in the dialogue. It seems certain that Malory was able to show things he could not have explained, and which he would have spoilt by attempting to explain.

But even so knowledgeable an explanation as we have seen above is rare. The narrator does not often tell us what is going on inside a character's mind,[18] and when he does describe emotions and traits of character, they are usually conveyed in single (often stock) phrases, carrying the sort of judgement which an ordinary man can infer from ordinary behaviour. And even such judgements as these are reduced in number from his sources. Malory tends to eliminate phrases like "le coeur lui eschauffe dyre" which occur in the French romances.[19] The explicit judgements on people in the *Morte Darthur* are quite unremarkable, whether they come from the narrator, or from one of the characters:

> "Thys ys a passynge good knyght and the beste that ever y founde, and moste of worship withoute treson, trechory, or felony." [V 64.1]

> And whan he sawe their countenaunce he dredde hym sore. . . .
> The grounde had quaked a lytyll; therewithall he feared.
> [V 280.9, 21]

Malory is making the same sort of judgements on his characters as they make on each other. And because his own interjections and his factual chronicle style separate the facts from him as narrator, his comment that X was "a semely man" or "a myghty kynge of men" becomes the observation of fact by a bystander. We might contrast Malory's acceptance of facts which "the Frensshe boke saith" with Sir Thomas More's frequent use of "hearsay phrases" like "Wise men said", in his *Richard III*. It was a technique More had learnt from Tacitus,[20] and More's phrases, while they distance him from the facts, simultaneously put him above them. They imply that he has sufficient wisdom to sift the evidence and to judge even the wise men.

Complex emotion in the *Morte* is only to be inferred from dialogue: it is not described, hinted at, or analysed by the narrator. Malory leaves his characters their mental privacy, and even allows them the irony he does not himself use:

> "That is overmuche seyde," sir Launcelot seyde, "of the at thys tyme." [V 265.31]

> "And therefore I woll do that I come fore." [V 84.7]

> "And wyte thou well, thou sir Palomydes Sarezyn, that we shall so handyll the or that thou departe that thou shalt wysshe that thou haddyst be crystynde." [V 717.36]

Malory's story can in this way be more subtle than his narrator's comments. We have noticed already that Mark's relationship with Tristram shows characteristics of obsession of which there is no hint in Malory's commentary, but almost any scene between Lancelot and Guenivere would equally well display Malory's silent insight. This absence of explicit knowledge further strengthens the chronicle verisimilitude of his book.

For these reasons, and because so many of Malory's knights are obviously taciturn, capable men of action, worthy of respect, they seem to stand independent of an author who only observes them from the outside, much as they might observe one another. The narrator's admiration for Lancelot comes to seem more like that of a man for his friend than the affection of a puppet-master for an interesting puppet.

It is appropriate to this spectator, who is so limited in ironic superiority and psychological insight, that he should have little to say about the way of the world at large. So little does the narrator intrude into the story with generalisations that it can be startling to find him able and willing to explain as much of the causes of things as:

> For oftetymes thorow envy grete hardynesse is shewed that hath bene the deth of many kyd knyghtes; for thoughe they speke fayre many one unto other, yet whan they be in batayle eyther wolde beste be praysed. [V 223.9]

There is more *savoir-faire* here than the rest of the story had taught us to expect from the narrator, even in military matters. Normally, the story seems wiser than the story-teller.

The narrator is not much more forthcoming with explanations of particular events than of life in general. We have seen that he does not use that kind of knowledge which would only be available to an author to explain the thoughts of his characters: neither does he use it to explain the development of the action. Normally we are given the facts without explanation, and left to fill in the causes and the details from our own imaginations. The explanations we receive are generally incomplete, and most of them come from the characters. Arthur will die in battle because of his sins, and Lancelot lies in a coma for twenty-four days because of the twenty-four years of his adultery.[21] But these are by no means the full explanation of the story; they merely point more tantalisingly to an unexpounded scheme of justice and judgement behind the story as a whole. So in "Balin", the story is bound up with fate and "because"s which are not explained. Why is the vicious invisible Garlon at the court of Pelles; what does Balin mean by "I am the pryse, and yet am I not dede;" and why "because of the dethe of that lady thou shalt stryke a stroke moste dolerous that ever man stroke, excepte the stroke of oure Lorde Jesu Cryste"?[22] Similarly, how does Lancelot know:

> "Hit ys nat my swerde; also, I have no hardines to sette my honde thereto, for hit longith nat to hange be my syde. Also, who that assayth to take hit and faylith of that swerde, he shall resseyve a wounde by that swerde that he shall nat be longe hole afftir."
> [V 856.21]

We do not know the answers, but our impression from all this is of an inescapable net of doom in which advice is disregarded and disaster follows inevitably, yet the situation is the more impressive because it is comprehended little more by the narrator who chronicles the facts than by the characters in whose lives the pattern of destiny is worked out. The full story is beyond the author's knowledge as it is beyond his control; and the characters of the *Morte Darthur* are able to take on a tragic stature because they are not overshadowed by the narrator.[23]

This lack of control is confirmed when Malory as narrator takes to explanation. The natural order of events is not adequate for complicated relationships, and these cause Malory many difficulties. The two most striking of these are misfit clauses and "trailing sentences" in which

F

"for . . . for . . . for. . . ." sequences unroll backwards towards a First
Cause. Both phenomena come from thinking only one clause at a
time.[24] Misfit clauses temporarily lead us astray by their order in the
sentence. For instance:

> And the name of thys knyght was called Balyne, and by good
> meanys of the barownes he was delyverde oute of preson, for he
> was a good man named of his body, and he was borne in
> Northehumbirlonde. [V 62.36]

After the initial shock of trying to discover why Arthur's barons
should give special favour to Northumbrian knights, the reader adjusts
himself to an apparent *naïveté* on the part of the author. Some other
examples have been quoted above.[25] Occasionally the effects can be
worse than this; as when Malory seems, because he had not thought far
enough in advance, to try to exculpate a coward:

> So whan sir Ector saw sir Gawayne downe, he drew hym asyde
> and thought hit no wysedom for to abyde hym, and also for
> naturall love, for because he was hys uncle. [V 981.28]

Malory's clauses of explanation are rarely successful unless simple, as in
Lyonesse's proud statement:

> "Brothir . . . I can nat telle you, for hit was nat done be me
> nother be myne assente, for he is my lorde and I am his, and he
> muste be myne husbonde. Therefore, brothir, I woll that ye wete
> I shame nat to be with hym nor to do hym all the plesure that I
> can." [V 334.10]

Because of the fundamentally paratactic nature of Malory's syntax, a
compensatory weight is placed on those words which do assert
relationship and function, as we see in the example above. A more
complex and rather less coherent explanation is found in the "Grail":

> "Alas!" seyde kynge Arthure. . . , "ye have nygh slayne me for
> the avow that ye have made, for thorow you ye have berauffte me
> the fayryst and the trewyst of knyghthode that ever was sene
> togydir in ony realme of the worlde. For whan they departe frome
> hense I am sure they all shall never mete more togydir in thys worlde,
> for they shall dye many in the queste. And so hit forthynkith nat me

a litill, for I have loved them as well as my lyff. Wherefore hit shall greve me ryght sore. . . , for I have had an olde custom to have hem in my felyship." [V 866.19]

One feels that Malory is here, as so often, getting the strength of his weaknesses, and that it is not by deliberate art that the rambling backward extension of Arthur's search into his own motives mimes successfully the incoherence of real grief. And he can reach directly back several removes into causes:

For, as the Freynshe booke seyth, the kynge was full lothe that such a noyse shulde be uppon sir Launcelot and his quene; for the kynge had a demyng of hit, but he wold nat here thereoff, for sir Launcelot had done so much for hym and for the quene so many tymes that wyte you well the kynge loved hym passyngly well. [V 1163.20]

This is one of Malory's most successful sentences of explanation. It breaks emphatically at "but", balancing against the preceding clause another co-ordinate with it, which then extends itself in casual dependents until it far outweighs the original. The very movement of the sentence imitates Arthur's feelings. In dialogue a touch of manly incoherence testifies to the force of emotion behind the speech, as for example, when Lancelot refuses an offer of illicit love in the "Lancelot". In explanation by the narrator, on the other hand, it characterises him with a certain *naïveté* and marks him as a man who does not comprehend, let alone control, his world.[26] It is thus a further guarantee of truth. The logic of the famous "love and summer" passage may be almost impossible to disentangle.[27] but the reader cannot doubt the urgency and importance with which its conclusions are presented. When resolved into a modern translation it loses its force as well as its charm.[28]

Malory is again the antithesis of Thackeray in his relationship with his reader. Thackeray continually swivels his moral judgement to let fly at both reader and himself:

In a word everybody went to wait upon this great man—everybody who was asked: as you the reader (do not say nay) or I the writer hereof would go if we had an invitation.[29]

Malory as narrator is always present, but he faces towards the story. In a much quoted passage, drawn presumably from his own experience, he applies his knowledge of prison to Tristram without mention of himself at all. We only infer the personal application from other knowledge.

> So sir Trystram endured there grete payne, for syknes had undirtake hym, and that ys the grettist payne a presoner may have. For all the whyle a presonere may have hys helth of body, he may endure undir the mercy of God and in hope of good delyveraunce; but whan syknes towchith a presoners body, than may a presonere say all welth ys hym berauffte, and than hath he cause to wayle and wepe. Ryght so ded sir Trystram whan syknes had undirtake hym, for than he toke such sorow that he had allmoste slayne hymselff. [V 540.28]

Here we see Malory avoiding obtruding himself into the story. We find some information about the author in the *explicits* of "Arthur", "Gareth", and the "Morte", where he asks for prayers for his deliverance from prison. These are the only pieces of personal revelation in the *Morte Darthur* except his statement in the *explicit* of "Lancelot & Guenivere":

> So I leve here of this tale, and overlepe grete bookis of sir Launcelot, what grete adventures he ded whan he was called "le Shyvalere de Charyot".... And bycause I have loste the very mater of Shevalere de Charyot I departe frome the tale of sir Launcelot; and here I go unto the morte Arthur. . . .
> [V 1154.1–14]

The information that he is a prisoner is an unexpected and personal addition to the conventional relationship of reader and author, but it is placed where personal remarks were often found in the literature of his time, and the information is part of his normal and eminently practical request for prayers. These passages are not integral with the text. They are only part of the *Morte Darthur* in the way in which a dedication is part of a modern book, or a curtain-call, where the actors' expressions may to a limited extent reflect their own feelings, is part of a play. And even here, as with the curtain-call, there are formalities to be observed. Malory only uses the personal pronoun "I" of himself in three of his *explicits*. He normally refers to himself by his full title, or in his function as author, or in the third person, and scraps of French and Latin and of English verse are put in for the sake of dignity.[30] There is a propriety to be observed here, and especially in prayer, which prohibits any degree of intimacy with the reader.

But if Malory has no personal relationship with the reader in the *explicits*, he has one in the body of the story as narrator. The story is seen through his eyes, and no sharp dividing line can be drawn between narration and commentary. Whenever one of the characters is not speaking, it is the narrator's voice we hear, in all-pervading terminology and occasional comment. He is without complete knowledge of or control over his story, and his extraordinary stylistic simplicity, compounded of normative vocabulary and elementary syntactical patterns, is so unobtrusive as to convince the reader of the truth of what he is being told. The *persona* which emerges from the pages is naïve enough to be trusted implicitly. His only mannerism appears to be avoiding mannered writing, and his formulaic style allows attention to be concentrated on the facts, rather than on the writing or the writer.

> And than they dressid their shyldis and spearys, and cam togydyrs with all her myghtes of their horsys. And they mette so fersely that bothe the horsys and knyghtes felle to the erthe, and as faste as they myght avoyde there horsys and put their shyldis afore them, and they strake togedyrs with bryght swerdys as men that were of myght, and aythir woundid othir wondirly sore, that the bloode ran oute uppon the grasse. [V 568.28]

Even here, the formula "as men that were of myght" delivers a judgement by the author. But it is a brief and formulaic judgement, and exactly the one which his characters would have given. All these things render it inconspicuous, as on the frequent occasions when the narrator and characters echo one anothers' phrases.[31]

This unity of style brings the narrator very close to the action, yet keeps him so factual and impersonal that it takes an effort to notice his interruptions of the action, whether with factual information, as in:

> And kynge Pellam lay so many yerys sore wounded, and myght never be hole tylle that Galaad the Hawte Prynce heled hym in the queste of the Sankgreall. For in that place was parte of the bloode of oure Lorde Jesu Cryste, which Joseph off Aramathy brought

into thys londe. And there hymselff lay in that ryche bedde. And that was the spere whych Longeus smote oure Lorde with to the herte. And kynge Pellam was nyghe of Joseph his kynne, and that was the moste worshipfullist man on lyve in tho dayes, and grete pité hit was of hys hurte, for thorow that stroke hit turned to grete dole, tray and tene. [V 85.21]

or with comment:

Here men may undirstonde that bene men of worshyp that man was never fourmed that all tymes myght attayne, but somtyme he was put to the worse by malefortune and at som tyme the wayker knyght put the byggar knyght to a rebuke.
[V 484.18]

The narrator has strong feelings and opinions, which correspond to the characters'; only once does he leave the camouflage of his normal style to become an individual in his own time, turning his attention completely from his noble knights to his readers:

Thus was kynge Arthur depraved and evyll seyde off. . . .
Lo ye all Englysshemen, se ye nat what a myschyff here was? For he that was the moste kynge and nobelyst knyght of the worlde, and moste loved the felyship of noble knyghtes, and by hym they all were upholdyn, and yet myght nat thes Englyshemen holde them contente with hym. Lo thus was the olde custom and usayges of thys londe, and men say that we of thys londe have nat yet loste that custom. Alas! thys ys a greate defaughte of us Englysshemen, for ther may no thynge us please no terme.
[V 1229.2]

But even here we may notice that Malory's materials are those available to the other writers of his time. Most of them are used, though not so well, in this lament for Humphrey of Gloucester by the "G" continuator of *The Brut:*

Here may men mark what this world is! this Duke was a noble man and a grete clerk, and had worsshippfully rewled this reame to the Kinges behove, and never coude be found faute in him, but envy of thame that wer governoures, and had promised the Duchis of Anges and therldome of Maigne, caused the destruccion of this noble man; for thei drad him, that he wold have enpesshed that deliverance.[32]

Malory is a little simpler in organisation, and a little more repetitive, so that as narrator he seems more desolated. But the main strength of his outburst comes from its context, its placing after the rest of the *Morte Darthur*. It continues to add to the weight of key words used many times before, and gives the support of a personal appearance by the narrator to them.

This famous and passionate outburst is unique, but throughout the *Morte Darthur* the narrator's strong feelings pervade his vision in the narrative, in evocative terminology and emotive tone. These define what he shows life to be. Life in the *Morte Darthur* is a moral matter, judged according to a chivalric code. What Malory saw first in a knight was not whether he was tall, or avaricious, or happy, but whether he was noble, with all that implied. Malory is using a literary form which makes it seem that the events are independent of their narrator, and in which the events are retold so simply that it seems unthinkable that they should have been distorted in any way by the factual chronicling voice. Nevertheless, the whole vision which we readers receive is indelibly tinctured with Malory's emotional reactions, and principally with his passion for chivalry. It is integral to his guileless vision of Arthur's days. Knights are noble, ladies fair, and so on. This is in keeping with Malory's basic reactions to the Arthurian story. His fundamental concern is to transmit his enthusiasm for knightliness. This we see in his periodic comments in his own person; but more subtly and more powerfully, he is forcing our response in ordinary narrative. Good and bad are clearly marked and made as desirable and repellent as is compatible with their seeming real. Gawain's liking for apples is nearly irrelevant: Gawain's vindictiveness is important and is plainly marked as repulsive.[33] The tragedy of Lancelot's adultery is the inextricable mixture of good and bad in it. The best of knights is trapped by his own weaknesses into a betrayal of chivalry.

It is because of this order of priorities that the physical surroundings of the story are so vague, except on those rare occasions, generally at crucial points in the narrative, when the author's imagination is more active than normally. It is at one such point that we see the adder in the heath-bush. This varied intensity of realisation gives a structural emphasis to the story, and the combination of limited facts and massive prescribed emotional response gives Malory much of his literary power. This power is the stronger because of the cumulative effect of the repetitive stock phrases. The reader can only accept that, without his noticing it, his reaction to the story is being controlled; or rebel, as Mark Twain did, and reject the story. Where Thackeray speaks from complete knowledge and his reactions to good and bad are compassion and contempt, Malory speaks from incomplete knowledge and his reactions to good and bad (the terms in which he saw life) are reverence and fear. These we are forced to share because we look through his eyes. And this creates the final paradox of Malory's art. Because the narrator in the *Morte Darthur* ignores us, our relationship with him is more intimate, if not more useful, than our relationship with Thackeray can ever be.

We are now in a better position to answer the question we posed at the beginning of this book: the question of how Malory looks when his style is seen in perspective against his age and ours. And the evidence suggests a similar impression at both times. Malory's narrative was simpler and more colloquial than that of his French sources, and Caxton's *Prologues and Epilogues* shows at least one writer of the time trying to reach a more involved and decorated English style than Malory's. Later, Lord Berners apologised for his translation of *Arthur of Little Britain*, "not presumynge that I have reduced it in to fresshe ornate polysshed Englysshe, for I knowe myselfe insuffycyent in the facond-yous arte of rethoryke. . . ."[34] And we have seen some other examples of artistic prose in earlier chapters. Modern readers find Malory lacking in pictorial vividness, and comparison with his sources showed him reducing this element in them. Caxton's preface to the *Morte Darthur* reveals that the moral aspect of the story impressed him as it does us.[35] We cannot be equally sure about the impression of Malory's dialogue, but I would argue that the formal characteristics of knightly speech which I have tried to distinguish would have made his knights a unified group for a fifteenth-century audience, and would probably have differentiated them from common experience, if not so much from the fictional speakers in the literature of the time. We will be much more aware than Malory's contemporaries of the *naïveté* of the narrator of the story, but even that impression may still have been there to some degree. This last factor is the most uncertain, for the course of English literature since Malory has largely been an exploration of human individuality in increasing depth. But it seems likely that the factors which we find distinctive and attractive in Malory may well have been those which had the same effect on his own age. The fifteenth century lacked the literary critical techniques of the twentieth, but it is possible to be affected by a Mozart sonata without being able to analyse sonata form. Although a fifteenth-century reaction could not prescribe our own, a coincidence would give us confidence both in our own judgement and in the enduring appeal of the *Morte Darthur*.

No consideration, however close, of past and present, will enable us to predict the future of a work of art. Meaning and response change with time, and with locality as well. It has been found impossible to expound *Jane Eyre*, as it has normally been understood, in a polygamous society in Nigeria. The audience finds nothing strange or horrifying in a bigamous marriage for the heroine. How readers of the future will evaluate Malory, we cannot foresee, but a writer who appeals both to his century and to ours calls upon something deep in human nature. To discover some of the ways in which this happens has been the purpose of the present study.

Because human judgement, though it be gradually gaining upon certainty, never becomes infallible; and approbation, though long continued, may yet be only the approbation of prejudice or fashion; it is proper to inquire, by what peculiarities of excellence [he] has gained and kept the favour of his countrymen.[36]

APPENDIX I

Some possible Neologisms in Malory: see p. 60

		NED	MED
abated	1104 abait (set on)	v 1, only citation	v, 1470 (not Malory)
actually	165 vigorously	adv 2, only citation	adv 2(b), only citation
alygeaunce	1093 satisfaction [theol]	this sense not cited	n (2), 2a, 1333 ff.
amyvestyall	151 [meaning unknown]	not cited (see V n.)	adj, only citation
arace	1119 raze	v, 1523 ff.	v 1, 1333 ff.
avayle	1193 [have at] advantage	sb 1, 1471 ff.	n 5(b), only M cited
aventre	89 level [a spear]	v, 1557 ff.	v, 1400 ff.
barget	1095 small boat	sb, 1471 ff.	n, only M cited
bayne	1085 bath	sb 1, 1475 ff.	n (a), M and later
bedaysshed	1122 adorned	v, 1564 ff.	only M cited
burde	1134 trapdoor	this sense uncited	this sense uncited
byverd	30 bever (tremble)	v², 1471 ff.	v, 1250 ff.
chafflet	1069 scaffold-platform	sb, only citation	n, 1440 ff.
constraynte	1097 constraint	sb 1, 1534 ff.	n 1(a), 1420 ff.
one of thes dayes	117 soon	sb 5b, 1535 ff.	n 12b(f), only citation
debate	104 armed conflict	sb¹ 1b, 1553 ff.	n 37, 1375 ff.
draughtes	1130 recesses	not cited	not cited, cf. draught chambir, 1435 ff.
enbraydyst	1190 upbraid	v, 1481 ff.	not cited
forecaste	1171 plan, plot	sb 2b, 1535 ff.	not cited
frycke	1085 vigorous	not cited, but cf. fresh, aj 10a	not cited, but cf. frecche, adj (b)
holdith	1163 possess sexually	v 6a, no other certain use in	v 8(b), 1325 ff.

menour	1174	mainour (being taken in the act)	sb² 1532: but used by Caxton in 1481.*
rasure	1119	scratch	sb¹1, 1471 ff.
fecche his raunge	160	measure his distance	sb¹5, 1471 ff.
shortecomyng	1202	misadventure	this sense uncited
be skyffe of	126	be rid of	v 18, 19d, 1567 ff.
stoon	106	break, crush	v, only citation
sure handyls	143	swordhilt guards	not cited
thirled	106	flow, gush	this sense uncited
unbecaste	1104	cast about for scent	v 4, only citation in this sense, but see Edward of York, The Master of Game, p. 83

* This is a legal technicality, not, as V's glossary has it, "behaviour" in a broad sense. V. The History of Reynard the Fox, tr. William Caxton, ed. E. Arber, p. 8.

These thirty-one words are not cited by NED before Malory. Twenty-one of them are in the range of MED, of which eight are cited before Malory, one ("abated") contemporary with him. A further word ("unbecaste"), which NED only cites from Malory, occurs in a work before him (c. 1405). Dr Rioux's list of words "created" by Malory is as follows:

"advaunte-garde", "araged", "attempt" (vb.), "barget", "bavoure", "chafflet", "enstraunge" (vb.), "flagon", "muffle", "orgulyte", "overgarment", "overgoverned", "overhasty", "pees" (sb. qty of liquid), "present" (sb., gif), "question" (vb.), "questing", "surcyngle", "track" (sb., of animal).

It gives us no confidence in the rest of the list to realise that of the eight words so far dealt with by the MED, "araged", "attempt", "bavoure", and "chafflet" are all exemplified in it from before 1425, and "enstraunge" and "flagon" each from two works before 1460. "Advaunte-garde" is cited from a work probably earlier than the Morte Darthur, and only "barget" remains to be attributed to Malory as its first user.

The Distribution of Certain Stock Phrases in the Morte Darthur

	Number of Pages	Number of Phrases	Not by Knights
"Arthur"	180	34	3
"Lucius"	63	Nil	Nil
"Lancelot" & "Gareth"	111	20	2
"Tristram" (to p. 518)	158	48	5
"Grail"	188	19	8
"Lancelot & Guenivere"	110	51	7
"Morte"	100	72	4
Total	910	244	29

APPENDIX III

The French Prose Tristan

1. MS B.N. fr 334, f 225ᵛ, col 2. Cf. V 515. 11–27.

Quant il sont issuz horz du chastel . il viennent en une moult bele
praierie . ou il avoit mei*n*t biau paveillon tendu . et meinte tente riche
et noble . ou les chevaliers tournoianz devoient cele nuit dormir . ceuls
qui ne povoient avoir ostel dedenz le chastel . et a lendemein sanz
nule faille devoit estre la veille du tournoiement . et sachiez que en cele
praierie saloient deduisant ces ch*evalier*s de Norgales et moult dautres
chevaliers estranges et aloient brisant lances les uns encontre les autres.
Palamedes meesmement saloit deduisant en cele compaingnie . et brisant
lances non mie de sa volente . mes ausint comme a force . car les uns et
les autres qui trop estoient durement desirement desirrant de veoir la
haute chevalerie de lui len avoient tant prie que il ne sen peust mie
legierement escondire ne bel . et pour ce saloit il entreuls deduisant . et
brisant lances tout ausi*n*t comme feisoient les autres qui la estoient . la
ou il saloient entreuls deduisant tout ainsint p*ar*mi la praierie Palamedes
le regarde et voit lescu persydes . et tout meintenant que il lapercoit il le
reconnoist si dist adoncques a soi meesmes . or voi je ici persydes venir .
ce est il sanz nule faille ne il ne me veult nul bien ne je a lui autresint .
Lors prent il une grosse lance et se tourne vers lui . et dist a un escuier
qui devant lui estoit . va ten fet il a ce chevalier que tu vois la . qui porte
cel escu tout vert a ce lyon dor rampant qui est tout fres et tout nouvel .
et li di que se il veult jouster . je en sui touz apareilliez . Si orraz lors q*ue*
il te dira . et se il te demande qui je sui . onques ne li di autre chose fors
que je sui un chevalier errant tout ainsint comme il est . et quant li
varlez entent le commandemant que Palamedes li fet. il ni fet nul autre
delaiement ancois sen vet tout droit a persydes . et li dist les paroles que

Palamedes li mandoit . et puis li moustre Palamedes . tout meintenant
que Persydes voit palamedes et il le reconnoist . li cuers li eschaufe tot
dire et de duell . si pensse un petit . et quant il a un petit pensse . il dist au
varlet . or va dire a Palamedes et si ne li cele mie . que puis que il ma
apele de la jouste . je ne len faudrai mie or viengne avant tout seurement
car il trouvera persydes (f 226ʳ, col. 1) tout apareille de la jouste . Li
varlez sen remet a palamedes . et si li conte trestout ce que persydes li
mande . lors torne palamedes hors de la compaingie . et sadresce envers
persydes . et la criee lieve tout meintenant de toutes parz . et dient tuit
veez la jouste veez la jouste . palamedes qui encontre persydes avoit gros
cuer si hurte le cheval desperons . et sen vient parmi lui . et li donne .i.
si grant cop enmi le piz . que persides na ne force ne povoir que il en
sele se puisse tenir . ancois vole du cheval a terre moult felonnessement
. et la criee lieve tot meintenant desus lui . or sus or sus sire chevalier
trop mauvesement vos estes tenu . quant palamedes voit persydes aba tu
. il ne regarde plus ancois leisse courre de celui poindre meesmes a
trystam qui de la jouste ne sestoit encore point apareillez . et il le
seurprent si soudainement a tout le grant cop que il li donne . que il le
porte tout meintenant a terre tout envers .

2. MS B.N. fr 103, f 191ʳ, col 1. Cf. V 515.11–518.4.

Lors se font armer . puis montent . et sen yssent hors en une moult belle
praerie ou il avoit maint riche paveillon tendu . ou les chevaliers qui ne
povoient avoir la nuit hostel en chastel devoient herbergier . A lande-
main sans faille devoient (f 191ʳ, col 2) estre les vespres du tournoiement
. ces chevaliers de norgales et autres saloient deduisant aval celle praerie
et brisant lances par deduit . Palamedes se deduisoit avec eulx et en
brisoit aussi non mie de sa volente . mais aussi comment par force . car
moult len avoient prie pour veir sa haulte chevalerie . et il ne les
escondeist pas volentiers . La ou palamedes se deduisoit avec les autres
il se regarde . et voit lescu persides si le congnut tantost si dit . Vecy
persides qui ne me veult nul bien . ne je a lui . Lors prent une grosse
lance puis dit a .i. escuier . va ten a cil chevalier qui porte cel escu vert
a cel lyon dor rampant . et lui dy . sil veult jouster que je suis tout
appareillie . Lors si orras quil dira . et si demande qui je suis dy luy que
Je suis ung chevalier errant aussi comment il est . Lescuier sempart . et
vient a persides et lui dit les paroles que palamedes lui mandoit . Quant
persides ouy parler lescuier le coeur lui eschauffe dyre et de deul si dit a

lescuier . or va . puis quil mappelle de jouste si lui dy que je ne lui
fauldray pas . Lescuier sen revient a palamedes et lui dit ce que persides
lui mande . Lors tourne palamedes hors de sa compagnie . Et sadresce
a persides tant comment cheval peult aler . et luy donne si grant coup
enmy le pis quil le fait voler du cheval a terre . Et la criee lieve sur lui .
Or sus or sus dans chevalier mauvaisement vous estes tenu . palamedes
sen passe oultre . et leisse courre a tristan de cellui poindre qui nestoit
pas appareillie de jouste . ne garde ne sen prenoit . et lui donne (f 191ᵛ,
col 1) si grant coup quil le porte tout envers a terre . Et le cry lieve
autrefois . Or sus . or sus chevalier mauvaisement vous saves tenir .

   Quant tristan entent que ceulx le vont gabant il se relieve molt
vistement si courouchie quil cuide bien esrager tout vif . Si vient a son
cheval . et monte . et dit . a ung varlet qui devant lui estoit . Varlet fait
tristan va a palamedes . et lui dy quil fist villennie de moy sourprendre
quant il mabati . Mais dy lui que je lui pry quil vienne une autre fois
jouster a moy . Et sil me peult abatre il aura conquis plus grant los quil
ne cuide . le varlet sempart . et conte a palamedes les paroles que tristan
lui mandoit . et Palamedes lui dit . puis que je lay abatu je ne jousteray
plus a lui . Et sache il bien que je ne le fis pour nulle male volente . Sil
est courouchie de ce fait si sen seuffre . et sil sen veult demain venger
au soir me trouvera devant le chastel as pucelles La ne luy fauldray je
mye de jouste . le varlet sen retourne a tristan . et lui conte mot a mot les
paroles que palamedes lui mandoit . Tristan est trop courouchie de
ceste responce sy commence durement a penser . Entretant quil pensoit
. Atant et vous venir dynadam qui le recongnut au cheval Et estoit venu
au tournoiement seulement pour veir les merveilles que tristan feroit .
Il avoit bien veu comment palamedes lavoit souspris a celle jouste . et
comment tristan lui avoit mande la jouste . et comment palamedes
lavoit refusee . Dynadam qui (f 191ᵛ, col 2) est moult lie de ce fait .
nonmie pour haingne quil ait a tristan fors pour ce quil ait achoison de
le gaber vient a tristan et lui dit . Ha tristan a quoy penses vous .
palamedes ce mest advis vous a apris ung tour de jouste plus que vous
ne savies . Il pert bien a vostre heaume . Il ne sera huymais heure qui ne
vous en doye souvenir de lui . Ce sceis je bien dynadam fait tristan Ainsi
va des adventures . Nul ne peult longuement jouster quil ne couviengne
aucune fois cheoir . Et se palamedes ma fait orendroit dolent une
autrefois me fera lie . Ce ne me desconforte point Et sachies quil ne donna
oncques en sa vie coup qui si chier lui fust rendu comment cist sera . En non
dieu fait dynadam comment quil en adviengne Il en a le premier
honnour.

Entretant quilz parloient ainsi atant et vous yssir du chastel ung chevalier arme de toutes armes . Et avec lui deux escuiers . Et chevauchoit moult simplement . si tost comment tristan voit la contenance du chevalier il dit a dynadam . Or poues veir chevalier qui bel chevauche . Certes je croy quil soit preudoms et bon chevalier . Se maist dieu fait dynadam Ce peult bien estre . Le chevalier portoit son escu couvert dune houche noire . Ung chevalier qui estoit de norgales et avoit a nom brians . Et estoit en la compagnie palamedes . Quant il voit le chevalier si dit a ses compaignons . Vecy venir ung trop bon chevalier . Il na pas granment de temps quil me fist ung deshonnour trop grant . Et se je a ce point ne men venge dehais aye je (f 192ʳ, col 1) Lors appelle ung sien escuier . et lui dit . Voy tu cil chevalier la . Va si lui dy que je lui mand quil viengne jouster a moy . Et sil le reffuse si luy dy depar moy quil lui couvient jouster a moy vueille ou non . Le varlet sen va au chevalier et lui dit ce que son seigneur lui mande . Parfoy fait le chevalier ton sire me mande trop grant outrage . car puis quil veult jouster a moy par force viengne avant car je ne lui fauldray mie . Le varlet sen retourne . et conte ces nouvelles a son seigneur . le chevalier hurte cheval des esperons contre briant de norgales . et le fiert si durement en son venir quil le porte du cheval a terre . Et sachiez que cestoit lancelot qui sen aloit au tournoiement au plus priveement quil povoit .

Quant lancelot oult abatu briant . tristan parole a dynadam et lui dit . Dynadam que vous semble . cuidies vous que je ne face congnoistre ung chevalier . Par la foy que je vous doy je ne vy mais pieca chevalier que je prisasse autant Et sachies quil feroit la maint beau coup si besoing en estoit . Je le croy bien fait dynadam mais trop me merveil pour quoy il porte lescu de cornoaille . pour ce fait tristan quil lui plaist . Et sachies que vous pourres veir ad ce tournoiement que tous les meilleurs chevaliers du monde porteront escus de cornoaille . Dieu aide fait dynadam . Et pour quoy le font ilz . Ce ne sceis je fait tristan . mais encore sera sceu . Entre eulx quilz parloient ainsi . A tant et vous ung autre chevalier de norgales qui parent estoit (f 192ʳ, col 2) brians quant il vit brians abatu il en fu courouchie a merveille . Si hurte cheval des esperons droit a lancelot . Et lui crie tant comment il peult . Sire chevalier gardes vous de moy a jouster vous couvient une jouste seulement . Sire chevalier fait lancelot . puis que une jouste me demandes . et vous laures . Lors hurte cheval des esperons . et fiert si le chevalier en son venir quil le fait voler a terre . Et la criee lieve maintenant dune part et dautre et dient tous que mauvaisement le font les chevaliers de norgales . Le frere le Roy de norgales qui parloit a

palamedes voit que les chevaliers de norgales estoient abatus si en oult
trop grant deul . Et pour ce quil congnoissoit la prouesse des deux
chevaliers qui abatus estoient ne sose meitre en adventure contre
lancelot . car il lui est advis quencontre lui ne pourroit durer quant il a
abatus deux si bons chevaliers comment ceulx quil a abatus . Si dit a
palamedes en qui prouoesse il se fioit moult . palamedes fait il par
amours et par courtoisie Donnes moy ung don qui poy vous coustera .
Sire dit palamedes je le vous doing volentiers . Je vous demand fait il que
vous ales jouster a cil chevalier qui ces deux a abatus . Certes fait
palamedes je ne vy pieca chevalier que je prisasse autant comment je
fais cestui . et pour lamour de vous et de vostre priere je yray a lui
jouster . Lors dit a ung escuier . Va ten a cil chevalier qui la sen va . et
lui dy quil sappareille (f 192ᵛ, col 1) de jouster . car a moy le convient
jouster . le varlet vient a lancelot et lui dit toutes les paroles que
palamedes lui mande . Dy moy fait lancelot qui est le chevalier qui de
jouste me requiert . Se maist dieu dit le varlet cest palamedes le bon
chevalier . Ha dieu fait lancelot aoure soies tu . longtemps a que je
desire que je peusse venir en lieu ou je me peusse essaier a palamedes .
Lors se met enmy le chemin lescu au col le glaive en poing.

   Quant tristan voit lappareil si dit a dynadam . par mon chief dynadam
vous pourres la veir jouste fort et dure . se oncques congnu bon
chevalier palamedes sera a terre . Tristan fait dynadam ainsi va des choses
du monde que on ne peult bien dire de cellui a qui on veult mal . tu hes
palamedes . pour ce quil tabati orendroit . et pour ce nen puis tu bien
dire . Et si na pas long temps que je te oy dire que palamedes estoit ung
des meilleurs chevaliers qui fust en monde apres lancelot . Est il ore en si
poy de terme devenu mauvais . quil ne se pourroit delivrer dun seul
chevalier . Quant tristan entent ce si ne dit plus mot . car il redoubte
moult les paroles dynadam . Si regarde Palamedes qui sadresce au ferir
des esperons vers lancelot . et le fiert si grant coup comme il peult . mais
de selle ne le remue . Et lancelot le fiert si durement enmy le pis quil na
povoir quil puisse le coup soustenir . ains vole du cheval a terre . Et se le
haubert ne fust bon il eust este (f 192ᵛ, col 2) en adventure de mort . Et
lancelot sen passe oultre lie et joyant . et se met en son chemin . Quant
palamedes fu abatu il ny oult nul qui criast aussi comme devant . tous
beissent les testes vers terre aussi comme silz fussent tous mors . Dynadam
fait tristan que dites vous de palamedes est il a terre . oyl voir . mais ce
nest pas par vous . meilleur chevalier de vous la abatu . Ce peult bien
estre dit tristan . Et sil na este par moy abatu il y pourra bien recouvrer
avant que le tournoiement departe . Tristan fait dynadam vous le

menaciez de loing . aumains lui aves vous huymais tresves donnees .
Dynadam fait tristan . encore ne lui ay je pas tresves donnees que sil
vouloit orendroit jouster a moy que je ne joustasse a lui . Orendroit
fait dynadam vous croy je bien . mais devant pour quoy ne lassaillies
vous . Tristan tristan nous veon souvent advenir que le loup nest pas si
grant comme on le crie . ne le chevalier si preux comment on le
raconte . Ces paroles dy je pour vous tristan . car certes se vous fussies
tel chevalier comment on dit ja palamedes ne vous eust abatu.

Tristan est si honteux quil ne sceit quil doye dire . Et cuide bien que
dynadam lui dye ces paroles tout a certes . mais non faisoit mais par gieu
et par envoiseure . Dynadam fait tristan je sceis bien que je ne suis mie
si bon chevalier comme sont maint autres . sachies quil men poise
durement . mais par la foy que je doy a celle que jaim plus que moy
(f 193ʳ, col 1) meisme avant que trois (sic) soient passes me pourries
veir en tel lieu que vous ne my atendries poin toute la cite de kamaalot.
Tristan fait dynadam au hault mot que vous aves dit vous croy je que
vous cuidies estre en lostel le roy marc vostre oncle en cornoaille ou
vous soulies faire vos vantances . Vous ny estes pas sans faille . ains estes
en royaume de logres ou vous trouveres chevaliers . non mye telz
comment il a en cornoaille Et par la foy que doy vous je vous cuide en
tel lieu trouver dedens trois jours que vous seres si lasse et si travaillie a
cellui point que se vous esties cheval je vous cuideroie legierement la
queue nouer . Or regardes se jaroie lors hardement de vous atendre . Et
si est mestier que vous me leissies passebreul vostre destrier ains que le
tournoiement de parte pour estonner . Tristan ne sceit que il doye dire
quant il entent ceste parole . A tant es vous venir entre eulx persides qui
dit a tristan . Sire temps est huymais de retourner . Et se cil chevalier qui
a vous parole vouloit venir avec nous il me plairoit moult . Dynadan
fait tristan venes avec nous herbegier . Sire fait il non feray ore vostre
mercy . Je yray ca devant en une maison de religion ou ung mien amy
matent que je ne leisseroie mie volentiers . je vous commant a dieu . Je
sceis bien que je vous verray en tournoiement . et vous moy . Bien peult
estre fait Tristan . . . . Mais atant leisse le conte a parler de tristan et de
persydes . Et retourne a parler de lancelot du lac.

3. MS B.N. fr 103, f 71ʳ, col 1. Cf. V 427.24–429.30.

Ung jour advint le mardy apres la feste saint Jehan que le roy fist tendre
trois paveillons devant tintagnel a une praerie si y ala lui et la royne.

pour deduire a grant compagnie . Atant es vous venir deux chevaliers armes . et vindrent aux paveillons tout droit . La royne et tristan jouoient aux esches Et les chevaliers viennent au roy et le saluent . Et le roy leur rent leur salut . et leur prie quilz descendent . Sire font ilz la vostre mercy . nous ne descendron mie . mais sil vous plaist . monstres nous la royne . (f 71ᵉ, col 2) car maintes journees avon faictes pour la veir . Seigneurs fait le roy veir la poves . Veez la la ou elle joue aux esches avecques tristan . les chevaliers ainsi montes com ilz estoient vont celle part . ou ilz veoient tristan et la royne . Tristan et la royne entendoient a leur gieu . et non pas aux chevaliers . Les chevaliers regardent moult yseult Et quant ilz lourent asses regardee si dit lun a lautre . que vous semble Certes fait lun . se nous fussion entre nous deux en ung champ je vous monstrasse que ma dame est plus belle . Par mon chief dit lautre je croy bien que vous le me monstrissies . car vous estes meilleur chevalier que je ne suis . Mais par droit ceste est plus belle comment quil en doye advenir . Certes fait lautre . il na en toute cornouaille chevalier que ung tout seul sil disoit que yseult fust plus belle que ma dame que je ne len rendisse mensongier . Et lors se regarda tristan et dit . Seigneurs . vous nestes pas courtoys qui si me blasmes devant moy . Et se vostre dame est plus belle de moy je vouldroye quelle fust cent fois plus belle . a moy nen affiert de riens . Et se dieu vous aist qui est vostre dame . fait lun . la royne dorcanie . Certes fait yseult . oncques mais ne louy si loer . Sire dit elle qui estes vous et comment aves vous nom . Dame fait il . Je suis filz au roy pelinor de listernois . et si ay a nom lamourat de gales . Par foy fait elle . Vous fustes filz au plus preudome dont je ouy oncques parler . Vous deveries estre preudome par droit . Et cil autre . (f 71ᵛ, col 1) comment a nom . Dame il a nom Drians . et est mon frere et na pas gramment quil fu nouvel chevalier . Et se jay dit folie . Dame je vous prie que vous le me pardonnes . Je le vous pardoing bien pour lamour de vostre pere . et non pas pour lamour de vous . car vous nestes pas bien courtois . Dame bien peult estre . or me garderay bien une autreffois de dire villennie a dame . Atant prennent congie . et sen vont . et quant ilz furent esloingnies des paveillons . Lamourat dit a son frere quil ne se partira ja dilleuc jusques quil sara comment ceulx de cornouaille sceivent jouster . Lors vient a une damoiselle qui aloit aux paveillons si lui dit . Damoiselle dictes au roy que nous sommes ycy deux chevaliers estranges et sil a nul chevalier a sa court qui vueille jouster quilz viennent cha jouster a nous . Sire fait elle . ce luy diray je bien . Lors vient la damoiselle au roy et luy dit ce que cil lui avoit mande . Ha fait

le roy . cest de lorgueil du royaume de logres . Certes ja ne sen partiront
sans jouste se je meisme y devoye aler . Lors commande a deux
chevaliers quilz sarment et quilz voisent jouster aux deux chevaliers
estranges . Et ils font le commandement du roy . La royne dit a tristan .
or verres ja lances brisier . car deux de nos vont jouster aux deux
chevaliers estranges . Certes dit tristan . ce poise moy . car je sceis bien
que les nostres ny gaigneront rien . Les deux chevaliers vont jouster aux
deux estranges (f 71ᵛ, col 2) Et drians si abat le sien . Et lamourat le
sien si que a poy quil ne lui a brisie le bras . Quant le roy marc voit ses
deux chevaliers abatus si dit aux autres . Ore seigneurs que feres vous . se
cilz sen vont quilz ne soient abatus honnis estes . car ilz se gaberont par
toutes cours de vous . Et lors veissies qui mieulx mieulx chevaliers
amer (sic) . Et quant drians les voit si dit a lamourat de gales . Frere fit
il nous avon fait fole emprise ja en vendra ycy plus de cinquante . ne
vous chault frere dit lamourat . car ja tant ny en vendra quilz ne voisent
a terre se tristan ny vient . Et tristan vient au roy . et lui dit . Certes sire
bien vous honnissies qui pour deux chevaliers faictes armer cinquante
deux de vostres . Ainsi comment tristan parloit au roy il se regarde . et
voit comment deux de leurs estoient ja abatus et navres a mort . Quant
les deux chevaliers ourent leur lances brisies ilz dient . en tirant leurs
espees . Traies vous en sus . Et se plus voules jouster faictes nous
apporter lances . Et ilz si firent aplante . Que vous diroye je . tant firent
les deux chevaliers quilz abatirent dix des chevaliers de cornouaille Lez
autrez sen retournerent tous esbahis . Et dient quilz aimment mieulx que
les deux chevaliers sen voisent quictes et delivres quilz fussent ne mors
ne plaies . Quant le roy marc voit ce si dit . ha chetifs chevaliers de
cornouaille . honnis estes a tousjours mais quant pour deux chevaliers
estes desconfis . Lors dit a tristan (f 72ʳ, col 1) Tristan que feres vous
sen yront ilz ainsi quictes . Certes sire dit il ilz se doivent bien aler . car
bien ont monstre quilz sont preudommes . Et se je aloie a eulx qui sont
travaillies . et moy repose on le me tendroit a couardise . Et je vueil fait
le roy que vous y ales . quilz vous congnoissent . Et prenes avec vous
deux compaignons . et certes je sceis bien quilz seront desconfis . Sire
dit tristan je feray vostre volente . Et lors sarme tristan et monte . et sen
va tout seul aux deux chevaliers . Et si tost com ilz le virent . si dirent .
vecy tristan sans doubte . Lors leisse courre Drians a tristan et le fiert si
durement quil brise son glaive sans autre mal faire . Et tristan le fiert si
quil lui perche lescu et le haubert . et lui met le fer du glaive en coste
senestre mais non pas en parfont . et porta lui et le cheval a terre tout en
ung mont . Quant lamourat voit son frere abatu si leisse courre a

tristan et le fiert si grant coup que le glaive quil vola en pieces . Et
Tristan le fiert si durement que moult le navra et labati a terre . Quant
le roy marc voit ces deux coups si dit . Ha tristan . comment tu es
preudoms se tu ne fusses triatre envers moy ou monde neust ton pareil
se ne fust lancelot seulement . Lamourat q*ui* retourne estoit voit que
tristan sen aloit si lui crie . Retournes sire che*valier* si nous entre essaions
aux espees . pource que je suis abatu ne suis je pas oultres . Tristan
lentent bien . (f 72ʳ, col 2) mais nul semblant nen fait . Ains sen vient
aux paveillons et lamourat va apres lui tout esragie . et dit . Comment
tristan . noes vous mie que je vous appelle a la bataille . et vous ne me
responnes nul mot . Nous so*m*mes tous deux sains et haities essaion no*us*
aux espees et illeuc verra on le meille*ur* de nos deux . se vous le refuses
on vous le devra tenir a couardie et a mauvaistie . Tristan lui dit . Sire
chevalier je ne me vueil pas combatre a vous . car je ny voy nulle
achoison . Si a fait lamourat . puis que je vous appelle a la bataille . car
vous estes de gra*nt* renommee je le puis bien refuser fait tristan car je ne
suis pas des compaignons de la table ronde . mais se jen estoie je ne le
pourroie pas refuser se je nestoie navre a mort . Et pour ce le refuse
je . Par foy fait lamourat bien suis ho*n*ni par ung mauvais chevalier
recrea*nt* qui a moy ne sose combatre . Et puis dit . Ha tristan je te
tenoye par deva*nt* meilleur chevalier du monde . Ho*n*ny soye je se
jamais di bien de toy . Ata*nt* sempart . et dit . honny soit cornoaille et
tous les chevaliers qui y sont . co*m*ment les plus recreans qui soient en
tout le monde . Et tristan dema*n*de au roy quil lui semble de cil
che*valier* . Certes fait le roy il est preudo*m*me . car par ardeur de coeur
dit il les paroles quil dit . Voire vraiement dit tristan . il est bon chevalier
de son aage . et croy quil sera preudo*m*e sil vit longuement . Lamourat
sen vient a drians son frere et dit . Drians fait il beau frere . Tristan le
beau mauvais ne se veult abat*re* (f 72ᵛ, col 1) a moy . maudit soit cil
qui jamais le tendra pour preudomme . car il la fait par couardie . Certes
dit drians non a . mais pour ce que vous estes travaillie et il est repose .
Taisies vous fait lamourat . honny qui le croirra . Alon nous ent au
royaume de logres . et lors se vont vers la mer si encontrerent une
damoiselle qui portoit ung cor divire.

4. MS B.N. fr 103, f 72ᵛ, col 1 (modern punctuation, paragraphs, and
   capitals). Cf. V 429.30–430.8.

Si encontrerent une damoiselle qui portoit ung cor d'ivire, et estoit en

la compagnie d'un escuier empres une fontaine . Lamourat demande
s'il savoit nulles nouvelles de la maison le roy Artu.

"Sire," fait le chevalier, "nanil. Mais nous y alon au plus droit que
nous pourron."

"Et de nulle autre nouvelle saves vous?"

"Certes," dit le chevalier, "non. Mais se vous estes d'uy en huit
jours a la maison le roy Artu, vous y verres une adventure bien
merveilleuse. Car une damoiselle envoie au roy Artu ung cor le plus
bel et le plus riche qui soit en tout le monde, et est fait pour
boire. Mais il est si merveilleux que la dame n'y bevra qui ait fausse
son seigneur que le vin n'espande tout sur elle. Et celle qui oncques
ne geust avec autre que son seigneur y peult bien boire seurement.
Et par ce pourra le roy Artus bien congnoistre les bonnes dames de sa
court."

"Et se la royne Genievre," fait Lamourat, "avoit jeu avec ung autre
chevalier le saroit le roy par ce cor?"

"Certes, sire, oyl," fait le chevalier.

"Se Dieu m'aist," fait Lamourat, "celle qui l'envoie a la royne ne
l'aimme mye. Et je vous prie que vous me dictes qui ceste est."

"Non feray, beau sire," fait le chevalier.

"Certes," (f 72ᵛ, col 2) fait Lamourat, "se ne le me dites, mort
estes."

"Me cuides-vous espoventer?" fait le chevalier. "Certes vous ne le
sares mie ore."

"Dont vous appelle je a la bataille," fait Lamourat.

"Ja de ce," fait le chevalier, "ne vous fauldray."

Lors s'entredonnent grans coups des espees, mais en poy d'eure le
meinne Lamourat a sa volente.

Lors dit le chevalier a Lamourat: "Se tu me veulx quictier, je te diray
ce que tu me demanderas, et ce que tu me demandes."

"Certes," dit Lamourat, "tu diras ainchois que je suis meilleur
chevalier de toy, et puis me diras le nom de celle qui a court t'envoye.
Et puis yras ou je t'envoirray, et presenteras le cor a ung homme que je
poy aimme."

"Ce ne feray-je mie," fait le chevalier.

"En nom Dieu," fait Lamourat, "dont est tu mort."

Lors le fiert si durement qu'il le fait voler a terre, et lui chiet l'espee
de la main. Et quant il se cuide relever, si le fiert tellement qu'il lui fait
voler le heaulme de la teste. Quant cil se voit desarme, si oult paour de
mort, si dit:

"Pour Dieu, mercy! Ne m'occy pas! Je feray ta volente." Lors lui couvenance comment chevalier qu'il fera son commandement.

"Je vueil," fait Lamourat, "que tu me dies le nom de ta dame."

"Je suis," fait le chevalier, "a Morgain la Fee."

"Se m'aist Dieu," fait Lamourat, "vous estes a la plus desloyal femme du monde. Cest cor a elle establi pour mectre descort entre le roy Artu et la royne Genievre sa femme. Mais ce n'avendra ja, puis qu'il est venu entre mes mains. Je te command que tu t'envoises en Cornouaille et presenteras ce cor au roy (f 73ʳ, col 1) Marc. Et lui diras que ung chevalier qui petit l'aimme lui envoie pour esprouver la bonte des dames de sa court. Car la bonte des chevaliers fu esprouvee quant Tristan le Beau-Mauvais refusa la bataille encontre le chevalier estrange. Et sache Tristan que pour sa honte est envoie le cor en Cornouaille."

Bibliography

The books listed below form a bibliography to the argument of this one: so a few items are relevant to the non-stylistic aspects of late medieval authors, and a few to style in other periods. But as a whole, this is the most comprehensive available bibliograpy for the study of prose style in the English late middle ages and early renaissance. To supplement it, a reader will have to consult Josephine Miles (*infra*), Harold Martin (under Ohmann *infra*), Richard M. Bailey and Dolores Burton, *English Stylistics: A Bibliography* (MIT, 1968), and the standard bibliographies of English literature, and choose from the items they give.

The texts listed below often contain, either in themselves or in their editors' commentaries, observations on style as important as anything in the books listed as secondary material, and in a few cases the divisions I have made has been arbitrary. Abbreviations of titles of periodicals are as in the *PMLA* annual bibliography.

Section I — Texts

A — The Bible and Anonymous Works

Deonise Hid Divinite, ed. Phyllis Hodgson. EETS, 231, 1955.

Die Abenteuer Gawains, Ywains, und le Morholts mit den Drei Jungfrauen, ed, H. O. Sommer. Beihefte zur *ZRP,* 47. Halle, 1913.

Galahad and Perceval, ed. H. O. Sommer. *MP,* 5 (1907–08), pp. 55–84, 181–200. 291–341.

Howleglass. London, 1528.

La Mort le Roi Artu, ed. Jean Frappier. Paris, 1936.

La Queste del Saint Graal, Roman du XIIIᵉ Siècle, ed. Albert Pauphilet. Paris, 1923.

Le Haut Livre du Graal, Perlesvaus, ed. W. A. Nitze and T. A. Jenkins. 2 vols. Chicago, 1932.

Le Morte Arthur, ed. James D. Bruce. EETS, ES 88, 1903.

Le Roman de Balain, ed. M. D. Legge. Manchester, 1942.
Le Roman de Tristan en Prose, ed. R. L. Curtis. Munich 1963–   .
Le Roman en Prose de Tristan, le Roman de Palamède, et la Compilation de Rusticien de Pise, Analyse Critique d'après les Manuscrits de Paris, ed. Eilert Löseth. Paris, 1891.
Merlin, Roman en Prose du XIIIᵉ Siècle, Publié avec le Mise en Prose du Poème de Merlin de Robert de Boron, d'après le Manuscript ... Huth, ed. G. Paris and U. Jacob. 2 vols. Paris, 1886.
Merlin, ed. Henry B. Wheatley. EETS, OS 10, 21, 36, 112, 1865–99.
Merlin, tr. Harry Lovelich, ed. Ernst Kock. EETS, ES 93, 112, OS 185, 1904–32.
Morte Arthure, ed. Edmund Brock. EETS, OS 8, 1871.
The Brut, or the Chronicles of England, ed. F. W. D. Brie. EETS, OS 131, 136, 1906–08.
The Foure Sonnes of Aymon, tr. William Caxton, ed. Octavia Richardson. EETS, ES 44–5, 1884–85.
The Historie of the Arrivall of Edward IV in England and the Finall Recoverye of his Kingdomes from Henry VI, A.D. MCCCCLXXI, ed. John Bruce. Camden Soc.: London, 1838.
The History of Reynard the Fox, tr. William Caxton, ed. E. Arber. London, 1880.
The History of the Valiant Knight Arthur of Little Britain, tr. Sir John Bourchier Lord Berners, ed. Edward V. Utterson. London, 1814.
The Holy Bible. ... London, 1611.
"The Second Chronicle of Vitellius A xvi," in *Chronicles of London*, ed. C. L. Kingsford. Oxford, 1905.
"The Siena Fragment" [of the prose *Merlin*], ed. Alexandre Micha. *Rom*, 78 (1957), 37–45.
The Towneley Plays, ed. G. England and A. W. Pollard. EETS, ES 71, 1897.
The Vulgate Version of the Arthurian Romances, ed. H. O. Sommer. 8 vols. Washington, 1909–16.

B — Works by Named Authors

Aelfric. *Aelfrics Grammatic and Glossar*, ed. J. Zupitza. Berlin, 1880.
Ascham, Roger. *The Scholemaster*, ed. E. Arber. London, 1870.
Aubrey, John. *Brief Lives*, ed. O. L. Dick. London, 1949.
Barclay, Alexander. *Egloges*. London, circa 1530. (Prologue and Eclogues I–III)
——. *Certayne Egloges of Alexander Barclay*. ... London, 1570. (Contains Eclogue IV)
Barstow, Stan. *A Kind of Loving*. London, 1960.
Bekynton, Thomas. *Official Correspondence*. 2 vols. Rolls Series: London, 1872.
Berners, Sir John Bourchier, Lord ——. See Anon, *History of Arthur...* ; Froissart; and Guevara.
Bonaventure, Saint (attrib.). *Vita Christi*, ed. Jehan Petit. Paris, circa 1510.

Bunyan, John. *The Pilgrim's Progress*, ed. R. Sharrock. Oxford, 1960.

Capgrave, John. *The Chronicle of England*. Rolls Series: London, 1858.

Castiglione, Baldassare. *The Courtyer*, tr. Sir Thomas Hoby. London, 1561.

Cavendish, George. *The Life and Death of Cardinal Wolsey*, ed. R. S. Sylvester. EETS, 243, 1959.

Caxton, William. *The Prologues and Epilogues*, ed. W. J. B. Crotch. EETS, OS 176, 1928.

——. See also Anon, *The Foure Sonnes*. . . ; and *The History of Reynard*. . . .

Cely family. *The Cely Papers, Selections from the Correspondence . . . of the Cely Family . . . 1475–88*, ed. Henry E. Malden. Camden Soc.: London, 1900.

Chartier, Alain. *Les Oeuvres*, ed. André du Chesne Tourangeau. Paris, 1617.

Chaucer, Geoffrey. *The Complete Works*, ed. W. W. Skeat. 7 vols. Oxford, 1894–97.

Chesterfield, Philip Stanhope, 4th Earl of ——. *Letters Written by the Late Right Honourable Philip Dormer Stanhope, Earl of Chesterfield, to his Son*. . . . 2 vols. London, 1774.

Chrétien de Troyes. *Cligès*, ed. W. Foerster. Halle a.S., 1889.

De la Tour Landry, Geoffroy. *Le Livre du Chevalier de la Tour Landry*, ed. Anatole de Montaiglon. Paris, 1854.

——. *The Book of the Knight of La Tour Landry*, ed. Thomas Wright. EETS, OS 33, 1906.

Douglas, Gavin. *The Poetical Works*, ed. John Small. 4 vols. Edinburgh, 1874.

Dunbar, William. *The Poems*, ed. W. M. Mackenzie. London, 1932.

Elyot, Sir Thomas. *The Boke Named the Governour*, ed. H. H. S. Croft. 2 vols. London, 1880.

Fish, Simon. *A Supplication for the Beggars*, ed. E. Arber. London, 1880.

Fortescue, Sir John. *The Governance of England*. . . , ed. Charles Plummer. Oxford, 1885.

Fox, George. *The Journal*, ed. J. L. Nickalls. Cambridge, 1952.

Foxe, John. *Actes and Monuments*. London, 1563.

Froissart, Sir John. *The Chronicle of Froissart Translated out of the French by Sir John Bourchier Lord Berners*, ed. W. P. Ker. 6 vols. London, 1901–03.

Fullonius, *alias* Willem Grapheus. *Acolastus*, tr. John Palsgrave. London, 1540.

Gervase of Canterbury. *The Chronicle*, ed. W. Stubbs. 2 vols. Rolls Series: London, 1879–80.

Golding, William. *Pincher Martin*. London, 1956.

Guevara, Antonio de. *The Golden Boke of Marcus Aurelius, Emperour and Eloquent Oratour*, tr. Sir John Bourchier Lord Berners. London, 1535.

Hall, Edward. *The Union of the Two Noble and Illustre Famelies of Lancastre and Yorke*. . . . London, 1550.

Henry VIII. *Letters and Papers, Foreign and Domestic, Henry VIII*, vols. III and XIII.

Higden, Ralph. *Polychronicon*, tr. John Trevisa, ed. C. Babington. 9 vols. Rolls Series: London, 1865–86.

John of Ireland. *Meroure of Wissdome*, ed. C. Macpherson. STS, 1926.

John of Salisbury. *Metalogicon*, ed. C. C. J. Webb. Oxford, 1929.

Lawrence, David Herbert. *Kangaroo*, ed. J. Gribble. London, 1963.

Love, Nicholas. *The Mirrour of the Blessed Lyf of Jesu Christ*, ed. L. F. Powell. Oxford, 1908.

Lydgate, John. *The Fall of Princes*, ed. Henry Bergen. EETS, ES 121–124, 1924–27.

——. *The Serpent of Division*, ed. H. N. MacCracken. Yale, 1911.

Malory, Sir Thomas. *Le Morte Darthur...*, *a Rendition in Modern Idiom by Keith Baines, with an Introduction by Robert Graves*. London, 1963.

——. *The Morte Darthur, Parts Seven and Eight*, ed. D. S. Brewer. London, 1968.

——. *Le Morte Darthur by Syr Thomas Malory, the Original Edition of William Caxton now Reprinted*, ed. H. O. Sommer. 3 vols. London, 1889–91.

——. *The Works of Sir Thomas Malory*, ed. Eugène Vinaver. 3 vols. Oxford, 1967.

Mandeville, Sir John (pseud.). *Travels*, ed. M. C. Seymour. Oxford, 1967.

——. *The Bodley Version of Mandeville's Travels*, ed. M. C. Seymour. EETS, 253, 1963.

More, Sir Thomas. *The Workes*, ed. W. Rastell. London, 1557.

——. *The History of King Richard III*, ed. R. S. Sylvester. Yale, 1963.

Nevill, William. *The Castell of Pleasure*, ed. Roberta Cornelius. EETS, OS 179, 1930.

Paston family. *The Paston Letters, 1422–1509*, ed. James Gairdner. 4 vols. Westminster, 1900–01.

——. *The Paston Letters, a Selection in Modern Spelling*, ed. Norman Davis. London, 1963. This contains more letters than the same editor's original-spelling *Paston Letters* (Oxford, 1958).

Pecock, Reginald. *The Repressor of Overmuch Blaming of the Clergy*, ed. C. Babington. 2 vols. Rolls Series: London, 1860.

——. *The Donet*, ed. E. V. Hitchcock. EETS, OS 156, 1921.

——. *The Folewer to the Donet*, ed. E. V. Hitchcock. EETS, OS 164, 1924.

Pope, Alexander. *The Twickenham Edition of the Poems of Alexander Pope*, ed. John Butt. 11 vols. London, 1939–67.

——. *Peri Bathous, or Martinus Scriblerus his Treatise of the Art of Sinking in Poetry*. London, 1727.

Purvey, John (attrib.). Prologue to the Old Testament in *The Holy Bible ... by John Wycliffe and his Followers*, ed. Josiah Forshall and Frederic Madden. 4 vols. Oxford, 1850.

Shillingford, John. *Letters and Papers of John Shillingford, Mayor of Exeter, 1447–1450*, ed. Stuart A. Moore. Camden Soc.: London, 1871.

Skelton, John. *The Poetical Works*, ed. Alexander Dyce. 2 vols. London, 1843.

Thackeray, William Makepeace. *Vanity Fair*, ed. G. and K. Tillotson. London, 1963.

Thorpe, William. "The Examination," in Foxe, q.v.

Trevisa, John. "Dialogue between a Lord and a Clerk upon Translation" and "Epistle ... unto Lord Thomas of Barkley...," in *Fifteenth-Century Prose and Verse*, ed. A.W. Pollard. Westminster, 1903.

York, Edward "Plantagenet", 2nd Duke of ——. *The Master of Game*, ed. W. A. and F. Baillie-Grohman. London, 1904.

Section II — Secondary Material

Ackerman, Robert W. "Malory's 'Ironsyde'," *RS*, 32 (1964), 125–133.

Adamson, J. W. "The Extent of Literacy in England in the Fifteenth and Sixteenth Centuries," *Library*, 10 (1929), 163–193.

Angelescu, Victor. "The Relationship of Gareth and Gawain in Malory's Morte Darthur," *N&Q*, 206 (1961), 8–9.

Arnold, Matthew. *On the Study of Celtic Literature*. London, 1867.

Arnould, E. J. *Le Manuel des Péchés: Étude de Littérature Religieuse Anglonormande*. Paris, 1940.

Atkins, J. W. H. *English Literary Criticism: The Medieval Phase*. London, 1952.

Auerbach, Erich. *Mimesis: the Representation of Reality in Western Literature*. Princeton, 1953.

——. *Literary Language and its Public in Late Latin Antiquity and in the Middle Ages*. London, 1965.

Aurner, Nellie S. *Caxton, Mirrour of Fifteenth-Century Letters*. London, 1926.

Baldwin, C. S. *The Inflections and Syntax of the Morte Darthur of Sir Thomas Malory*. Boston, 1894.

——. "The Verb in the Morte Darthur," *MLN*, 10 (1895), 92–4.

——. *Medieval Rhetoric and Poetic to 1400*. New York, 1928.

Baugh, Albert C. *A History of the English Language*. 2nd ed. London, 1959.

Benham, Allen R. *English Literature from Widsith to the Death of Chaucer*. New Haven, 1916.

Bennett, J. A. W. (ed.) *Essays on Malory*. Oxford, 1963.

Bennett, Henry S. *The Pastons and their England*. Cambridge, 1922.

——. "Caxton and his Public," *RES*, 19 (1943), 113–119.

——. "Fifteenth-Century Secular Prose," *RES*, 21 (1945), 257–263.

——. *Chaucer and the Fifteenth Century*. Oxford, 1947.

——. "The Production and Dissemination of Vernacular Manuscripts in the Fifteenth Century," *Library*, 1 (1947), 167–178.

——. *English Books and Readers, 1475–1557*. Cambridge, 1952.

Bowra, C. M. *Heroic Poetry*. London, 1961.

Bradbrook, Muriel C. *Sir Thomas Malory*. Writers and Their Work Series, No. 95 (1958).

Brewer, D. S. (ed.) *Chaucer and Chaucerians*. London, 1966.

Brook, Stella. *The Language of the Book of Common Prayer*. London, 1965.

Bühler, Curt F. *William Caxton and his Critics*. Syracuse U.P., 1960.

Burrow, John. "The Audience of Piers Plowman," *Anglia*, 75 (1957), 373–384.

Byles, A. T. P. "William Caxton as a Man of Letters," *Library*, 15 (1935), 1–25.

Caplan, H. *Medieval Artes Praedicandi: A Handlist*, and *Supplement*. Cornell U.P., 1934, 1936.

Chambers, E. K. *Sir Thomas Malory*. English Association Pamphlet, 51 (1922).

——. *English Literature at the Close of the Middle Ages*. Oxford, 1945.

Chambers, R. W. *On the Continuity of English Prose*. EETS: London, 1932.

BIBLIOGRAPHY

Charland, Th.-M. *Artes Praedicandi: Contribution à l'Histoire de la Rhétorique au Moyen Âge.* Ottawa, 1936.

Chaytor, H. J. *From Script to Print.* Cambridge, 1945.

Crosby, Ruth. "Oral Delivery in the Middle Ages," *Speculum,* 11 (1936), 88–110.

Curtius, Ernst R. *European Literature and the Latin Middle Ages.* London, 1953.

Davis, Norman. "The Language of the Pastons," *PBA,* 40 (1954), 119–144.

——. "Styles in English Prose of the Late Middle and Early Modern Period," *Les Congrès et Colloques de l'Université de Liège,* 21 (1961), 165–184.

——. "The *Litera Troili,*" *RES,* 16 (1965), 233–244.

Deanesly, M. "Vernacular Books in England in the Fourteenth and Fifteenth Centuries," *MLR,* 15 (1920), 349–358.

Dekker, Arie. *Some Facts Concerning the Syntax of Malory's Morte Darthur.* Amsterdam, 1932.

Dillon, B. "Formal and Informal Pronouns of Address in Malory's Le Morte Darthur," *AM,* 10 (1969), 94–103.

Dobson, Eric J. *English Pronunciation 1500–1700.* 2nd ed. 2 vols. Oxford, 1968.

Eliot, T. S. *Selected Essays, 1917–1932.* London, 1932.

Enkvist, Nils E., J. Spencer, and M. Gregory. *Linguistics and Style.* London, 1964.

Faral, Edmond. *Les Arts Poétiques du XIIe et du XIIIe Siècle.* Paris, 1924.

Ferrier, Janet M. *French Prose Writers of the Fourteenth and Fifteenth Centuries.* Oxford, 1966.

Field, P. J. C. "Description and Narration in Malory," *Speculum,* 43 (1968), 476–486.

Fish, Stanley E. *John Skelton's Poetry.* Yale, 1965.

Fowler, Roger (ed.). *Essays on Style and Language.* London, 1966.

Frappier, Jean. *Étude sur la Mort le Roi Artu.* Paris, 1936.

French, W. H., and C. B. Hale (ed.). *Middle English Metrical Romances.* New York, 1930.

Galbraith, V. H. "The Literacy of the Medieval English Kings," *PBA,* 21 (1935), 201–238.

Gerould, Gordon H. *Saints' Legends.* Boston, 1916.

Gordon, Ian A. *The Movement of English Prose.* London, 1966.

Green, Vivian H. H. *Bishop Reginald Pecock, A Study in Ecclesiastical History and Thought.* Cambridge, 1945.

Greenwood, Alice D. "The Beginnings of English Prose," in *The Cambridge History of English Literature,* ed. Sir A. W. Ward and A. R. Waller (Cambridge, 1907–27), II, ch. iii.

——. "English Prose in the Fifteenth Century," ibid., II, chs. xii and xiv.

Gregory, Michael. "Old Bailey Speech in 'A Tale of Two Cities'," *REL,* 6 (1965), 42–55.

Hammond, Eleanor P. (ed.). *English Verse between Chaucer and Surrey.* Duke U.P., 1927.

Hay, Denys. *Polydore Vergil, Renaissance Historian and Man of Letters.* Oxford, 1952.

Hempl, George. "The Verb in the Morte Darthur," *MLN,* 9 (1894), 240–241.

Huizinga, J. *The Waning of the Middle Ages.* London, 1924.

Hulbert, James R. Rev. in *PQ*, 26 (1947), 302–306, of Joseph E. Mersand, *Chaucer's Romance Vocabulary.*

Jacob, E. F. "Florida Verborum Venustas: Some Early Examples of Euphuism in England," *BJRL*, 17 (1933), 264–290.

Jefferson, B. L. *Chaucer and the Consolation of Philosophy of Boethius.* Princeton, 1917.

Johnson, Samuel (ed.). *The Plays of William Shakespeare.* 8 vols. London, 1765.

Kennedy, Arthur G. *The Pronoun of Address in English Literature of the Thirteenth Century.* Stanford (California), 1915.

Ker, William P. *Epic and Romance.* London, 1897.

——. *Essays on Medieval Literature.* London, 1905.

——. *English Literature: Medieval.* London, 1912.

Kingsford, Charles L. *English Historical Literature in the Fifteenth Century.* Oxford, 1913.

Knowles, David. *The English Mystical Tradition.* London, 1961.

Krapp, George P. *The Rise of English Literary Prose.* New York, 1915.

Kurath, H., and Sherman Kuhn (ed.). *A Middle English Dictionary.* Ann Arbor, 1953– .

Legge, Mary Dominica. *Anglo-Norman Literature and its Background.* Oxford, 1963.

Levin, Samuel R. *Linguistic Structures in Poetry. Janua Linguarum,* 23 : 's Gravenhage, 1962.

Lewis, Clive Staples. Rev. in *MÆ*, 3 (1934), 237–240 of E. K. Chambers, *Sir Thomas Wyatt. . . .*

——. *A Preface to Paradise Lost.* Oxford, 1942.

——. *English Literature in the Sixteenth Century Excluding Drama.* Oxford, 1954.

——. "The English Prose Morte," in *Essays on Malory,* ed. J. A. W. Bennett, q.v.

——. *The Discarded Image.* Cambridge, 1964.

——. *Studies in Medieval and Renaissance Literature.* Cambridge, 1966.

Lewis, Edwin H. *The History of the English Paragraph.* Chicago, 1894.

Loomis, R. S. *Arthurian Literature in the Middle Ages.* Oxford, 1959.

Lot, Ferdinand. *Étude sur le Lancelot en Prose.* Paris, 1918.

Lubbock, Percy. *The Craft of Fiction.* London, 1926.

MacQueen, John. "Some Aspects of the Early Renaissance in Scotland," *FMLS*, 3 (1967), 201–222.

Matthews, William. *Later Medieval English Prose.* New York, 1963.

——. *The Ill-Framed Knight, A Skeptical Inquiry into the Identity of Sir Thomas Malory.* California U.P., 1966.

Miles, Josephine. *Style and Proportion: the Language of Prose and Poetry.* Boston 1967.

Miller, Brian D. H. Rev. in *MÆ*, 35 (1966), 71–8, of *The Bodley Version of Mandeville's Travels,* ed. M. C. Seymour.

Mitchell, R. J. *John Tiptoft.* London, 1938.

Moorman, Charles. "Internal Chronology in Malory's Morte Darthur," *JEGP*, 60 (1961), 240–240.

Morgan, Margery M. " 'A Talking of the Love of God' and the Continuity of Stylistic Tradition in Middle English Prose Meditations," *RES*, 3 (1952), 97–116.

———. "A Treatise in Cadence," *MLR*, 47 (1952), 156–164.

Morley, Henry. *English Writers*, IV–VI. London, 1889–90.

Mosher, Joseph A. *The Exemplum in the Early Religious and Didactic Literature of England*. New York, 1911.

Murphy, J. J. "A New Look at Chaucer and the Rhetoricians," *RES*, 15 (1964) 1–20.

Murray, Sir James A. H. *et al.* (ed.). *A New English Dictionary on Historical Principles*. Oxford, 1888–1933.

Murry, John Middleton. *The Problem of Style*. London, 1922.

Mustanoja, Tauno F. *A Middle English Syntax*. Helsinki, 1960.

Noguchi, S. "The Paradox of the Character of Malory's Language," *Hiroshima Studies in English Language and Literature*, 13 (1967), 115–134. (I have been unable to see this item.)

Oakeshott, Walter F. "A Malory Manuscript," *The* [London] *Times*, 25 August 1934.

Ohlander, Urban. "Omission of the Object in English," *SN*, 16 (1943–44) 105–127.

Ohmann, Richard M. "Prolegomena to the Analysis of Prose Style," in *Style in Prose Fiction*, ed. Harold C. Martin, *English Institute Essays, 1958*. New York, 1959.

Olmes, Antonie. *Sprache und Stil der Englischen Mystik des Mittelalters*. Halle a.S., 1933.

Orr, John. *Old French and Modern English Idiom*. Oxford, 1962.

Owst, G. R. *Literature and the Pulpit in Medieval England*. Oxford, 1961.

Pascal, Roy. "Tense and Novel," *MLR*, 57 (1962), 1–11.

Phillipps, K. C. "Contamination in Late Middle English," *ES*, 35 (1954), 17–20.

Pickford, Cedric E. *L'Évolution du Roman Arthurien en Prose vers la Fin du Moyen Âge*. . . . Paris, 1960.

Prins, Anton A. *French Influence in English Phrasing*. Leiden, 1952.

Rasmussen, Jens. *La Prose Narrative Française du XVᵉ Siècle*. Copenhagen, 1958.

Reiss, Edmund. *Sir Thomas Malory*. New York, 1966.

Rickert, Edith. "Chaucer at School," *MP*, 29 (1932), 257–274.

———. "King Richard II's Books," *Library*, 13 (1932–33), 144–147.

Rioux, Robert N. "Sir Thomas Malory, Créateur Verbal," *EA*, 12 (1959), 193–197.

Roberts, W. F. J. "Ellipsis of the Subject-Pronoun in Middle English," *London Medieval Studies*, 1 (1937), 107–115.

Robertson, D. W. "Frequency of Preaching in Thirteenth-Century England," *Speculum*, 24 (1949), 376–388.

Robins, R. H. *Ancient and Mediaeval Grammatical Theory in Europe*. . . . London, 1951.

Sandved, Arthur O. "A Note on the Language of Caxton's Malory and that of the Winchester Manuscript," *ES*, 40 (1959), 113–114.

——. *Studies in the Language of Caxton's Malory and that of the Winchester Manuscript.* Oslo and New York, 1968.

Schlauch, Margaret. "Chaucer's Prose Rhythms," *PMLA*, 65 (1950), 568–589.

——. "Chaucer's Colloquial English, its Structural Traits," *PMLA*, 67 (1952), 1103–1116.

——. *The English Language in Modern Times.* Warsaw, 1959.

Schneider, John P. *The Prose Style of Richard Rolle of Hampole.* Baltimore, 1906.

Schofield, William H. *English Literature from the Norman Conquest to Chaucer.* New York, 1906.

Scudder, Vida D. *Le Morte Darthur of Sir Thomas Malory: A Study of the Book and its Sources.* London and New York, 1921.

Sebeok, Thomas A. (ed.). *Style in Language.* London and New York, 1960.

Serjeantson, Mary S. *A History of Foreign Words in English.* London, 1961.

Seymour, M. C. "A Medieval Redactor at Work," *N&Q*, 206 (1961), 169–171.

Shaw, Sally. "Caxton and Malory," in *Essays on Malory,* ed. J. A. W. Bennett, q.v.

Sherman, L. A. "Some Observations upon the Sentence-Length in English Prose," *UNS* (1888), 119–130.

——. "On Certain Facts and Principles in the Development of Form in Literature," *UNS* (1892), 337–366.

Šimko, Ján. "A Linguistic Analysis of the Winchester Manuscript and William Caxton's Edition of Sir Thomas Malory's Morte Darthur," *ČMF-Philologica,* 8 (1956), 1–2.

——. *Word-Order in the Winchester Manuscript and in William Caxton's Edition of Thomas Malory's Morte Darthur (1485): A Comparison.* Halle a.S., 1957.

Sisam, Kenneth. *Fourteenth-Century Verse and Prose.* Oxford, 1921.

Smith, George G. *Specimens of Middle Scots.* Edinburgh, 1902.

——. "The Middle Scots Anthologies: Anonymous Verse and Early Prose," *Cambridge History of English Literature,* II, 267–285.

Spitzer, Leo. *Linguistics and Literary History: Essays in Stylistics.* Princeton, 1948.

Stauffer, Donald A. *English Biography before 1700.* Cambridge (Mass.), 1930.

Stendhal (Henri Beyle). "Du Style," in *Mélanges de Littérature,* ed. H. Martineau. 3 vols. Paris, 1933.

Stevenson, W. H. "The Introduction of English as the Vehicle of Instruction in English Schools," in *An English Miscellany Presented to Dr Furnivall* (Oxford, 1901), 421–429.

Stidston, Russell O. *The Use of Ye in the Function of Thou . . . in Fourteenth-Century England.* Stanford (California), 1917.

Sutherland, D. R. "On the Use of Tenses in Old and Middle French," in *Studies in French Language and Literature presented to Professor Mildred K. Pope.* Manchester, 1939.

Sutherland, James. *A Preface to Eighteenth-Century Poetry.* Oxford, 1948.

——. *On English Prose.* Toronto U.P., 1957.

Swieczkowski, Walerian. *Word Order Patterning in Middle English.* 's Gravenhage, 1962.

Thompson, James W. *The Medieval Library.* 2nd ed. New York, 1957.

——. *The Literacy of the Laity in the Middle Ages.* California, 1939.

Tilley, Morris P. *A Dictionary of the Proverbs in England in the Sixteenth and Seventeenth Centuries*. Ann Arbor, 1950.

Tucker, P. E. "Malory's Conception of Chivalry as it Appears in his Treatment of the Story of Sir Lancelot." Unpubl. B.Litt. thesis, Oxford, 1954.

Twain, Mark (Samuel L. Clemens). *A Connecticut Yankee in King Arthur's Court*, in *Works* (London, 1900), vol. 16.

Ullman, Stephen. *Style in the French Novel*. Cambridge, 1957.

——. *Language and Style*. Oxford, 1964.

Vinaver, Eugène. *Malory*. Oxford, 1929.

——. *Form and Meaning in Medieval Romance*. Presidential Address, Modern Humanities Research Association, London, 1966.

Visser, F. T. *An Historical Syntax of the English Language*. Leiden, 1963– .

Weiss, Roberto. *Humanism in England during the Fifteenth Century*. Oxford, 1957.

Wells, John Edwin. *A Manual of the Writings in Middle English, 1050–1400*. New Haven, 1916–51.

Whitehead, F. "On Certain Episodes in the Fourth Book of Malory's Morte Darthur," *MÆ*, 2 (1933), 199–216.

Whiting, B. J. *Chaucer's Use of Proverbs*. Harvard, 1934.

Williamson, George. *The Senecan Amble*. London, 1951.

Wilson, R. H. "Malory and the Perlesvaus," *MP*, 30 (1932), 13—22.

——. "Malory's Naming of Minor Characters," *JEGP*, 42 (1943), 364–385.

——. "Malory's 'French Book' Again," *CL*, 2 (1950), 172–181.

——. "Addenda on Malory's Minor Characters," *JEGP*, 55 (1956), 563–587.

Wilson, R. M. "Three Middle English Mystics," *E&S*, 9 (1956), 87–112.

——. "On the Continuity of English Prose," in *Mélanges de Linguistique et de Philologie, Fernand Mossé in Memoriam*. Paris, 1959.

Wimsatt, W. K. *The Prose Style of Samuel Johnson*. New Haven, 1941.

Winterbottom, Michael. "The Style of Æthelweard," *MÆ*, 36 (1967), 109–118.

Workman, Samuel K. *Fifteenth-Century Translation as an Influence on English Prose*. Princeton Studies in English, 18: Princeton, 1940.

Wroten, Helen I. "Malory's 'Tale of King Arthur and the Emperor Lucius, Compared with its Source, the Alliterative Morte Arthure." Ph.D. thesis, Illinois, 1950.

Wyld, Henry C. "Aspects of Style and Idiom in Fifteenth-Century English," *E&S*, 26 (1940), 30–44.

——. *A History of Modern Colloquial English*. 3rd ed. Oxford, 1953.

G

Notes

NOTES TO CHAPTER I

1. R. M. Ohmann, "Prolegomena to the Analysis of Prose Style," in *Style in Prose Fiction*, ed. H. C. Martin, *English Institute Essays 1958* (New York, 1959), pp. 1–24.
2. Nils E. Enkvist, J. Spencer, and M. Gregory, *Linguistics and Style* (London, 1964), pp. 10–28.
3. *On the Study of Celtic Literature* (London, 1867), pp. 135–141.
4. *Linguistics and Literary History: Essays in Stylistics* (Princeton, 1948), ch. iv. His theory of style is expounded in ch. i of the same book.
5. *V*. William Matthews, *The Ill-Framed Knight* (California, 1966).
6. "Du Style" (1812) in *Mélanges de Littérature*, ed. H. Martineau, 3 vols. (Paris, 1933), III, 110.
7. Ohmann, op. cit., pp. 13–14.
8. W. K. Wimsatt, *The Prose Style of Samuel Johnson* (New Haven, 1941), p. 11.
9. It is not necessary for us to enter into the details of the controversy over the unity of the *Morte Darthur* which has occupied Malory scholarship for the past twenty years. Except for a small school immediately around Professor Eugène Vinaver, who originally suggested that Malory's work was not one book but eight, the consensus of scholarly opinion is now firm that the book was intended to be and is a substantial unity, with no more lapses than might have been expected of a work composed in prison. A sensible if unexciting summary of the matter can be found in Edmund Reiss, *Sir Thomas Malory* (New York, 1966). Scholarly interest seems now to be turning to other aspects of Malory's work.
10. W. P. Ker, *Essays on Medieval Literature* (London, 1905), pp. 22–5.
11. Eugène Vinaver (ed.), *The Works of Sir Thomas Malory*, second edition (Oxford, 1967), 3 vols., paged consecutively, cited hereafter as V. The eight tales into which V is divided will be referred to as "Arthur", "Lucius", "Lancelot", "Gareth", "Tristram", "Grail", "Lancelot & Guenivere", and "Morte". The quotation above is from V lxiv.
12. The best assessments are E. K. Chambers' brief and factual but sometimes inaccurate account in his *English Literature at the Close of the Middle Ages* (Oxford, 1945), pp. 198–9, and D. S. Brewer's stimulating preface to his recent part-edition, *The Morte Darthur: Parts Seven and Eight* (London, 1968), pp. 12–19.

13. S. Ullmann, *Style in the French Novel* (Cambridge, 1957), p. 6. The first chapter of this book contains an excellent short history of modern stylistic theory.
14. "The Function of Criticism," in *Selected Essays, 1917-1932* (London, 1932), p. 23. Eliot's italics.
15. *The Plays of William Shakespeare* [ed. Samuel Johnson], (London, 1765), I, vi-vii.

NOTES TO CHAPTER II

1. *V. C. E.* Pickford, *L'Évolution du Roman Arthurien en Prose vers la Fin du Moyen Âge* (Paris, 1960). It was apparently also for Jacques d'Armagnac that the thirteen poems of the William of Orange cycle were made up into one long prose romance: *v.* H. J. Chaytor, *From Script to Print* (Cambridge, 1945), p. 88.
2. A summary description is given by J. Frappier, "The Vulgate Cycle," in *Arthurian Literature in the Middle Ages*, ed. R. S. Loomis (Oxford, 1959), pp. 295-318.
3. V 278-282; *Le Haut Livre du Graal, Perlesvaus,* ed. W. A. Nitze & T. A. Jenkins, 2 vols. (Chicago, 1932), I, 339-49; R. H. Wilson, "Malory and the Perlesvaus," *MP*, 30 (1932), 13-22.
4. *V.* Fanni Bogdanow, "*The Suite de Merlin...,*" in Loomis, op. cit., pp. 325-35.
5. Most speculations have assumed a French source, but W. F. Oakeshott suggested that "Gareth" might be of Malory's own writing (in "A Malory Manuscript," *The* [London] *Times,* 25 August 1934), and Robert W. Ackerman argued in "Malory's 'Ironsyde'," *RS*, 32 (1964), 125-133, that an English source might be involved at some point.
6. More precise information on the sources can be found in the notes to V.
7. *V.* Pickford, op. cit., pp. 176-185.
8. V cxlv. 22-3.
9. E. Vinaver, *Malory* (Oxford, 1929), pp. 30-1.
10. Balin, V 59-92; Fr. text *Le Roman de Balain,* ed. M. D. Legge (Manchester, 1942), cited as L. The word count includes the twelve folios omitted from L, printed in *Merlin...,* ed. G. Paris, 2 vols. (Paris, 1886), I, 245-75. Appendix III *infra* gives three passages of the French prose *Tristan*, from which Malory's reduction can be seen.
11. *Troilus*, II, 81-4. My references to Chaucer are from *The Complete Works of Geoffrey Chaucer*, ed. W. W. Skeat, 7 vols. (Oxford, 1894-97). V 375.17: Malory's "herde rede of" may be only a set phrase, but would still be evidence of his time or of one very shortly before it.
12. Chaytor, *From Script to Print*, pp. 5-21.
13. *Letters and Papers, Foreign and Domestic, Henry VIII,* III (1519-23), I, 1.
14. Sir Thomas Elyot, *The Boke Named the Governour,* ed. H. H. S. Croft, 2 vols. (London, 1880), I, 98-113.
15. Alain Chartier, *Les Oeuvres...,* ed. André du Chesne Tourangeau (Paris,

1617), p.316; Baldassare Castiglione, *The Courtyer*, tr. Sir Thomas Hoby (London, 1561), fol. H ii^v.

16. Most critics think much more highly than I do of *The Owl and the Nightingale*, but they are united in seeing it as a solitary oasis in a thirteenth-century desert.

17. R. W. Chambers, *On the Continuity of English Prose*, EETS (1932); cf. R. M. Wilson, "On the Continuity of English Prose," in *Mélanges de Linguistique et de Philologie, Fernand Mossé in Memoriam* (Paris, 1959), pp. 486–94, and N. Davis, "Styles in English Prose of the Late Middle and Early Modern Period," *Les Congrès et Colloques de l'Université de Liège*, 21, pp. 165–184.

18. E. J. Arnould, *Le Manuel de Péchés: Étude de Littérature Religieuse Anglo-normande* (Paris, 1940), p. 20.

19. D. W. Robertson, "Frequency of Preaching in Thirteenth-Century England," *Speculum*, 24 (1949), 376–88.

20. *V. H.* Caplan, *Mediaeval Artes Praedicandi, A Handlist* (Cornell, 1934) and *Supplement* (1936), and Th.-M. Charland, *Artes Praedicandi: Contribution à l'Histoire de la Rhétorique au Moyen Âge* (Ottawa, 1936).

21. M. M. Morgan, " 'A Talking of the Love of God' and the Continuity of Stylistic Tradition in Middle English Prose Meditations," *RES*, 3 (1952), 97–116.

22. V. R. M. Wilson, "Three Middle English Mystics," *E&S*, 9 (1956), 87–112.

23. *V. Deonise Hid Divinite*, ed. P. Hodgson, EETS 231 (1955), pp. xlvii–lvii.

24. Wilson, op. cit.

25. M. Deanesly, "Vernacular Books in England in the Fourteenth and Fifteenth Centuries," *MLR*, 15 (1920), 349–58.

26. William Matthews (ed.), *Later Medieval English Prose* (New York, 1963), pp. 5–6. On the vexed question of the relationship of the English translations of Mandeville, see K. Sisam, *Fourteenth-Century Verse and Prose* (Oxford, 1921), pp. 240–2. More recent work is cited in B. D. H. Miller, rev. of *The Bodley Version of Mandeville's Travels*, ed. M. C. Seymour, in *MÆ*, 35 (1966), 71–8.

27. *Metalogicon*, ed. C. C. J. Webb (Oxford, 1929), pp. 82–3.

28. *Meroure of Wissdome*, ed. C. Macpherson, STS (1926), p. 164.

29. John Aubrey, *Brief Lives*, ed. O. L. Dick (London, 1949), p. 226.

30. V. J. W. H. Atkins, *English Literary Criticism: the Medieval Phase*, 2nd ed. (London, 1952), pp. 99–103.

31. Willem Grapheus *alias* Fullonius, *Acolastus* (London, 1540), fol. A iv^r.

32. Pp. 144–172.

33. Foxe, p. 170.

34. Op. cit., p. 145.

35. H. S. Bennett, "Fifteenth-Century Secular Prose," *RES*, 21 (1945), 257–263.

36. *The Folewer to the Donet*, ed. E. V. Hitchcock, EETS, OS 164 (1924), pp. lxv ff.

37. *The Repressor*, ed. C. Babington, Rolls Series, 2 vols. (1860), II, 554–5.

38. V. Deanesly, op. cit., p. 353.

39. Samuel K. Workman, *Fifteenth-Century Translation as an Influence on English Prose* (Princeton, 1940), p. 150.
40. Nicholas Love, *The Mirrour of the Blessed Lyf of Jesu Christ*, ed. L. F. Powell (Oxford, 1908), p. 8.
41. Love, p. 103.
42. Bonaventure (attrib.), *Vita Christi*, ed. Jehan Petit (? Paris, 1510), fol. D vii^r.
43. Love, pp. 164–5.
44. *Mandeville's Travels*, ed. M. C. Seymour (Oxford, 1967), p. 4: *v.* note on the real relationship of the English, French, and Latin texts, p. 231.
45. For French, *v.* Janet M. Ferrier, *French Prose Writers of the Fourteenth and Fifteenth Centuries* (Oxford, 1966), pp. ix–xii and *passim*, and at greater length, Jens Rasmussen, *La Prose Narrative Française du XVe Siècle* (Copenhagen, 1958).
46. *V.* M. D. Legge, *Anglo-Norman Literature and its Background* (Oxford, 1963), p. 216.
47. M. Deanesly, "Vernacular Books in England in the Fourteenth and Fifteenth Centuries," *MLR*, 15 (1920), 349–58.
48. E. Rickert, "King Richard II's Books," *The Library*, 13 (1932–33), 144–7.
49. H. S. Bennett, *The Pastons and their England* (Cambridge, 1922), pp. 261–2.
50. A. A. Prins, *French Influence in English Phrasing* (Leiden, 1952), pp. 18–20. Cf. J. Orr, *Old French and Modern English Idiom* (Oxford, 1962).
51. C. S. Lewis, *English Literature in the Sixteenth Century excluding Drama* (Oxford, 1954), p. 61. *V.* E. Faral, *Les Arts Poétiques du XIIe et du XIIIe Siècle* (Paris, 1924), and C. S. Baldwin, *Medieval Rhetoric and Poetic to 1400* (New York, 1928).
52. E. Auerbach, *Literary Language and its Public in Late Latin Antiquity and in the Middle Ages* (London, 1965), ch. ii; cf. M. Winterbottom, "The Style of Æthelweard," *MÆ*, 36 (1967), 109–118.
53. *Chronicle*, Rolls Series, 2 vols. (1879–80), I, 87.
54. E. F. Jacob, *Florida Verborum Venustas*, *BJRL*, 17 (1933), 264–90.
55. *Official Correspondence*, Rolls Series, 2 vols. (1872), I, 116.
56. The rest of the paragraph depends on Workman, *Fifteenth-Century Translation*, chs. iv–vii.
57. Rolls Series (London, 1858), p. 47.
58. Workman, p. 150, n. 9.
59. *The Governour*, ed. Croft, I, 243–69, II, 370.
60. *The Poems*, ed. W. M. Mackenzie (London, 1932), 5–20.
61. R. M. Wilson, "Three Middle English Mystics," *E&S*, 9 (1956), 87–112.
62. R. Crosby, "Oral Delivery in the Middle Ages," *Speculum*, 11 (1936), 88–110.
63. *Canterbury Tales*, I 43 (Parson's Prologue); B. L. Jefferson, *Chaucer and the Consolation of Philosophy of Boethius* (Princeton, 1917), pp. 25–46. Chaucer does in fact use alliterative effects in verse: notably in the jousting in the *Knight's Tale* and in the battle of Actium in the *Legend of Dido*.
64. In *Fifteenth Century Prose and Verse*, ed. A. W. Pollard (Westminster, 1903), p. 209. Pollard gives "*needful* meaning": I give the alliterating phrase from MS BM Stowe 65, fol. 216^r, col. 1.

65. *The Serpent of Division*, ed. H. N. MacCracken (Yale, 1911), p. 54.

66. Prol. to *Eneydos*, in *The Prologues and Epilogues*, ed. W. J. B. Crotch, EETS, OS 176 (1928), pp. 107–110.

67. A. D. Greenwood, "English Prose in the Fifteenth Century," in *The Cambridge History of English Literature* (Cambridge, 1907–27), II, 333.

68. Caxton praised Skelton for the "polysshed and ornate termes" which he had culled from reading "the ix. muses", in *Prologues*, p. 109.

69. *The Poetical Works*, ed. A. Dyce, 2 vols. (London, 1843), I, 208–9. There is a discussion of Skelton's opinions on language in S. E. Fish, *John Skelton's Poetry* (Yale, 1965), pp. 16–25.

70. *Letters and Papers, Foreign and Domestic, Henry VIII*, XIII, p. 430.

71. B. L. Jefferson, *Chaucer and the Consolation of Philosophy*, pp. 25–46; Margaret Schlauch, "The Art of Chaucer's Prose," in *Chaucer and Chaucerians*, ed. D. S. Brewer (London, 1966), pp. 140–163.

72. Quoted in G. R. Owst, *Literature and the Pulpit in Medieval England* (Oxford, 1961), p. 137.

73. Loc. cit.

74. V. H. Galbraith, "The Literacy of the Medieval English Kings," *PBA*, 21 (1935), 201–38, and James W. Thompson, *The Literacy of the Laity in the Middle Ages* (California, 1939).

75. J. W. Adamson, "The Extent of Literacy in England in the Fifteenth and Sixteenth Centuries," *Library*, 10 (1929), 163–193.

76. H. S. Bennett, "The Production and Dissemination of Vernacular Manuscripts in the Fifteenth Century," *Library*, I (1947), 167–178; and J. A. Burrow, "The Audience of Piers Plowman," *Anglia*, 75 (1957), 373–84.

77. *Apology* (1533) in *The Workes of Sir Thomas More*, ed. W. Rastell (London, 1557), p. 850.

78. V. A. T. P. Byles, "William Caxton as a Man of Letters," *Library*, 15 (1935), 1–25, and C. F. Bühler, *William Caxton and his Critics* (Syracuse U.P., 1960).

79. Deanesly, "Vernacular Books."

80. Ed. Charles Plummer (Oxford, 1885), p. 149.

81. R. Weiss, *Humanism in England during the Fifteenth Century* (Oxford, 1957), chs. iii, iv, and vii.

82. Ibid., pp. 68–9, 118–119.

83. Edward "Plantagenet", *The Master of Game*, ed. W. A. & F. Baillie-Grohman (London, 1904).

84. Ibid, p. 6. The text, from BM MS Vespasian B XII, gives "*with* hiundes bene vanchasours...," clearly a scribal error. I follow MS Bodl. 546, fol. 8ᵛ and Bodl. MS Douce 335, fol. 4ᵛ in reading "which".

85. *The Union of the Two Noble and Illustre Fameiles of Lancastre and Yorke*.... (London, 1550), Henry IV, fol. 24ʳ. The dormouse is one of the less common symbols for the deadly sin of sloth: M. W. Bloomfield, *The Seven Deadly Sins* (Michigan, 1952), pp. 245–249 and index.

86. *Prologues*, ed. Crotch, pp. 88, 108.

87. *The Brut, or the Chronicles of England*, ed. F. W. D. Brie, EETS, OS 131, 136 (1906–08), I, 54. This edition prints "everyche anone, everyche" from

Bodl. MS Rawl. B. 171. I follow the collated MSS Bodl. Douce 323 and Trin. Coll. Dublin 490 in omitting the repeated word.

88. *The Paston Letters, a Selection in Modern Spelling,* ed. N. Davis (London, 1963), pp. 27–8; *The Brut,* I, 221–3.

89. London, 1694. Critical ed. by J. L. Nickalls (Cambridge, 1952).

NOTES TO CHAPTER III

1. *Canterbury Tales,* B 4401.
2. Ibid., A 859.
3. Margaret Schlauch, "Chaucer's Colloquial English, its Structural Traits," *PMLA,* 67 (1952), 1103–16.
4. *The Cely Papers.* . . , ed. Henry E. Malden (London, 1900), pp. 58–9.
5. Ibid., p. 57; *The Paston Letters,* ed. Norman Davis (London, 1963), pp. 10–13.
6. Workman, *Fifteenth-Century Translation,* p. 3.
7. *The Holy Bible* . . . *by John Wycliffe and his Followers,* ed. J. Forshall and F. Madden, 4 vols. (Oxford, 1850), I, 57. Cf. Capgrave's practice, pp. 24–5, and example from Malory quoted p. 41 *infra.*
8. H. S. Bennett, *Chaucer and the Fifteenth Century* (Oxford, 1947), p. 199.
9. L. A. Sherman, *Some Observations upon the Sentence-Length in English Prose* (Nebraska, 1888), p. 121.
10. Edwin H. Lewis, *The History of the English Paragraph* (Chicago, 1894), pp. 73–6. He suggests Tyndale as the first English writer to use the paragraph as a "stadium of thought".
11. *V.* MED, "for"; C. S. Baldwin, *The Inflections and Syntax of the Morte Darthur* (Boston, 1894), pp. 135, 139.
12. I.e. the account up to 1333, before the successive continuators take over (vol. I of Brie's ed.). Of the continuators, B and G are syntactically more capable than the others.
13. Cf. Erich Auerbach, *Mimesis, the Representation of Reality in Western Literature* (Princeton, 1953), ch. v, for the effects of asyndetic parataxis in the *Chanson de Roland,* especially pp. 99–100.
14. *Canterbury Tales,* A 2599–2620.
15. Especially 2612–14. Cf. the famous scene of the Temple of Mars (A 1975–1994).
16. A solitary small example in Malory is at V 285.10–12.
17. V 515.11–22; cf. MS BN fr. 334, fol. 226^r given in Appendix III, pp. 163–4. This gives a further element to the climax in the French, where the audience is silenced when its favourite is unhorsed.
18. See p. 44–5 below and Auerbach, *Mimesis,* pp. 99–100.
19. K. C. Phillipps, "Contamination in Late Middle English," *ES,* 35 (1954), 17–20.
20. Another example V 513.25. Caxton emends the first: to the chynne that he fylle. . . . S 115.4, and not the second.
21. Mustanoja (p. 142) cites none comparable, but *v.* examples in W. F. J. Roberts, "Ellipsis of the Subject-Pronoun in Middle English," in *London Medieval Studies,* I, (1937), 107–115.

22. Nothing strictly comparable is cited in Urban Ohlander, "Omission of the Object in English," *SN*, 16 (1943), 105–127. Caxton emends the case we have quoted: chaced hym oute of your countrey, by whome. . . . S 731.24.

23. Workman, *Fifteenth-Century Translation*, ch. ii and *passim*.

24. Cf. *Paston Letters*, ed. Davis, p. 162 and note 1.

25. W. H. French and C. B. Hale (ed.), *Middle English Metrical Romances* (New York, 1930), p. 17.

26. Caxton emends this: Launcelot wallop alle that he myghte. S 786.1.

27. Another fifteenth-century English version of this passage avoids the dangers by staying very close to the French original. See *Merlin*, ed. Henry B. Wheatley, EETS, OS 10, 21, 36, 112 (text paged consecutively), p. 96, and Sommer, II, 80.

28. I here give the Winchester MS reading of Vinaver's first (1947) ed. Caxton reads: Soo that day. . . . (S 287.7), which Vinaver accepts in his second ed. This would reduce but not remove the confusion.

29. Caxton emends: Whan the kynge of the Cyté whiche was cleped Estorause sawe the felaushyp. . . . (S 722.4), which unfortunately is still ambiguous.

30. *Paston Letters*, ed. Davis, p. 245. Cf. *The Brut*, ed. Brie, I, 88.25.

31. George Cavendish, *The Life and Death of Cardinal Wolsey*, ed. R. S. Sylvester, EETS (1959), p. 135.

32. Other examples V 1104. 19–25, 1150.28, 1212.29. Caxton emends all four cases: S 672.29, 764.23, 29, 793.16, 832.1.

33. Ed. Baillie-Grohman, p. 10. The editor argues that the hare, which is the subject of the passage, was thought to be bisexual, and that this caused the variation of pronoun.

34. An account of the whole process is given in Mustanoja, pp. 437–40, 583–619.

35. Quoted in H. C. Wyld, *A History of Modern Colloquial English*, 3rd ed. (Oxford, 1953), p. 89

36. In the French as well as the English. The historic present is not mentioned in C. S. Baldwin, *The Inflections and Syntax of the Morte Darthur* (Boston, 1894), or in Arie Dekker, *Some Facts Concerning the Syntax of Malory's Morte Darthur* (Amsterdam, 1932).

37. Mustanoja, pp. 485–8.

38. Ed. Octavia Richardson, EETS, ES 44–5 (1884–85). The historic present appears sporadically throughout.

39. *Paston Letters*, ed. Davis, p. 113 (Margaret Paston); *Middle English Metrical Romances*, ed. French and Hale, p. 18; cf. in one short passage of the *Morte*, V 310.13, 322.32, 345.11, 362.16, 376.8, 392.3, 444.30, 445.22, 448.31, 450.14, 466.2.

40. Caxton emends to: fought . . . fought, S 109.17.

41. Cf. V 310.15, 907.23.

42. S 666.35, 667.26.

43. S 186.1, 623.27.

44. A modern example of the use of the historic present as the dominant tense in a novel is Stan Barstow's *A Kind of Loving* (London, 1960), where

the colloquial effect is striking. The various uses of the present are examined in Roy Pascal, "Tense and Novel," *MLR*, 57 (1962), 1–11.

45. Wyld, *Modern Colloquial English*, pp. 362–3. The references which follow are to Gairdner's ed.

46. Robert N. Rioux, "Sir Thomas Malory, Créateur Verbal," *EA*, 12 (1959), 193–7.

47. This was the first (1947) edition; the second edition, which I use elsewhere in this book, contains some 75 new words.

48. *V. J. R.* Hulbert, Rev. of Joseph E. Mersand, *Chaucer's Romance Vocabulary, PQ*, 26 (1947), 302–6.

49. See any standard history of the language, e.g. A. C. Baugh, *A History of the English Language* (London, 1959), pp. 200–22.

50. Evidence for this statement and the rest of the paragraph will be found in Appendix I, p. 160.

51. *Paston Letters*, ed. Davis, pp. 14, 43, 121, 46, 252, 257.

52. N. S. Aurner, *Caxton, Mirrour of Fifteenth-Century Letters* (London, 1926), p. 144; M. P. Tilley, *A Dictionary of the Proverbs in England in the Sixteenth and Seventeenth Centuries* (Ann Arbor, 1950), J4.

53. *Canterbury Tales*, A 247.

54. A. A. Prins, *French Influence in English Phrasing* (Leiden, 1952), p. 18.

55. *V.* Sally Shaw, "Caxton and Malory," in *Essays on Malory*, ed. J. A. W. Bennett (Oxford, 1963), pp. 114–145.

56. *V.* especially V 1211–12 and *Le Morte Arthur*, ed. J. D. Bruce, EETS, ES 88 (1903), ll. 2540–2600.

57. Workman, *Fifteenth-Century Translation*, p. 8.

58. *Supra* pp. 43–4. He also resists his sources in denying himself the historic present (*supra* pp. 53–7).

59. E.g. *La Mort le Roi Artu*, ed. J. Frappier (Paris, 1936), 47.14, 10.14.

60. *Merlin*, ed. Wheatley, e.g. p. 92; cf. Sommer, II, 77. In a forthright critical generation, W. H. Schofield said of Malory: "the splendid distinction of his style appears heightened when compared with that of his fellow, the servile translator of the whole, or, indeed, with the tiresome metrical version prepared about 1450 by the skinner Lovelich, whose trade seems to have occupied him too little." (*English Literature from the Norman Conquest to Chaucer* [New York, 1906], p. 250.) Schofield did not enlarge on the bad effects of servility, but we must.

61. *The Chronicle of Froissart Translated out of the French by Sir John Bourchier Lord Berners*, 6 vols. (London, 1901–03), I, 6.

62. Cf. V 459.13, 826.22, 832.24, 845.33; Caxton, *Prologues*, ed. Crotch, pp. 92, 105; and Berners in another translation, speaking of a sword "called Traunchfer, that is for to say, cutter of yron." *The History of the Valiant Knight Arthur of Little Britain*, ed. E. V. Utterson (London, 1814), p. 208, cf. p. 252.

63. For instance, *v.* Geoffrey de la Tour Landry, *The Book of the Knight of La Tour Landry*, ed. Thomas Wright, EETS, OS 33* (1906), p. 128, and cf. *Le Livre du Chevalier de la Tour Landry*, ed. Anatole de Montaiglon (Paris, 1854), p. 190. And this stencil translation is from the better of the fifteenth-century attempts: the other (Caxton's) was so literal that it would be

easily possible from its Gallicisms and infelicities to identify the very manuscript used (Wright's ed., p. xvi).
64. *Merlin*, ed. Wheatley, p. 117. MED records "affichen" previously, but in a different sense.
65. *V.* Sommer, II, 94. 4–5.
66. *Merlin*, p. 162; Sommer, II, 119.30.
67. *Merlin*, p. 134; Sommer, II, 103. 18–19.
68. Sommer, II, 85.4; *Merlin*, p. 103; V 15.24.
69. Margaret Schlauch, "The Art of Chaucer's Prose," in *Chaucer and Chaucerians*, ed. D. S. Brewer, p. 147.
70. The source, which is in the subjunctive, but does not use this construction, is cited in V's note; cf. V 180.22.
71. See NED, "that", conj. 3c; F. T. Visser, *An Historical Syntax of the English Language* (Leiden, 1963–   ), II, 806; *Paston Letters*, ed. Gairdner, III, 172 and Supp., 75; *Howleglass* (London, 1528), sig. E iiiᵣ.
72. See notes to V 451.20, 470.19, 551.32, 866.25, 885.30, 973.16, 1000.18, 1001.27, 1014.27, 1065.23, 1135.2, 1139.1, 1153.1.
73. Eugène Vinaver, "Sir Thomas Malory," in *Arthurian Literature in the Middle Ages*, ed. R. S. Loomis (Oxford, 1959), p. 548.
74. But for a few examples of stencil translation in Malory, see V 1534–36.

NOTES TO CHAPTER IV

1. Lydgate, *Fall of Princes*, ed. H. Bergen, 4 vols., EETS ES 121–124 (1924–1927), VI, 102–4; Alexander Barclay, *Egloges* (London, ? 1530), prologue l.38; William Nevill, *The Castell of Pleasure*, ed. Roberta Cornelius, EETS OS 179 (1930), p. 113.
2. *Certain Egloges of Alexander Barclay* (London, 1570), IV, 15–20.
3. *Cligès*, ed. W. Foerster (Halle a. S., 1889), l. 41. "For of the Greeks and Romans no one speaks—little or much—any longer; their word has ceased and their bright flame is put out."
4. To accept the historicity of Lucius was not to be absurdly credulous. In his savage and witty *Supplication for the Beggars* (1529), Simon Fish, an educated and sceptical cleric, was able to quote Arthur's campaign against Lucius beside half a dozen historical conquests in a list of the greatest military achievements recorded (ed. E. Arber [London, 1880], p. 5). Lord Chief Justice Fortescue, who was probably the judge who committed Malory to prison on several occasions (Matthews, *The Ill-Framed Knight*, pp. 28–30), also accepted the traditional story of Arthur. Fortescue, a shrewd constitutional lawyer, cites "gret Artour" in a completely matter-of-fact way among the kings who had ruled by what he calls "*Ius Regale*" (*Governance*, ed. Plummer, p. 115 and note).
5. E. R. Curtius, *European Literature and the Latin Middle Ages* (London, 1953), pp. 455, 83; cf. E. Faral, *Les Arts Poétiques du XII⁰ et du XIII⁰ Siècle* (Paris, 1924), pp. 52–4 and *passim*; C. S. Baldwin, *Medieval Rhetoric and Poetic to 1400* (New York, 1928), pp. 206–27. Cf. Tony Hunt, "The Rhetorical Background to the Arthurian Prologue," *FMLS*, 6 (1970), 1–23.

6. *English Verse Between Chaucer and Surrey*, ed. Eleanor P. Hammond (Duke University Press, 1927), pp. 169–171 gives some dozen examples and further references.
7. Curtius, op. cit., pp. 82–3, 92–4; *Mort Artu*, ed. Frappier, p. 138.
8. Curtius, op. cit., pp. 159–162.
9. *Paston Letters*, ed. Gairdner, II, 318.
10. E.g. V 177.19, 373.30, 385.14, 387.27, 387.36, 419.36, 1048.8, 1080.19.
11. Hardly a critic has failed to quote this passage as an example of the beauty of Malory's style, but the anaphora was first pointed out by D. S. Brewer in his ed., *The Morte Darthur, Parts Seven and Eight* (London, 1968), p. 14. *V.* also J. J. Murphy, "A New Look at Chaucer and the Rhetoricians," *RES*, 15 (1964), 1–20.
12. *V.* op. cit., ch. iii, n. 55.
13. *V.* parallel texts in Helen I. Wroten, "Malory's Tale of King Arthur and the Emperor Lucius Compared with its Source, the Alliterative Morte Arthure," Illinois Ph.D. dissertation (1950).
14. W. P. Ker, *Essays on Medieval Literature* (London, 1905), p. 25. More recently I. A. Gordon has firmly asserted that Malory was a conscious stylist, but without producing any evidence for his view: *The Movement of English Prose* (London, 1966), pp. 59, 67.
15. J. Frappier, *Étude sur la Mort le Roi Artu* (Paris, 1936), pp. 372–97; *Le Roman de Tristan en Prose*, ed. R. L. Curtis, I (Munich, 1963), p. 11.
16. V 85 (L 81); V 68 (L 17).
17. See Caxton's praise of Chaucer's brevity in the epilogue to his edition of the *House of Fame*, in *Prologues and Epilogues*, ed. Crotch, p. 69; and E. R. Curtius, *European Literature*, pp. 487–94.
18. Wroten, pp. 79–80.
19. V 1538–39.
20. William Matthews, *The Ill-Framed Knight*, pp. 94–8.
21. Rioux, "Sir Thomas Malory, Créateur Verbal," p. 196. We may also note here that the curious gender of "*Le Morte Darthur*" is recorded in Anglo-Norman. I am grateful to Miss M. A. Muir for information on this point.
22. None of Malory's French sources shows any marked tendency to alliteration. See, for instance, Appendix III *passim* for sections of the French prose *Tristan*.
23. Pope, *The Dunciad*, B I.31. My references to Pope's poetry are from *The Twickenham Edition of the Poems of Alexander Pope*, ed. J. Butt, 11 vols. (London, 1939–67).
24. "Malory's 'Tale of King Arthur'," pp. 38–47.
25. S. R. Levin argues that it is the natural effect of doublets, particularly compound ones, to bring out any such similarities possible: "Linguistic Structures in Poetry," *Janua Linguarum*, 23 (1962), p. 35.
26. C. S. Lewis, "The English Prose *Morte*," in *Essays on Malory*, ed. J. A. W. Bennett, p. 23.
27. *Mirrour*, ed. Powell, pp. 92–3; cf. Bonaventure, *Vita Christi*, sig. D. iii^v.
28. *The Union of Lancastre and Yorke*, Henry V, fol. 3^v.

29. E.g. Hall's narrative of and moralising over rebellion, ed. cit., Henry IV, fol. 25ʳ.
30. Roger Ascham, *The Scholemaster* (1570), ed. E. Arber (London, 1870), p. 112.
31. For another similar case see V 309.23.
32. Worship V 63.18, 25, 26, 27, 64.3, 28, 65.27, 70.22, 26, 73.27, 75.30, 76.10, 78.12; Proues V 64.28, 67.12, 26, 68.4, 11, 70.27, 74.16, 75.5, 10, 77.10, 78.21, 87.1, 5, 88.38.
33. "For" and "so" often have little meaning in Malory: see Baldwin, *Syntax*, pp. 135, 139, and V 1237.32.
34. See R. H. Wilson, "Malory's Naming of Minor Characters," *JEGP*, 42 (1943), 364–85; and "Addenda on Malory's Minor Characters," *JEGP*, 55 (1956), 563–87.
35. V 1177.24, 1178.15, 16, 1183. 4, 1191.30, 1205.1, 1233.8, 1236.7, 1239.30, 1251.9, 1254.38, 1259.28.

NOTES TO CHAPTER V

1. Cf. William Golding's *Pincher Martin* (London, 1956) where the status of all that has been apprehended in the novel is retrospectively altered by its last incident.
2. Robert Graves, pref. to K. Baines (ed. & tr.), *Le Morte Darthur: King Arthur and the Legends of the Round Table: A Rendition in Modern Idiom.* . . . (London, 1963), p. xiv. The "white" abbeys may be of white (Cistercian) monks as against black (Benedictine) ones, rather than of white stones, but this merely reinforces his point.
3. C. S. Lewis, *The Discarded Image* (Cambridge, 1964), pp. 9, 205–12.
4. E. K. Chambers, *Sir Thomas Malory*, English Association Pamphlet, 51 (1922), pp. 6–8; H. S. Bennett, *Chaucer and the Fifteenth Century* (Oxford, 1947), p. 202; E. Vinaver, *Malory* (Oxford, 1929), pp. 50–1; and Lewis, *supra*.
5. Not in the French *Merlin* (ed. Paris, II, 125). Vinaver believes the phrase to be the product of Malory's misunderstanding of the French (V 119.14n). But whether invented or misunderstood, its presence is the product of a decision by Malory.
6. V 185.12, 293.16, 1048–49.
7. V 1082.34, 1048–49.
8. For all his awareness of words, the first set-piece description in Hall's Chronicle is of the former kind, and comes after 112 large pages: *Union of Lancastre and Yorke*, Henry V, fol. 23ʳ.
9. *V.* the list of French phrases in J. Frappier, *Étude sur la Mort le Roi Artu*, pp. 373–4.
10. *V.* p. 64 *supra* and Appendix III, pp. 164, 166.
11. *A Preface to Paradise Lost* (Oxford, 1942), ch. iv.
12. P. E. Tucker, "Malory's Conception of Chivalry as it Appears in his Treatment of the Story of Sir Lancelot," unpubl. B.Litt. thesis (Oxford, 1954), ch. ii, esp. pp. 22–3.

13. Apart from the excellent but inaccessible work above, the subject of Malory's scale of values is best pursued in V. D. Scudder, *Le Morte Darthur of Sir Thomas Malory, A Study*. . . . (London, 1921), pp. 177–362; C. S. Lewis, review of E. K. Chambers, *Sir Thomas Wyatt*. . . . in *MÆ*, 3 (1934); R. T. Davies, "Malory's Launcelot and the Noble Way of the World," *RES*, 6 (1955), 356–64; id., "Malory's 'vertuouse love'," *SP*, 53 (1956), 459–69; id., "The Worshipful Way in Malory," in *Patterns of Love and Courtesy*, ed. J. Lawlor (London, 1966), pp. 157–177; M. C. Bradbrook, *Sir Thomas Malory*, Writers and Their Work Series (London, 1958); Tucker's epitome of his thesis in *Essays on Malory*, ed. J. A. W. Bennett, pp. 64–103; S. J. Miko, "Malory and the Chivalric Order," *MÆ*, 35 (1966), 211–30; V lxxiii–xcix; and *The Morte Darthur, Parts Seven and Eight*, ed. D. S. Brewer, pp. 23–35.

14. E.g. V 401.17, 407.18, 408.1, 460.1, 470.16,30, 485.26, 489.34, 514.31, 545.17, 557.3, 606.11, 639.29, 698.25, 715.28, 742.1,15,25, 745.20, 755.6, 784.22, 791.27, 792.19, 796.1, 797.10, 808.11, 832.12, 844.32; and 1187.27, 1192.18, 1214.10, 1215.30, 1249.18.

15. V 193.23; not in *Morte Arthure*, ed. E. Brock, EETS, OS 8* (1871), l. 611.

16. V 86–8 (L 91–5); V 73–4 (L 31–5).

17. Appendix III, p. 164 (my punctuation).

18. Sommer, V, 100.9 (my punctuation).

19. *Mort Artu*, ed. Frappier, 90.25.

20. Ibid., 90.18.

21. *The Foure Sonnes of Aymon*, I, 60–1. I have supplied the full stops.

22. E.g. V 69.26, 71.23, 79.15.

23. *Arthur of Little Britain*, ed. Utterson, p. 163.

24. Ibid., pp. 170–3.

25. V 73.13 (L 54).

26. V 273; Sommer V, 306.

27. V 430.2, cf. Appendix III, pp. 172–3.

28. V 515.26, cf. Appendix III, p. 165.

29. V 760.2–3, and note citing source passage.

30. *Historie of the Arrivall of Edward IV in England and the Finall Recoverye of his Kingdomes from Henry VI, A.D. MCCCCLXXI*, ed. John Bruce, Camden Soc. (London, 1838).

31. Ed. cit., pp. 27–8.

32. V 526.15, 1070.19.

33. V 202–203.

34. M. C. Seymour, "A Medieval Redactor at Work," *N&Q*, 206 (1961), 170.

35. *The Bodley Version of Mandeville's Travels*, ed. M. C. Seymour, EETS 253 (1963), 105.10–15. I have emended this sentence in accord with B. D. H. Miller's review, *MÆ*, 35 (1966), 73–4.

36. V 187.11–13, *Morte Arthure*, ll. 171–213.

37. *Canterbury Tales*, A 4211–13.

38. *The Pilgrim's Progress*, ed. R. Sharrock (Oxford, 1960), pp. 250–1.

39. Pickford, *L'Évolution du Roman Arthurien*, p. 42; *Mort Artu*, ed. Frappier, p. 179.

40. L 34–5, 38–9, 11, 77, 107.

41. L 21, 6, 85.
42. Vinaver puts an exclamation mark at the end of this sentence: I feel it is unjustified.
    The image Malory uses is also found in the raciest and most colloquial part of Chaucer's *Miller's Tale* (A 3759). This does not imply that Malory had read Chaucer: rather that both drew on a common culture.
43. Auerbach, *Mimesis*, p. 114.
44. V 270.5, 271.17, 271.37 (not in Sommer, V, 210–213).
45. Mark Twain [Samuel L. Clemens], *A Connecticut Yankee in King Arthur's Court* (London, 1900), p. 117–118.

NOTES TO CHAPTER VI

1. "Dialogue" here is used to include monologue: the sense is established in NED.
2. Scudder, *Le Morte Darthur*, p. 393.
3. V 83.28, 331.19, 719.11, 738.28, 744.5. It is also uncommon in the French: for one example *v.* the *Tristan* MS in Appendix III, p. 163.
4. Margaret Schlauch, *The English Language in Modern Times* (Warsaw, 1959), pp. 35–6.
5. V 137, 1104; cf. V 682–683.
6. The most important are V 16, 71, 86, 99, 109, 114, 140, 151, 198, 255, 271, 329, 352, 393, 441, 500, 701, 734, 748, 819, 910, 1125. The ambiguous status of dwarves in romances is shown by R. O. Stidston, *The Use of Ye in the Function of Thou* (Stanford, California, 1917), p. 78.
7. V 701.5, 1125.28.
8. *V.* Norman Davis, "The *Litera Troili*," *RES*, 16 (1965), 243–4, for a useful bibliography of recent work on the two pronouns.
9. V 90.9, 1230.11, 1259.9. Failure to understand this category distorts the otherwise excellent work of B. Dillon: "Formal and Informal Pronouns of Address in Malory's Le Morte Darthur," *AM*, 10 (1969), 94–103.
10. An excellent summary history of this will be found in R. Brown and A. Gilman, "Pronouns of Power and Solidarity," in *Style in Language*, ed. T. A. Sebeok (M.I.T., 1960), pp. 253–76. The authors notice that modern French mountaineers change from the respectful to the intimate pronoun above a certain altitude.
11. Arthur later says "he desyred his sustynance, . . . and thereby we demed many of us that he was nat com oute of a noble house." (V 339.35)
12. *The Cely Papers*, ed. Malden, pp. 5–6.
13. N. Davis, "The Language of the Pastons," *PBA*, 40 (1954) p. 131.
14. *Paston Letters*, ed. Gairdner, III, 50.
15. Stidston, op. cit. n. 6 *supra*, pp. 70–81.
16. The results are tabulated in Appendix II, p. 162.
17. Regular V 276.14, 399.2, 494.7, 885.3, 888.8, 929.9, 1168.16; irregular V 116.7, 143.1, 144.13, 1122.30, 1171.23.
18. I doubt whether any other valid general statement can be made about the

effect of Malory's prose rhythms on his style and on the *Morte Darthur*
as a whole. Many critics have spoken perceptively of this phrase or that,
but an account of the attempts to generalise would read like Browning's
"Childe Roland to the Dark Tower Came."

19. V 246.6–14, 186.4–23.
20. V 505.36, 1176.20, 1252.24, 1256.32.
21. *V.* Helen Wroten, "Malory's 'Tale of King Arthur'," pp. 65–7.
22. *Essays on Malory*, ed. Bennett, p. 24.
23. Charles Moorman has suggested that Malory felt the normal expressions
    of courtly love were exaggerated, and is here parodying them: *ELH*, 27
    (1960), 163–176. I find this unlikely and unproved.
24. V 669.18, 688–697, 38.20, 231.23; cf. 259.32, 533.18, 647.27, 668.14.
25. *Arthur of Little Britain*, pp. 290–1.
26. V 506, cf. 508.7, 599.35, 605.1 and note, 657.17, 665.24, 688–697, 705.20,
    749.35, 757.31.
27. But for one example see *Arthur of Little Britain*, p. 138.
28. V 22.7; 200.14, 204.7; 225.26; 281.21; 304.35, 306.34, 310.36; 462.12,
    465.24; cf. V 73.29, 101.27, 163.19, 191.8, 199.11, 221.9, 265.31, 299.17,
    304.1, 398.29, 418.33, 597.31, 666.12, 717.3, 718.2, 888.3, 926.30, 971.3,
    1066.5, 1070.23, 1087.27, 1125.14.
29. V 926.30, 888.3.
30. V 717.36, 304.1.
31. V 109–114.
32. V 1176.16; *Mort Artu*, ed. Frappier, 97.9, cf. 80.21.
33. John Paston I also becomes much more incisive and fluent under emotional
    stress, especially when he loses his temper, *v. Paston Letters*, ed. Davis,
    pp. 105–9. Both his logic and his use of figures of speech improve.
34. V 67.2 (L 14); V 61.33 (L 4).
35. V 515–516; source in Appendix III, p. 165.
36. V 324.34.
37. V 395.15. Lancelot uses the same formula in a very similar situation
    (V 281.21).
38. V 928.1–13.
39. V 210.14, 353.14, 732.14, 744.31.
40. See below, p. 129.

NOTES TO CHAPTER VII

1. V 579.35, 754.34.
2. References are to Gairdner's ed.
3. V 1259.9n, apparently followed by D. S. Brewer, *The Morte Darthur,
   Parts Seven and Eight* (London, 1968), p. 157n; *Paston Letters*, ed. Davis,
   p. 210n. See also *supra*, pp. 69–73.
4. Gavin Douglas, *The Poetical Works*, ed. John Small, 4 vols. (Edinburgh,
   1874), III, 206.
5. Douglas, *Works*, II, 221–2.

6. For examples of the opposite extreme in translating Homer, see James Sutherland, *A Preface to Eighteenth Century Poetry* (Oxford, 1948), pp. 88–9.

7. In *Minor Poems*, pp. 41–2.

8. *Peri Bathous, or Martinus Scriblerus, his Treatise of the Art of Sinking in Poetry*, in [Swift–Pope] *Miscellanies, The Last Volume* (London, 1727), p. 67. His own "Imitation" is more clearly condemned by these words than anything Malory or Chaucer wrote.

9. Ibid., p. 29.

10. E.g. V 304–10.

11. V 330.4 ff.

12. V 1122.14, 1104.34, 360.6. *V*. Tilley, W419.

13. V 114.3, 1054.20, 1172–73.

14. Quoted by Owst, *Literature and the Pulpit*, pp. 420 ff.

15. V 11.36, 18.19, 64.12, 77.18fn., 97.26, 120.10, 131.28, 144.6,9, 158.15, 217.26, 223.9, 246.11, 295.2,7, 306.2, 358.10, 360.6, 388.34, 396.9,15, 410.23, 421.35, 422.26, 429.15, 447.36, 510.11, 516.3,4,5 550.14, 619.6, 687.30, 712.23, 745.32, 792.14, 796.22, 896.5, 906.8, 932.3, 934.11, 955.28, 988.8, 1002.2, 1047.19, 1084.5, 1106.8, 1114.27, 1120.2, 1126.5, 1127.13, 1128.16,17, 1133.28,29, 1169.26, 1175.12, 1219.18, 1228.6, 1237.5, 1251.13, 1254.12.

16. *Letters Written by the Late Right Honourable Philip Dormer Stanhope, Earl of Chesterfield* . . . . 2 vols. (London, 1774), I, 147 (cf. I, 464).

17. 1477, 1479, 1489. Another and more accessible translation is ed. Curt F. Bühler, EETS (1941).

18. *Paston Letters*, ed. Davis, pp. 130, 173, 209, 219 (Margaret), and 232, 233, 260; ed. Gairdner, I, 189, 195, 423, 444, II, 22, 23, 73(4), Supp., 68, 93, 124, 139; and Tilley B740 (Margaret), C42, C868, C907, H638, M112, M371 S66, T496.

19. *Cely Papers*, ed. Malden, p. 14; cf. Tilley E177, P366.

20. *V*. B. J. Whiting, *Chaucer's Use of Proverbs* (Harvard, 1934), pp. 75, 152–4.

21. J. Huizinga, *The Waning of the Middle Ages* (London, 1924), pp. 209–11.

22. V 144.6,9; 1133.28; 1047.19.

23. *V*. Wyld, *Modern Colloquial English*, p. 21.

24. V 116–117.

25. E.g. V 879–881, 889.8–30, 990–994.

26. *V. supra* p. 55. The Pastons could be better at this: e.g. *Paston Letters*, ed. Gairdner, I, 193 (James Gloys).

27. Cf. V 1054.5–12, 1199.12–17.

28. *Paston Letters*, ed. Davis, p. 101.

29. *Paston Letters*, ed. Gairdner, I, 12.

30. V 944–945.

31. Gawain's words are not in *Le Morte Arthur*, ll. 3073, 2889–97.

32. V 1258.4, 1017.6.

33. See *supra*, pp. 78–82.

34. The source is cited in Vinaver's note.

35. *The Towneley Plays*, ed. G. England and A. W. Pollard, EETS, ES 71 (1897), p. 234.

36. *Canterbury Tales*, A 2630, A 57.

37. V 339.18, 295.7.
38. *V. F.* Whitehead, "On Certain Episodes in the Fourth Book of Malory's 'Morte Darthur'," *MÆ*, 2 (1933), 199–216.
39. B. J. Whiting, "Gawain: his Reputation, his Courtesy, and his Appearance in Chaucer's Squire's Tale," *MS*, 9 (1947), 189–234.
40. V 1077–80, cf. *Mort Artu*, ed. Frappier, pp. 19–20. The other English version also has a respectable Gawain: *Le Morte Arthur*, ed. Bruce, ll. 570–615.
41. V 146.18, 191.27.
42. V 1086.22, 1075.38.
43. E.g. V 422–423.
44. For source, see Appendix III, pp. 170–1.

NOTES TO CHAPTER VIII

1. H. J. Chaytor, *From Script to Print* (Cambridge, 1945), pp. 11–13.
2. *V.* John Lawlor, "The Earlier Poems," in *Chaucer and Chaucerians*, ed. D. S. Brewer, pp. 39–64.
3. W. M. Thackeray, *Vanity Fair*, ed. G. and K. Tillotson (London, 1963), pp. 19–20.
4. Ibid., p. 318.
5. Ibid., p. 15.
6. *V.* Percy Lubbock, *The Craft of Fiction* (London, 1926), ch. vii, and Thackeray, op. cit., pp. 315, 142, 328.
7. *V.* Ruth Crosby, "Oral Delivery in the Middle Ages," *Speculum*, 11 (1936), 88–110.
8. There have been two ingenious attempts to explain minor contradictions in the *Morte* by postulating a complicated internal chronology: Charles Moorman's in *JEGP*, 60 (1961), 240–9, and R. M. Lumiansky's in *TSE*, 5 (1955), 29–40. Both leave too many small points unresolved.
9. E.g. *Mort Artu*, ed. Frappier, 207, 218–19; cf. the comparable phrase "Que vous diroye je?" in the prose *Tristan* (Appendix III, p. 170).
10. V 403.25, 405.5, 1050.2, 1055.11, 1076.14, 1119–20, 1121, 1147.2, 1165.13, 1174.20, 1229.6, 1258.32 (Cf. example quoted p. 53 *supra*).
11. V 7.1, 855.12, 1232.18, 1260.7.
12. Caxton omits the last element: S 363.19.
13. R. H. Wilson, "Malory's 'French Book' Again," *CL*, 2 (1950), 172–181.
14. *Supra*, pp. 31–3.
15. *English Verse between Chaucer and Surrey*, ed. E. P. Hammond (Duke University Press, 1927), p. 195, ll. 50–60. "To" (l. 57) means "so that".
16. Damsell V 64.11, Merlin's prophecies V 68.8, 72.5,16,25, 73.23, 75.11,16, 78.9,16, 79.3, 85.31, 91.21,28, independence V 76.16, 91.15.
17. Twenty-eight references to this phrase in the "Tristram" alone are given in ch. v, n. 14 *supra*; see also V 415.31, 428.11, 466.23, 489.34, 517.3, 526.9, 534.4, 625.24, 626.3, 648.12, 738.1,26, and V 408.25, 526.22, 744.30, 745.12–35, and especially Tristram's tributes to Lancelot, V 745, 755–756 and notes.

18. *V. supra*, p. 103.
19. E.g. MS B.N. fr. 103, fol. 191ʳ, col. 2 (Appendix III, p. 164).
20. Sir Thomas More, *The History of King Richard III* ed. R. S. Sylvester (Yale, 1963), p. xcvi.
21. V 44.27, 1017.16.
22. V 83–4, 88.11, 72.25.
23. The limitations of this style are shown by D. H. Lawrence, who claims to comprehend, though he does not control, his world in *Kangaroo* (ed. Gribble [London, 1963]). Both writers use vague and emotive terms, colloquial syntax and phrases, and echoes of themselves, but Malory is not trying to draw a diagram of the world: he is accepting rather than explaining it. The coarsely ironic "rather"s with which Lawrence explains marriage (ch. ix, p. 170) are alien to Malory. To use the style they share to explain the universe exposes the thought embodied in that style as a preposterous pretence—to use Lawrence's own words—"like sex in trees" (ch. x, p. 180).
24. *V.* Workman, *Fifteenth-Century Translation*, ch. i. A less convincing explanation has been put forward by I. A. Gordon, who suggests that the baneful influence of French prose caused English writers to desert the mainstream of Alfredian English (*The Movement of English Prose*, pp. 50–7, 66). Even if it were credible that a writer would choose incompetence rather than competence, the surviving English prose seems to me rather to point to an attempt, often unconscious, to recreate a standard which did not exist (*v.* ch. ii *supra*). No doubt English writers, whether translating or writing original prose, often made the same mistakes as their French counterparts, when faced with ideas beyond their capacity for expression. In languages so similar, this was inevitable. But as Workman has shown, it is precisely when the translators desert their originals that they get into trouble.
25. *V. supra*, pp. 46–8.
26. E.g. V 270–271, 295.31–35.
27. V 1119–1120.
28. *V.* Baines (ed.), *Le Morte Darthur*, p. 458.
29. *Vanity Fair*, ed. cit., p. 458.
30. V 180, 363, 845, 1037, 1154, 1260.
31. *V. supra*, pp. 78–82.
32. *The Brut*, ed. Brie, II, 513.
33. V 360.33, *v.* V. Angelescu, "The Relationship of Gareth and Gawain in Malory's Morte Darthur," *N&Q*, 206 (1961), 8–9.
34. Ed. Utterson, p. iv.
35. V cxliii–cxlvi.
36. Johnson's *Shakespeare*, I, viii.

Index

62624

823.2
M29
F45

Date Due

NOV 21 '78			
DEC 12 72			
OCT 1 1 1983			
OCT 2 5 1983			
12 14 90			
AP 25 02			

NYACK COLLEGE LIBRARY
NYACK, NEW YORK

BRO
DART Printed in U.S.A.